Mark Hagger is Lecturer in Medieval History at Bangor University. He is the author of *The Fortunes of a Norman Family: The de Verduns in England, Ireland and Wales 1066–1316* and has published a number of articles on Norman aristocracy, law and government.

WILLIAM
KING AND CONQUEROR

MARK HAGGER

I.B. TAURIS
LONDON · NEW YORK

Published in 2012 by I.B.Tauris & Co. Ltd
6 Salem Road, London W2 4BU
175 Fifth Avenue, New York, NY 10010
www.ibtauris.com

Distributed in the United States and Canada Exclusively by Palgrave Macmillan
175 Fifth Avenue, NY 10010

ISBN: 978 1 78076 354 5

A full CIP record for this book is available from the British Library
A full CIP record for this book is available from the Library of Congress

Library of Congress catalog card: available

Typeset in Perpetua by A. & D. Worthington, Newmarket, Suffolk
Printed and bound in Sweden by ScandBook AB

This book is dedicated to the memory of my mother, Mrs J.E. Hagger, 1932–2007, and to my father, in the hope that it might in some way comprise a return on his investment.

CONTENTS

ILLUSTRATIONS

Maps

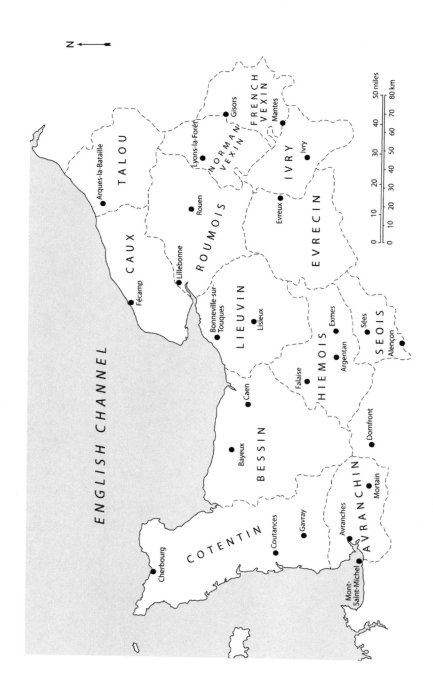

Map 1. The counties of Normandy in the eleventh century.

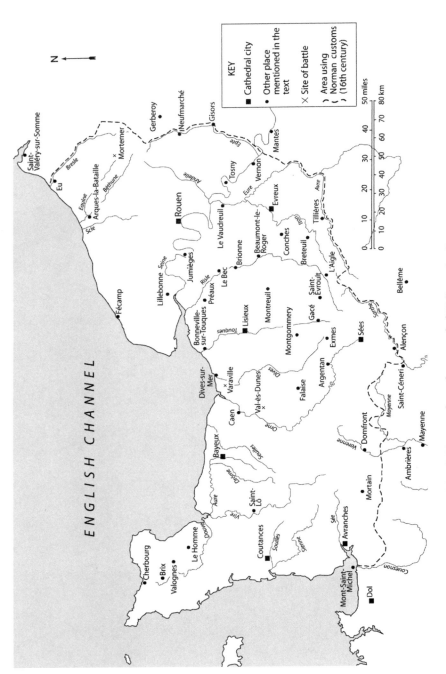

Map 2. Normandy in the time of of William the Conqueror.

ENGLISH CHANNEL

KEY

■ Cathedral city

● Other place mentioned in the text

✕ Site of battle

⟩ Area using
⟨ Norman customs
⟩ (16th century)

50 miles
80 km

N

Map 3. England, 1066–87.

†

PREFACE

This book aims to provide an accessible introduction to the life and career of William the Conqueror, as well as the Norman Conquest of 1066, for both undergraduates and the general reader. It is also intended to place William's life in the context of the times, and I have sketched in some incidental details about what it was like to live in England and Normandy in the eleventh century, which I hope will add an extra dimension to this biography. I must add a caveat that the events and episodes of William's life and times are not always clear-cut – there is debate and uncertainty about a good many things – but by drawing on a number of sources, whether contemporary or near-contemporary documents and narratives, or the work of more recent historians, it is possible to construct a coherent portrait of this iconic figure.[1]

I have written this book so that William retains centre stage throughout. It is about what *he* did, what *he* wore, how *he* governed the territories under his rule. This has provided a way to filter information, but it does mean that some interesting topics have been left out. For example, as William was a king, not a queen, I have not written about the role of queenship or women more generally; as he was not a monk I have not looked in detail at life in monasteries. I hope that the book spurs those who are disappointed by such omissions into further researches of their own, and that the notes and bibliography provide some useful starting points for that work.

This book was originally commissioned in 2007, but publication was subsequently delayed for a number of reasons, and it eventually became clear that a new publisher would have to be found. I am therefore extremely grateful to Lester Crook at I.B.Tauris not just for agreeing to take the book on but also for his enthusiasm about it. I must also thank Ann Williams of the University of East Anglia, who generously read through the whole of the manuscript and offered many useful insights and corrections; Leonie Hicks of the University of Southampton for a useful (and timely) suggestion; my colleagues at, and several generations of students of, Bangor University, who have provided a relaxed and stimulating environment in which to work; and Kate Waddington, for making everything so much better. My mother died while this book was being written, and so it is dedicated to her memory. It is also dedicated to my father whose support has been constant.

PROLOGUE

A MOST WORTHY KING

In November or December 1066, following the submission of the English leaders who had not been killed at Hastings, William, duke of the Normans, entered London in triumph. The city is famously described by William fitz Stephen, who included the portrait in his *Life* of Thomas Becket, himself a Londoner, towards the end of the twelfth century:[1]

> Among the noble and celebrated cities of the world that of London, the capital of the kingdom of the English, is one which extends its glory farther than all the others and sends its wealth and merchandise more widely into distant lands ... It has on its east the palatine fortress, very great and strong: the keep and walls rise from very deep foundations and are fixed with a mortar tempered by the blood of animals. On the west there are two castles, very strongly fortified, and from these there runs a high and massive wall with seven double gates and with towers along the north at regular intervals. London was also once walled and turreted on the south, but the mighty Thames, so full of fish, has with the sea's ebb and flow washed against, loosened, and thrown down those walls in the course of time. Upstream to the west there is the royal palace which is conspicuous above the river, a building incomparable in its ramparts and bulwarks. It is about two miles from the city and joined thereto by a populous suburb.

In 1066 the king's palace at Westminster stood on an island – the island of Thorney – and was separated from the 'populous suburb' by the branching channels of the Tyburn stream and the adjacent marshes. The palace stood on the bank of the Thames, with the buildings clustered around the great hall. It was here that Edward the Confessor had died in January, and William would continue to use his predecessor's hall throughout his reign. It was only in the 1090s that his son and heir, William Rufus, would pull down the old wooden building and put in its place a great stone hall, some 73 metres (240 feet) long. That hall still stands today, albeit heightened, refaced and re-roofed in the fourteenth century. When William Rufus first saw it in 1099, he characteristically complained that it was not large enough by half,[2] but it was still probably the largest stone hall in Europe at that time.

Across from the royal palace stood the new abbey, the West Minster, a monastery that would quickly give Thorney a new name. The abbey was founded originally by St Dunstan, archbishop of Canterbury, in *c*. 960, but it was rebuilt and enlarged by Edward the Confessor *c*. 1050. The *Life of King Edward* reports that:

> The king ... being devoted to God, gave his attention to that place, for it both lay hard by the famous and rich town and also was a delightful spot, surrounded by fertile lands and green fields and near the mouth of the main channel of the river, which bore abundant merchandise of wares of every kind for sale from the whole world to the town on its banks. And, especially because of his love of the Prince of the Apostles ... he decided to have his burial place there ... And so at the king's command the building, nobly begun, was made ready, and there was no weighing of the cost, past or future, as long as it proved worthy of, and acceptable to, God and St Peter. The house of the principal altar, raised up with most lofty vaulting, is surrounded by dressed stone, evenly jointed. Moreover, the circumference of that temple is enclosed on both sides by a double arch of stones ... Next is the crossing of the church, which is to hold in its midst the choir of God's choristers, and, with its twin abutments from either side, support the high apex of the central tower. It rises simply at first with a low and sturdy vault, swells with many a stair spiralling up in artistic profusion, but then with a plain wall climbs to the wooden roof which is carefully covered with lead.

The surviving eleventh-century nave at Jumièges in Normandy might give an indication of what Edward's Westminster Abbey looked like when it was completed, although the relationship between the two buildings remains less than certain. According to the 'C', 'D' and 'E' versions of the *Anglo-Saxon Chronicle* the church was consecrated just a week before Edward died, on 28 December 1065, although construction continued until *c*. 1080.[3] The Bayeux Tapestry, which provides the only contemporary representation of the church, shows a man fixing an elaborate weather-vane to the east end which probably commemorates this event. Round about the abbey stood a small village. Domesday Book records perhaps 61 households, as well as another 25 houses of the abbot's men-at-arms and others – perhaps royal officials – with fields and woodland too.

1. The abbey of Jumièges, dedicated in 1067, and perhaps the
model for Westminster Abbey.

If the church was modelled on that at Jumièges, Duke William might have
felt rather at home as he entered the building in state on Christmas Day 1066
for his coronation as king of the English. The account in the 'D' version of the
Anglo-Saxon Chronicle is brief, and provides little in the way of detail:

> Then on midwinter's day Archbishop Ealdred consecrated him king in
> Westminster; and he gave his hand on it and on Christ's book, and also
> swore, before he [Ealdred] would set the crown on his head, that he would
> hold this nation as well as the best of any kings before him did, if they would
> be loyal to him.

The 'D' text of the *Chronicle* was, it is thought, composed by someone from
Archbishop Ealdred's circle, and that is why it is expressly noted that the
archbishop extorted a promise of good lordship from William *before* he would
crown him. The writer wanted it to be known that Ealdred had done his
best to curb William's aggression before making him king. And William
was crowned by Archbishop Ealdred of York because the archbishop of

Canterbury, Stigand, who would usually have performed the ceremony, was an excommunicate pluralist, and William did not want his coronation to be tarnished by that prelate's involvement.

The coronation service is likely to have followed the form set out in the Third English Coronation Ordo, although historians are divided on the question of whether the Second or Third Ordo was used.[4] The ceremony would have begun with William prostrating himself before the altar. He then made a triple promise to protect the Church and people, to punish wrongdoers and to judge justly, and was acclaimed king. According to William of Poitiers, Archbishop Ealdred of York, followed by Geoffrey of Montbray (often Anglicized as Mowbray), bishop of Coutances, asked the English and French respectively if they were willing for William to become king. They all shouted their approval. There followed a benediction and then William's hands, breast, shoulders, elbows and head were anointed with blessed oil. His head was anointed again, this time with chrism (oil mixed with balsam). He was given the sword and other regalia. The crown was blessed and set on his head. The ring was put on his finger, and the sceptre and rod were placed in his hands. Finally he was enthroned before those of his subjects who remained in the abbey. There may not have been many, for during much of the ceremony a fire raged through Westminster.

What caused the fire? The story is told to us by a chronicler called Orderic Vitalis.[5] He notes that guards had been posted outside the abbey during the service to prevent any violence or disorder,

> but at the prompting of the Devil, who hates everything good, a sudden disaster and portent of future catastrophes occurred. For when Archbishop Ealdred asked the English, and Geoffrey, bishop of Coutances, asked the Normans, if they would accept William as their king, all of them gladly shouted out with one voice, if not in one language, that they would. The armed guard outside, hearing the tumult of the joyful crowd in the church and the harsh accents of a foreign tongue, imagined that some treachery was afoot, and rashly set fire to some of the buildings. The fire spread rapidly from house to house; the crowd who had been rejoicing in the church took fright and throngs of men and women of every condition rushed out of the church in frantic haste. Only the bishops and a few clergy and monks remained, terrified, in the sanctuary, and with difficulty completed the consecration of the king, who was trembling from head to foot. Almost all the rest made for the scene of the conflagration, some to fight the flames and many others hoping to find loot for themselves.

These words are taken from Orderic's *Ecclesiastical History*, the bulk of which was written in Normandy between 1123 and 1137, although it was not completed until 1141, shortly before he died. It is interesting that Orderic saw the fire at Westminster as a 'portent of future catastrophe'. It is not clear what events Orderic was thinking of here, but it is possible that he was referring to the rebellions that William would face, and the actions that this first Norman king would take to quash the resistance to his rule – particularly the so-called 'harrying of the north' (see Chapter 5). In contrast, the source from which Orderic borrowed most of his account, *The Deeds of William*, written by William of Poitiers in the 1070s, makes no reference at all to the Devil, or to people leaving the ceremony, or to William trembling.[6] Instead Poitiers blames the fire solely on the rashness of the nervous soldiers and then moves on. So why did Orderic add these words? William of Poitiers was a secular clerk writing for King William with the intention of praising and defending his rule. Orderic, in contrast, was writing some time after events when legends might have grown up around them, had a more ambivalent attitude to the king and, as a monk, was prone to see the Devil at work where others might see only human fallibility. But although Orderic embroiders his tale, and although his *Ecclesiastical History* must often be treated with caution, it should not be written off altogether. It is a rich source of material on life and events in Normandy in the eleventh and twelfth centuries, and Orderic is a great storyteller.

Although their accounts of the coronation differ in drama and emphasis, both Orderic and Poitiers agree that William went on to rule well. William of Poitiers thought that William performed good works after his coronation with an even greater zeal than before. 'He was,' Poitiers says, 'inspired to great and noble undertakings, as a most worthy king.' Orderic, immediately after his dramatic account of the coronation, opined that William 'reigned well and justly in prosperity and adversity for twenty-eight years, eight months, and sixteen days' – although elsewhere he was more critical.

Although the coronation was, perhaps, the highlight of William's career, it could only happen because William had struggled to make his rule effective in Normandy, and had cowed (or outlived) the adversaries of his youth. He had also played the hand he had been dealt well, and he had been lucky. Nor did William's career end with his coronation. He ruled as king and duke for another 21 years, struggling to overcome a succession of rebellions and wars. Here, faced with a more youthful opposition and with more ground to cover, he was not always so successful, even if some of his greatest monuments – the White Tower of the Tower of London or Domesday Book – date from this period. This book, then, will examine William's reign, as both duke of the Normans and king of the English, it will attempt to sketch his character, it will look at the times in which he lived, and it will suggest that, although he had flaws, he was indeed a 'most worthy king'.

†

CHAPTER 1

FIRE AND SWORD EVERYWHERE, c. 1027–47

In 1026 Duke Richard II of Normandy (d. 1026) gave the county of the Hiémois (see Map 1) to his second son, Robert. One of the castles within the district was constructed on the rock that gives the town of Falaise its name, and it was during one of his stays here that Robert spied an under-taker's daughter by the name of Herleva.[1] According to William of Malmes-bury, another Benedictine monk who was, like Orderic Vitalis, writing about a century after events,

> her beauty had once caught his eye as she was dancing, and he could not refrain from sleeping with her; and henceforward he loved her above all others, and for some time kept her in the position of a lawful wife. The son she bore him was called William after his great-great-grandfather.

William of Malmesbury's words suggest that he was aware that Robert and Herleva's union would have been recognized as a lawful marriage by many living in Normandy at the time, and they would probably have seen William as Robert's legitimate son. But to others, especially ecclesiastics living outside the duchy, he was illegitimate, and he was thus known by his non-Norman contemporaries as William the Bastard.

When was William born? Robert succeeded his brother as duke of the Normans in 1027 in suspicious circumstances: it was rumoured that Robert had poisoned his brother to bring this about. As it is unlikely that Robert resided at remote Falaise for any length of time after his succession, William was probably born either in 1027 or 1028 – dates which fit in with Malm-esbury's assertion that William was seven in 1035.[2] It is also the case that Robert's succession brought to an end his (unblessed) marriage with Herleva.

1

Now that Robert was duke, the daughter of an undertaker would no longer suffice as a bride. Herleva was thus put aside, but was looked after, being married to a knight called Herluin of Conteville. The couple subsequently had two sons, Robert and Odo, who were both to be elevated to positions of the highest honour by their half-brother. As to Duke Robert, he might afterwards have married a sister of King Cnut of the Danes and the English before his premature death.[3]

There is almost no record of William's early childhood years, although we do know that he was sometimes at court and that he was treated as his father's heir, despite his birth out of wedlock. Otherwise he is almost invisible until 1035, when his father suddenly announced that he intended to undertake a pilgrimage to Jerusalem. The reasons for this decision are unknown, although later writers speculated that it was due to remorse for murdering his brother. Duke Robert consequently summoned Archbishop Robert of Rouen, his uncle, and the other great men of his duchy to his court and made his scheme known to them. According to William of Jumièges, a Benedictine monk at the monastery of Jumièges on the River Seine, who was writing only a few years after events:

> All were greatly astonished by his words for they feared that his absence would lead to the country being disturbed in various ways. He presented them with his only son, William, and earnestly besought them to choose him as their lord in his place and to accept him as military leader. In spite of the boy's tender years everyone in the town rejoiced in his encouragement and in accordance with the duke's decree readily and unanimously acclaimed him their prince and lord and pledged him their fealty with inviolable oaths. When he had accomplished this as he wished, the duke entrusted him to tutors and guardians.

Robert left a Normandy braced for disturbances during his absence. But no one could have anticipated that he would never return. He succeeded in reaching Jerusalem, and prayed at the Holy Sepulchre for eight days, but on the journey home he fell sick and died at Nicaea (now Iznik) in present-day Turkey, and was buried in the church of St Mary there.

And so William, aged seven or eight, was now duke of the Normans, a people who had a reputation for fickleness and a penchant for rebellion. Orderic Vitalis has King William speak these words on his deathbed:

> If the Normans are disciplined under a just and firm rule they are men of great valour, who press invincibly to the fore in arduous undertakings and,

2. The castle at Falaise, where William was probably born.

proving their strength, fight resolutely to overcome all enemies. But without such rule they tear each other to pieces and destroy themselves, for they hanker after rebellion, cherish sedition, and are ready for any treachery.

If these are really William's words, he was speaking from bitter experience. It must certainly have been clear to everyone that his first years would be difficult. As a child, he had little authority of his own. He was entirely reliant on the loyalty of his subjects, and on the ability of his guardians to maintain order in his name until he should come of age. At first, Archbishop Robert of Rouen was able to hold Normandy together. Justice was done. Some of the wrongs of the turbulent reign of Robert the Magnificent were put right. Bishop Hugh of Bayeux, for example, was able to recover some of the lands that his cathedral had lost by the judgement of the archbishop and other of the 'best men' of Normandy. But it was not to last. The death of Archbishop Robert in 1037 may have been a turning point; it has certainly been seen as such by modern historians. In the view of William of Malmesbury, however, the key event was the murder of Duke William's guardian, Gilbert of Brionne, in *c.* 1041. Malmesbury wrote: 'When … Gilbert was killed by his cousin Ralph, it was fire and sword everywhere.'

Even before Gilbert's death, however, it is clear that law, order and justice were under siege. William of Jumièges noted that as soon as Duke Robert's death became known,

> many Normans built earthworks in many places and erected fortified strongholds for their own purposes. Having dared to establish themselves securely in their fortifications, they immediately hatched plots and rebellions and fierce fires were lit all over the country.

Indeed Gilbert himself took the opportunity offered by the duke's minority to reopen a dispute that Duke Robert had settled. Orderic Vitalis, who lived close to the places concerned, tells us that during the reign of Duke Robert, Gilbert had attempted, without success, to wrest the village of Montreuil from the Giroie family. The tables were turned on him, however, because not only did he fail to secure Montreuil, he also lost another village, Le Sap, to the same family in the feud. When he became Duke William's guardian, and there was no one to gainsay him, he decided that the time was right to regain Le Sap. But he had again misjudged his adversaries. Not only did the Giroie family unite once more against him, but they were joined by Ralph of Gacé, the son of Archbishop Robert of Rouen and a man who might well have felt that he should have become guardian of the young duke instead of Gilbert. And so this time, instead of merely losing his property, Count Gilbert lost his life. The Giroie family, on the other hand, kept Le Sap and Montreuil, and Ralph of Gacé was chosen by Duke William to be his guardian and the leader of his military forces.

Some historians have portrayed William's minority as a time of real danger for the young duke.[4] Orderic claims that, for fear of his kinsmen and to save him from discovery by traitors who sought his death, he would be smuggled secretly out of his chamber in the castle at night by his uncle Walter (one of Herleva's brothers) and taken to the cottages and hiding places of the poor. It is a dramatic image, but it is not clear that it has any basis in reality. Indeed it might have been intended to echo the uncertain youth of Julius Caesar, as told by the Roman writer Suetonius.[5] Such allusions to classical models are quite common in eleventh- and twelfth-century narratives, and were intended to associate their subjects with great figures from Antiquity. In any case, William of Jumièges, who was much closer to events, does not mention that the young duke was personally in danger at any point. Indeed there is just one occasion when William is placed at the scene of an outrage, and again only by Orderic:

Osbern too, steward of the ducal household, son of Herfast, brother of Countess Gunnor, unexpectedly had his throat cut in his bed one night by William, son of Roger of Montgommery, while he and the duke were sound asleep in the duke's chamber at Vaudreuil. At that time, Roger was in exile in Paris because of his perfidy, and his five sons Hugh, Robert, Roger, William and Gilbert were in Normandy deeply engaged in the commission of horrible crimes. But not long afterwards William, because of this crime, repaid his debt to God and was justly punished. For Barnon of Glos, Osbern's *prévôt*, who wished to avenge the unjust murder of his lord, one night gathered a band of ready warriors, entered the house where William and his accomplices were sleeping, and instantly killed all of them at the same time.

Orderic's account is dramatic, but its accuracy is open to some doubt. We have here a stealthy night-time attack on the sleeping Osbern, but although we do know from other sources that Osbern was indeed murdered, we also learn that at least one of his men was seriously injured at the same time. This might suggest a brawl or a skirmish; it certainly makes much less probable the murder-in-the-dark of Orderic's account. Montgommery's failure to seize such an opportunity and kill William also makes it unlikely that the young duke's life was really threatened, and in all fairness it should be noted that Orderic does not say that it was – this is something that later historians have simply assumed was the case. Instead Orderic relates the story of Osbern's murder simply as an example of the disturbances that afflicted Normandy during William's minority, and his words make clear what William of Montgommery's intention was. William was not after the duke; he was acting out a personal vendetta. Osbern had helped to bring down his father, who had usurped ducal lands and was subsequently driven from Normandy as a result. William killed Osbern as an act of revenge for his part in his father's downfall.[6] But this just started another feud, which apparently ended only when Barnon of Glos avenged his lord in a tit-for-tat killing spree.

Other feuds, although disruptive, did not directly involve men so close to the duke. There was, for example, a conflict along the River Risle in which members of the long-established Tosny family unsuccessfully attempted to prevent the rival house of Beaumont from eroding their power and influence in the region. Hugh of Montfort and Walkelin of Ferrières indulged in a private war against each other, too, and both were killed for their trouble. But, unfortunately for the young William, it was not only his subjects who attempted to take advantage of his youth and weakness. King Henry of the French took the opportunity offered by the duke's vulnerability to demand the destruction of the border castle at Tillières, on the River Avre, which had been constructed at the very southern limit of the duchy by Duke Richard II around the year 1000. William and his counsellors agreed to the king's demand, but Gilbert Crispin, who had been appointed custodian by Duke Robert, refused to surrender and fortified it against the French. It was only when William appeared at Tillières and commanded Crispin to surrender the fortress in person that he capitulated. King Henry then set fire to the castle and left. But, not content with the concessions afforded him, or perhaps smelling blood, he attacked and burned the settlement at Argentan, which he pillaged. He then returned to Tillières and rebuilt and garrisoned the castle, in flagrant breach of the terms of surrender agreed with William.[7]

It would be easy to think that these various episodes revealed that the young William was weak and vulnerable. But some of the turmoil might actually have been caused by a growth in ducal power, rather than resulting from weakness at the centre. Osbern was killed because he had taken action on Duke William's behalf to recover estates that had been lost to Roger I of Montgommery. Equally William's supporters could successfully drive into exile the *vicomte* of the Hiémois, Thurstan Goz, when he rebelled against the duke, and fortified the castle at Falaise against him, in *c.* 1043. William, then, was able to exercise effective control even in parts of the duchy that were remote from the centre (at Rouen). His power is also reflected in the frequent presence at William's court of two men from the west of Normandy, Ralph Taisson and Nigel of the Cotentin. As such, perhaps we should trust William of Poitiers, the duke's biographer, when he notes that during the 1040s many men wished to follow the duke, and that he, growing older, developing his skills and listening to wise counsel, was restoring peace to Normandy.

Poitier's words also suggest that William was by now ruling in his own right, and it seems likely that he had done so from shortly after King Henry's invasion of his territories. David Bates has recently suggested that William's personal rule began in around 1042.[8] About this time William began to gather around him the men who were to remain his closest advisers and stalwart adherents for the rest of their lives, and who formed something of a ruling clique. These included William fitz Osbern, the son of William's murdered steward, and Roger II of Montgommery, whose brother was responsible for the murder but whose father had later succeeded in restoring himself to his lands and to the duke's confidence. Roger of Beaumont was also frequently at the duke's court in the 1040s, and he, too, was to remain important in the duke's counsels.[9]

The formation of this close-knit clique at the centre of government could be nothing other than exclusive, and some of those who were excluded did not like it. One such was Count Guy of Burgundy. He was William's cousin, the son of William's aunt, Adeliza, and Count Reginald of Bourgogne-outre-Sâone. To ensure that he could rely on Guy's loyalty, William had given him the fortresses at Vernon, on the Seine, and Brionne, on the Risle. But this was not enough. As a scion of the ducal house, Guy no doubt felt that he should have been at the very centre of government. But the witness lists of the acts issued in William's name suggest that the duke took a different view and ruled without his advice. Guy thus determined on rebellion.

Another disaffected lord was Nigel II of the Cotentin. His father, who had died in *c.* 1042, had been the main instrument by which the dukes from Richard II onwards had made their authority known in the Cotentin peninsula. Even before his death, however, the dukes had been creating new avenues through which to express their power over the region. Important pieces in the jigsaw of political control were put in place when the bishop of Coutances, Robert, returned to his episcopal city in around 1026 (his predecessors had ruled *in absentia*, living for the most part in Rouen, for the previous 75 years), and when the dukes constructed three castles in the Cotentin, at Cherbourg, Brix and Le Homme (now the Isle Marie). It is also possible that Duke William continued to build up ducal power in the region in the years immediately before 1046, forging relationships with other lords of the Cotentin, such as Thurstan Haldup (his surname means 'the deaf'), lord of le Plessis and Créances, whose son, Eudo, married Muriel, William's half-sister. The result was that Nigel II was marginalized, like Count Guy, and thus he decided to rebel – although Guy still had to purchase his support first by giving him the castle of Le Homme.

The threat of a powerful duke of the Normans making his authority in the west of the duchy a reality might have caused a groundswell of discontent that led others to join Guy in rebellion in 1046–47, just as King John's interference in the north of England, following the loss of Normandy in 1204, contributed to the civil war that would end in Magna Carta.[10] That said, the other two leading rebels named by William of Poitiers, Ranulf of Bayeux and Haimo 'the Toothy', seem to have had other reasons for rebellion. Ranulf had been unjustly deprived of lands on Guernsey by William's father, while Haimo may have rebelled because he had been frustrated in his attempts to reconcile the duke with his kinsman, Thurstan Goz, by more peaceful means.

But whatever the motivations of the rebels, William of Poitiers portrays the rebellion as a battle between the peace and justice of the duke, and the intemperance and injustice of overmighty lords, describing the events of 1046–47 in these words:

> When these beginnings were already restoring to Normandy the splendour and tranquillity of its ancient state ... some people preferred to enjoy their accustomed liberty, retaining their own possessions and seizing those of others at their pleasure. The man who stood out as promoter of these mad schemes was Guy, son of Reginald count of Burgundy, who held the mighty castles of Brionne and Vernon by gift of the duke, with whom he had been brought up from childhood in the same household. But he desired to get either the ducal office or the greater part of Normandy. He associated with himself in this wicked conspiracy Nigel, governor of the *pagus* [county] of Coutances, Ranulf *vicomte* of Bayeux, Haimo nicknamed 'toothy', and other powerful men ... The rebels killed many innocent people whom they tried in vain to convert to their cause, or whom they recognized as major obstacles to their plans ... So the conspiracy grew little by little from this beginning until the perjured rebels were strong enough to challenge their lord openly at Val-ès-Dunes, disturbing all the country round with their tumult.

When the rebellion finally broke, William was at Valognes. According to the Norman poet Wace, who was writing during the 1160s and 1170s, the duke was roused in the middle of the night, and warned that he should leave immediately. His enemies were arming themselves and if he did not leave straightaway he would not get out of the Cotentin alive. William dressed and galloped down the peninsula, crossed the River Vire and, avoiding the main road to Bayeux, went to Ryes where the lord, Hubert of Ryes, had his sons conduct the duke to Falaise, avoiding the towns on the way. In the meantime Hubert himself led the duke's pursuers on a wild goose chase. As Ryes is a few miles north-east of Bayeux and as he chose to take refuge at Falaise, it would seem from this episode that William could still count on the support of at least some of the lords of Lower Normandy. Roger of Montgommery must surely have been among them.

With the rebellion now out in the open, the counties of the Bessin and Cotentin appear to have been lost to the duke. This is certainly suggested by the names of the known rebels. Further, Bishop Hugh of Avranches and the count of Avranches are conspicuous by their absence, and the fact that the count, William Werlenc, was, in the 1050s, to be deprived of the western half of his county and then exiled from Normandy altogether might also indicate that he had not wholeheartedly supported the duke at this time of crisis. Smaller fish, such as Hubert of Ryes and Ralph Taisson, who were surrounded by enemies, would not have been able to support the duke openly. But even though much of Lower Normandy was against him, William still had support. The lords of Upper Normandy rallied to his cause, although the loyalty of the citizens of Rouen seems to have been in doubt for a time, as did King Henry of the French, who led an army into Normandy to help him – a *volte face* perhaps explained by the king's concerns about Anjou and Burgundy.[11]

The French assembled their army at Valmeray just off the road from Caen to Saint-Pierre-sur-Dives and about mid-way between the two. The knights prayed in the church and then rode on to the battlefield, known as Val-ès-Dunes, forming up along the river bank (probably the River Muance). The duke led his forces up from Argences, three kilometres to the north of Valmeray, and followed the river until he joined with the French on the field. Wace confirms what these dispositions would lead us to think: that William had the right wing and King Henry the left, and that the army was facing west. Wace paints a terrific picture of the battle, of the knights riding up and down the lines to organize their troops, of the standards flying in the wind and the brightly painted shields, of sunlight glancing off helmets. He describes the battlecries – the 'God help' of the duke's men and the 'Holy Saviour' of Nigel of the Cotentin's unit – and the thunder of the hoofs as the two lines rushed towards each other. Nigel's knights attacked the French. They charged in tight formation with couched lances and, when these broke, fought sword-to-sword. King Henry was knocked from his horse, although his coat of chain mail saved him from injury; Wace shows us the struggle as the rebel Normans attempted to pull him off while his French knights tried to hold him on. The duke's men pushed forward, with William at their head. The rebel line collapsed. Ranulf the *vicomte* and others fled the field, escaping west, past Fontenay-le-Marmion and Fleury-sur-Orne, crossing the Orne as best they could. Many were caught in the attempt and were cut down where they stood. So many were killed or drowned, Wace tells us, that the water mills at Borbeillon were brought to a standstill.

The rebels suffered a variety of different fates, which do not necessarily reflect their part in the revolt. By the end of the battle, Haimo 'the Toothy' had been killed, although he had fought so valiantly that he was given a splendid funeral by his erstwhile enemies. Nigel of the Cotentin fled to Brittany,

3. The earthworks of Grimoult of Le Plessis-Grimoult's castle.

although he had managed to recover some of his estates, if not his position, by 1054. Grimoult of Le Plessis-Grimoult, who is said to have been the man who had intended the duke's death at Valognes, forfeited his estates and was imprisoned in fetters at Rouen. He remained there in chains until his death 30 years later. Ranulf, *vicomte* of the Bessin, perhaps because he had just reason to rebel, apparently escaped unpunished, and he and his family continued in office for decades to come. Count Guy, the leader and instigator of the revolt, retreated to his castle at Brionne – on an island in the river, and not on the hill where the later ruins stand today – where he was besieged for another three years until he surrendered. He was then permitted to leave Normandy and return to Burgundy. Poitiers, as is his wont, makes much of the duke's merciful treatment of his enemy.[12]

The battle of Val-ès-Dunes was a momentous event for the young Duke William. William of Jumièges declares, a little optimistically, that after William's victory all the other nobles of Normandy 'gave hostages and bent their stiff necks to him as their lord. And thus after the fortresses had been destroyed everywhere no rebel dared to rise against him anymore.' William of Poitiers, whose work perhaps owes something to that of William of Jumièges here, also celebrates the duke's triumph:

> All the conquered Normans submitted at once to their lord. And many gave hostages. Next they hastened at his command to destroy utterly all the new fortifications which they had constructed in their eagerness for change. The citizens of Rouen had to abandon the insolence that they had presumptuously shown in defiance of the young count. Henceforth the Church rejoiced,

because it was possible to celebrate the divine mystery in peace; the merchant rejoiced at being able to go where he would in safety; the farmer gave thanks for being able to plough the fields and scatter seed, instead of hiding from the sight of soldiers. Men of every condition and order praised the duke to the skies, and wished him long life and health with all their hearts.

Such then was Normandy after Val-ès-Dunes. William's reign and life were beginning a new chapter. He was now about 20 years old.

†

CHAPTER 2

THE UNDEFEATED DUKE, 1047–66

After Val-ès-Dunes, the very fact of his victory meant that William was more secure than ever. But Val-ès-Dunes did not usher in a period of peace; it did not allow William to reign untroubled. There was still a great deal that he would have to do before his position was truly secure. The events of 1047–66 thus saw William fighting off invasions and rebellions from one side of Normandy to the other, not continuously, but at regular intervals until 1060. But the period also saw a change. After 1060 William was crossing the frontiers of Normandy and campaigning in Maine and Brittany; fighting his enemies on their soil, not his. These 20 years were consequently a time of vigorous renewal and expansion.

One man who caught the mood of the time was the Benedictine monk, William of Jumièges (c. 1000–c. 1070). He began work on his *Gesta Normannorum Ducum* (*The Deeds of the Dukes of the Normans*), celebrating William and his predecessors, in the 1050s and wrote for a decade before putting his quill down in around 1060. He returned to his work in the period 1067–70, perhaps at William's own request, to provide details of William's reign as king of the English.[1] We know nothing more of the man himself, although on one interpretation of his nickname, Calculus, he suffered from kidney or bladder stones. His work was popular and survives today in more than 50 medieval manuscripts, and it is important, too, because it provides an account of William's rule in Normandy before 1066 that was contemporaneous with the events it describes. And the very fact that he thought that there was reason to celebrate the line of Norman dukes reveals that William and Normandy were no longer on the back foot, and that contemporaries felt a new sense of optimism.

13

William's first move following his victory at Val-ès-Dunes was to build up relations with the counties of Flanders and Ponthieu, which lay to the east of Normandy. Shortly after the battle, William's sister, Adelaide, married Count Enguerrand of Ponthieu, bringing that small neighbouring county into his orbit. But William's determination to secure peace with his eastern neighbours is best seen in his own choice of spouse. According to William of Jumièges,

> now that the duke, flourishing in the strength of his youth, was past the age of adolescence, his magnates urgently drew his attention to the problem of his offspring and succession. When he heard that Baldwin of Flanders had a daughter called Matilda, a very beautiful and noble girl of royal stock, he took counsel and sent envoys to ask her father for her hand.

The marriage was highly advantageous. The counts of Flanders proved time and again to be dangerous enemies, before, during and after William's reign. Neutralizing this threat through marriage, at least until the death of his brother-in-law in 1070, was no mean feat. And the fact that it took place at all tells us that Count Baldwin V believed that William was now secure in his duchy, for he would surely not have allowed the marriage to go ahead if he had not been certain of the duke's prospects.

The marriage, however, was not made without a hitch. Both William of Jumièges and William of Poitiers hide the controversy, although Jumièges was concerned enough about it to state categorically that the marriage was made 'lawfully'. The details are only provided by the twelfth-century historians. The problem was that William and Matilda were related.[2] In the eleventh century the Church forbade marriage between anyone related to within seven degrees (sixth cousins).[3] As this applied to William and Matilda's situation, the proposed marriage was discussed at an ecclesiastical council held at Reims by Pope Leo IX in October 1049. There it was condemned. This German pope's hostility, although based on canon law, might have been made all the more implacable if he had interpreted the marriage as part of a rebellion against the German king, Henry III, that had begun in 1047 and in which Baldwin of Flanders was involved.[4]

But William had no intention of giving up on the marriage, or his alliance with Flanders, so easily, and in spite of the pope's condemnation he married Matilda at Eu, a town on the eastern border of Normandy, in late 1049 or 1050. The fact that the marriage had gone ahead put William in a stronger negotiating position *vis-à-vis* the pope's objections, but he still needed to gain a dispensation that would legitimize the marriage. In the meantime William faced opposition at home, as some Norman prelates spoke out against the union. Lanfranc, prior of the abbey of Le Bec, was accused of criticizing the match by some of William's courtiers who had an axe to grind. Archbishop Malger of Rouen might also have voiced objections. William of Malmesbury says that the archbishop was deposed in 1054, while the dispute was ongoing, because he 'had found it intolerable that two blood relations should share the same marriage bed, and had aimed the weapon of excommunication against his nephew and that nephew's consort'. But although the marriage unsettled the Church in the duchy, and threatened the legitimacy of any heir, William was unable to achieve a rapprochement until after Leo IX's death in 1054. His successor, Pope Nicholas II, was a different matter. He needed the support of the Normans in southern Italy, who were still closely connected to Normandy. He had not forbidden the marriage himself, and this, too, might have made him more flexible than his predecessor. And so, Orderic tells us, perhaps sensing that the times had changed,

> Duke William sent legates to the pope in Rome to take his counsel in this matter. The pope then wisely pointed out that if he were to order a divorce this might cause a serious war between Flanders and Normandy. Therefore absolving husband and wife of any charge he laid a penance upon them. He ordered both to found a monastery where monks and nuns should zealously pray for their salvation. Thus, putting his orders into action, they founded an abbey dedicated to the Holy Trinity as well as one dedicated to the protomartyr St Stephen at Caen.

The two churches are still there to this day, albeit subject to later rebuilding and restoration. Holy Trinity stands on a hill to the east of the town centre, and St Stephen dominates the skyline to the west. Together they are lasting memorials not only to the marriage and the power of William and his wife but also to William's desire to develop Caen as the capital of Lower Normandy – a position it still holds today.

To the south of Normandy there were a number of small, independent counties and lordships: the Dunois, the Perche, Bellême, Maine and Brittany. These formed a buffer between Normandy and its main rival to the south, Anjou. The counts of Anjou had been growing in power during the eleventh century, something which probably accounts for King Henry's willingness to assist William in 1047. By 1051 Count Geoffrey of Anjou had succeeded

in drawing into his orbit the lords of Bellême, and, either at their own voli-
tion or by coercion, they had given the count possession of the towns of
Domfront and Alençon. Of these, only Alençon had been held from the duke,
but neither could now be allowed to remain in the hands of Count Geoffrey.[5]
And so Duke William marched his army to Domfront and invested it. He
constructed a ring of four siege castles around the fortress and settled down
to starve the garrison into submission.[6]

While William was besieging Domfront, news came that Count Geoffrey
was approaching with a large army:

> When William learned of this, he hastened against him, leaving proven
> soldiers in charge of the siege. Roger of Montgommery and William fitz
> Osbern, both of them strenuous young men, were sent ahead as scouts to
> discover the arrogant intention of the enemy by talking with him. Geoffrey
> made known through them that he would rouse William at Domfront with his
> trumpet call at first light of dawn on the morrow. He announced in advance
> what horse he would ride in the battle and described his shield and clothing.
> They replied that there was no need for him to tire himself by travelling
> further, for the man he wished to fight would be on the spot immediately. In
> their turn they described the horse, clothing and arms of their lord.

William of Poitiers thus makes it clear that this battle was not to be some
sudden skirmish, and provides some interesting details about how warfare
was conducted in this period. A time and place for the fight were set. Details
of the horses and appearance of the chief protagonists were provided so that
they could be recognized on the battlefield, and would not be accidentally
killed by the enemy – this was, of course, in the days before heraldry. But
despite having gone to all this trouble, Count Geoffrey failed to attack, allowing William of Poitiers to crow about his lack of valour and how he was terrified of the Normans.

Aware that the count had left the region, William launched a surprise
attack on Alençon, acting on a tip-off that he could easily take the town if
he attacked it at that moment. He rode through the night and arrived before
the walls at dawn. William of Jumièges, who gives the earliest account, says
that William met with some resistance from the defenders of a fortification
across the River Sarthe, and reports that William was mocked by the defenders as he reconnoitred it. Orderic adds more detail, remarking that the men
who were defending the walls beat animal pelts and shouted insults, all of
which was designed to remind William that his mother's family had been

4 and 5. William's abbey
of Saint-Etienne of Caen,
showing the west front
(with later spires) and the
nave.

mere undertakers. This might seem a minor insult today, the sort of boorish posturing that could be shrugged off without any loss of face, but it was not so to William. This was a great affront to his dignity, an unforgiveable act in an age in which men were proud and boastful and quick to anger at any slight. And so when William took the fortress he had all of those who had mocked him brought before him, and then he had their hands and feet cut off 'under the eyes of all the inhabitants of Alençon'. The town was surrendered to William soon afterwards, as the citizens were afraid that a similar punishment might be visited on them if they did not yield quickly.

William of Jumièges does not raise an eyebrow at this. He does not suggest that the mutilation of these men was an act of outrageous cruelty. He might have been of the same mind as Orderic, who later put a speech into the mouth of Odo of Bayeux that tells us something about how rulers were meant to behave:

> Whoever ought to have the rule of the kingdom and the people of God, who differ greatly from one another in their conduct, needs to be both gentle and severe as occasion requires. He should be gentle as a lamb to good men and to the obedient and humble, but harsh as a lion to evil men and rebels and law-breakers.

And these men were not just rebels but also traitors. They had mocked the duke, which made them guilty of the crime of *lèse majesté*.[7] Their punishment was deserved and was the same as that inflicted in *c.* 996 on a band of rebellious peasants, while in 1075 each member of the rebel garrison of Norwich lost a foot.[8] Furthermore, it is also possible that William of Jumièges's version of the event, or William's behaviour during it, was influenced by a story found in Caesar's *Gallic War*. Caesar had besieged the town of Uxellodunum (perhaps Puy d'Issolu on the Dordogne) and, by diverting the river and thereby depriving the citizens of water, had brought about its surrender:

> Caesar knew that his leniency was universally known, and so he was not afraid that if he acted somewhat harshly he would appear to have done so out of any innate cruelty ... For this reason he decided upon making an example of the townspeople in punishing them, so as to deter the rest. He allowed them to live, therefore, but cut off the hands of all those who had carried arms against him.[9]

Caesar, then, calculated that he could afford to act harshly on occasion if it furthered his conquest and so long as he did not behave in such a manner all

6 and 7. The castle at Domfront. The keep is the work of Henry I, the walls are later. In the valley below stands the eleventh- and twelfth-century church of Notre-Dame sur l'Eau.

the time. Caesar was held up as a role model for medieval warriors and rulers, and as William, too, had a similar need 'to deter the rest', Jumièges may have seen some parallels between what happened at Uxellodunum and Alençon. In any event, there was nothing cruel or blameworthy in what William did there, according to contemporary standards, and the fact that William of Poitiers does not mention the incident need be indicative only of the fact that he wanted to downplay the resistance that William had faced. In any event, the taking of Alençon effectively brought the campaign to an end. When William returned to Domfront, the burgesses swiftly surrendered, either because rumours of William's harshness had reached them or because the departure of Count Geoffrey left them without an ally.

Almost as soon as William had taken Alençon and Domfront, an unexpected rebellion broke out in Talou (see Map 1). Count William of Arques had been closely allied with his nephew in the years up to 1052. We know nothing about their relationship, other than that Duke William apparently trusted him – otherwise he would not have given him the county of Talou. William of Poitiers claims that the count had borne a grudge against the duke for years, which seems highly unlikely, given that he had staunchly supported him throughout his minority. Poitiers also highlights his overbearing arrogance, and here he may well have a point. In his acts, Count William liked to style himself 'William, count by the grace of God, son of Richard II duke of the Normans', which smacks of pretension and self-importance. He also appears in some diplomas to be acting alongside William, rather than allowing William to take precedence, as was his right as duke.[10]

Count William, then, was a little over-mighty. He was a man with a high opinion of himself. And this is probably why he rebelled. In 1051–52 the count had gone to the southern border of the duchy to help the duke besiege Domfront. William of Poitiers says that during the siege the count slipped away from William's army without asking permission and threw off his loyalty to the duke, refusing to remain his vassal any longer:

> On account of this and his countless bold enterprises the duke, warned by the event and suspecting that he would attempt even more greater outrages, seized the fortifications of the lofty refuge where he thought himself most secure [the castle at Arques], and put in a guard, but in no other way diminished his right … But not long afterwards the faithless guards, worn down by countless pleas of all kinds, surrendered the powerful castle to its founder for the promise of rewards. Straightaway on his return his fury,

growing fiercer than ever, drove him to exact vengeance as though he had suffered injuries and loss of property. It caused great wretchedness in the province and all around. Disturbances, pillage and rapine, rage unchecked, threatening devastation. The castle is equipped with arms, men, provisions, and everything necessary for such an enterprise; the ramparts, already strong, are made still stronger. No place remains for peace and rest. In brief, a most dire rebellion is prepared.

Orderic suggests that Count William rebelled on account of William's illegitimate birth, but this is Orderic's stock explanation for rebellion against the duke and can be discounted. It is more likely that, while he was before Domfront, Count William had seen at first hand that there was no longer a place for him in the duke's inner circle. Roger of Montgommery and William fitz Osbern, men of an age with the duke, had already risen to prominence. Count William, like Count Guy before him, was now excluded. And more importantly, others could see that Count William was excluded. This was probably enough in itself to drive William to rebellion. But worse still, the count's authority in the east of Normandy was being undermined by Duke William's dealings with Flanders and Ponthieu. The count had manufactured his own alliance with Ponthieu by marriage to one of Count Enguerrand's sisters, and he may now have seen that relationship brought to nothing, and his own authority in the region retreating before that of his nephew. And so Count William rebelled.

When news of the rebellion reached the duke, he set out from the Cotentin for Arques, riding with such speed that all but six of the horses of his companions dropped from exhaustion.

News of the rebellion had also reached Rouen and a force of 300 men was dispatched to see if they could intercept supplies being delivered to the castle. They soon learned, however, that large forces were assembled there, and so the leaders held back, chiefly because they did not trust their own men not to join the rebels. They may have had good reason to worry, as it was rumoured that most of the region had defected to William of Arques. Duke William did not trouble himself with this hearsay, however, and rode directly to the castle, where he launched an impromptu and near single-handed attack on Count William, whom he had spotted on a hill outside the fortress. But the count managed to escape into the castle, forcing Duke William to besiege him. He built a siege castle at the bottom of the hill, garrisoned it, and then left, confident that his lieutenants would be able to bring matters to a satisfactory

8. The castle at Arques. The towers are twelfth century and later, but the impressive ditches and some of the wall date from the eleventh century.

conclusion in his absence.

What the duke did not know, however, was that King Henry I of France had decided to support Count William, and had set out for Arques with a royal army. This was the first sign that relations between King Henry and Duke William had broken down. Within a year of Val-ès-Dunes William had attended a great council held at Senlis by King Henry, and soon afterwards had marched with the king against Count Geoffrey of Anjou, assisting him in the siege of the castle at Mouliherne. Although they would not have realized it at the time, this was the last occasion that the duke and King Henry were to work together. From 1052 onwards William and the king were at loggerheads. Why did this happen? Part of Henry's change of policy must have been due to William's growing power, which would have caused the king to view Normandy as a greater threat than Anjou. Two developments in particular may have led King Henry to reach this conclusion. First, William had defeated Count Geoffrey at Domfront and Alençon, and, secondly, he had married Matilda. Both of these events might have caused Henry to conclude that the duke of the Normans needed to have his wings clipped.

Things did not go well for the king, however – something that was to become a tendency in his dealings with Duke William. First, part of his army was tricked and ambushed by a Norman force before it even arrived at Arques. Count Enguerrand of Ponthieu, allied through marriage to both Duke William and William of Arques, died in this skirmish. King Henry, with the remainder of his army, did at least reach Arques, and once there he launched an unsuccessful attack on the siege castle. He also resupplied Count William and his men. And having achieved no more than this, Henry left – 'shamefully retreated' is how William of Jumièges puts it – having learned that Duke William was approaching, and being reluctant to give battle. The duke then invested Arques for a second time and starved Count William into surrender.

> What a sad spectacle! What a wretched end! French knights, famous such a little while before, come out with the Normans as fast as their failing strength permits, hanging their heads as much from shame as from starvation; some clinging to starved mounts, whose hooves hardly ring out or stir the dust; some wearing greaves and spurs, advancing in strange company, most of them carrying their horse's saddle on their bowed and weary backs, some staggering and barely keeping upright.

Thus William of Poitiers crows over the defeat of William of Arques.[11]

Count William gave up his castle, left Normandy as an exile, and spent the remainder of his days at the court of the count of Boulogne, from whom he received food and clothing. The proud Count William must have found his reliance on this charity utterly humiliating. He was not replaced. Instead, Duke William retained the castle at Arques in his own hands, and appointed a *vicomte* to administer the county for him.[12]

Embarrassed by his failure to relieve Arques, and perhaps increasingly wary of the power that Duke William wielded, King Henry returned to Normandy early in 1054 in concert with his new ally, Count Geoffrey of Anjou. The king led a force past Evreux and then north towards Rouen. William of Jumièges says that the Normans met part of the French force around Mortemer, even as they were 'totally preoccupied with arson and rape of women'. Wace, who does not entirely disagree with this account, says that the Normans came up to Mortemer at dawn and set fire to the village as the French knights were sleeping after a night of drinking and rapine. The French armed themselves as best they could and tried to flee the flames, but their escape routes were blocked by Norman knights. The battle, if such it could be called, lasted from dawn to noon and resulted in the defeat of the French. It was a defeat that the Normans took great pleasure in announcing to the king and his army. Ralph of Tosny stood on a hill overlooking the French camp and, it may be supposed, dramatically silhouetted against the skyline, shouted in a loud voice:

> My name is Ralph of Tosny and I bring you dreadful news. Take your chariots and carriages to Mortemer to collect the bodies of your friends. The French came up against us to try out the Norman army, and they found it much stronger than they had expected. Their standard bearer, Odo, shamefully took flight, and Count Guy of Ponthieu was captured. All others were taken prisoner or were slain, and those who fled swiftly could escape only with difficulty. On behalf of the duke of the Normans, convey this news to the king of the French.

Once the news was duly conveyed to him, King Henry led his army out of Normandy and concluded what was to be a short-lived peace with the duke. Count Guy of Ponthieu was kept in prison for two years before being released. His power was now suborned to that of the Norman duke, so that when Harold Godwinson was forced to land in Ponthieu and was captured by Guy in 1064 or 1065, William was able to demand that he should be released into his custody.

What of Henry's ally, Count Geoffrey? After William had defeated the French at the battle of Mortemer, he turned his attention to the count. He led an army into the county of Maine, which lay to the south of the western half of Normandy and was at that time under Angevin control, and built a castle at Ambrières. This was a deliberate provocation, as well as an aggressive move, and something that Geoffrey could not ignore. He therefore attempted to take the castle. Something of the nature of what was entailed when an earth-and-timber castle like that at Ambrières was attacked is supplied by *The Deeds of Louis the Fat*, written by Abbot Suger of the French abbey of Saint-Denis, just outside Paris, in the middle of the twelfth century. He describes the attack on the castle at Le Puiset as follows:

> What a sight to behold! Arrows were raining down, sparks of fire were flashing from countless blows atop gleaming helmets, and shields were being pierced and broken with amazing speed. The enemy were pushed back through the gate into the castle; but once inside they hurled down from the ramparts and the palisade a surprising volley of missiles on our men, which even the boldest among them found almost unbearable. By dismantling roof timbers and throwing down the beams, the enemy began driving our men

back, but they did not succeed, for the royal forces called upon their own valiant strength of body and spirit and fought bitterly against their foes. When their shields had been broken, they crouched behind shingles [wooden tiles] from the roof, doors, and anything made of wood, and pushed against the gate. We had also loaded wagons with great piles of dry wood, greased with fat and lard, which would make them burst quickly into flames ... A brave band of our men, taking cover behind these great heaps of wood, set the wagons up against the gate. They planned to turn them into a fire that no one could extinguish. While our side took risks struggling to set the wagons on fire, and theirs to put them out, Count Theobald led a great host of knights and foot soldiers in an attack against the castle from a different side; namely the one facing Chartres. Mindful of the wrongs he had suffered, the count hurried into battle, encouraging his men to climb up the steep slope of the embankment. But he lost heart when they fell back down again with even greater haste; to be precise, they tumbled down in a heap ... He did his best to find out whether they had breathed their last under the shower of rocks falling upon them. The knights who were defending and circling the castle on swift horses came unexpectedly upon the men clinging to the palisade with their hands and cut them down. They slaughtered them and sent them to the ground with thuds; from the top of the wall to the very bottom of the ditch.[13]

The fighting, then, was desperate, *ad hoc* and at times, with the troops slipping down the ramparts, farcical. The attack on Ambrières was not much different. Wace reports that the Norman defenders of the castle taunted the Angevin troops who were attacking them, even going so far as to demolish a section of their own palisade in order to tempt the Angevins to attack. But although the Normans were ready for a fight, the Angevins were not. Count Geoffrey withdrew.

In 1057 King Henry and Count Geoffrey made war once again on Duke William. They advanced together from the south, through the county of the Hiémois, past Exmes and Saint-Pierre-sur-Dives, and then turned northwest, heading for Bayeux. From there, and apparently without even attempting to take the city, they turned east for Caen where they crossed the Orne. It is only now that we hear of any damage being done. The armies of the king and count laid waste the Pays d'Auge and the Lieuvin, perhaps with the intention of forcing William to do battle. In any event, the duke caught up with them at the River Dives, near the coast at Varaville, just as the French army was crossing the river. According to Wace, the duke attacked the tail of the army, pushing it back along the causeway that crossed the estuary and eventually onto a bridge, which collapsed under the weight. Neither William of Poitiers nor William of Jumièges talk of a bridge, however. They mention only a ford, although the effect is likely to have been the same. Pushed up against the river bank, the French had nowhere to go. Many were killed, some drowned and others were taken prisoner. And all the while the king and the remainder of his army, who had already crossed the river, looked on impotently.

After this disaster, King Henry and Count Geoffrey left Normandy, never to return. They died within a few months of each other in 1060. But before then, Count Geoffrey remained a potential ally to anyone coming under the duke's sway and who, like the rebels of 1047, resented the loss of their accustomed liberty. One such was Robert fitz Giroie. He was lord of Saint-Cénéri-le-Gérie, located in a border area which was not yet firmly part of Normandy. Duke William gave him a kinswoman as a wife, but this failed to win his loyalty. Indeed, aware that his independence was threatened, and concerned, too, by the growing power of his neighbour, and Duke William's friend, Roger of Montgommery, Robert rebelled and called on the count of the Angevins for aid. After Robert's death – Orderic says he died after eating poisoned apples – his nephew, Arnold of Echauffour, took up the baton of resistance. But unlike his uncle, Arnold held lands in Normandy and could thus be coerced to make peace. But this was not the end of the matter. Although all seemed to be well for a time, Roger of Montgommery and his wife, Mabel of Bellême, 'flattered the duke into taking their part and cunningly incited him to anger against their neighbours',[14] so that Arnold of Echauffour was exiled from the duchy. Orderic says that he was later murdered on Mabel's orders. He certainly died before he could recover his lands. On his death they passed not to his heirs but to Roger of Montgommery. It was by methods such as these that Roger, with the duke's connivance, extended his power on the southern frontier of the duchy.

The victory at Varaville, and the deaths of King Henry and Count Geoffrey, were real landmarks in William's reign. He had quelled internal rebellions and fought off external enemies. He had suborned the Normans to his rule, and his enemies were dead. France was ruled now by King Philip, who was a child of just eight years old and in no position to threaten Normandy, while in Anjou, Count Geoffrey was succeeded by Geoffrey the Bearded, whose rule was challenged by his brother, Fulk, for eight years until Geoffrey was deposed. All of this meant that when Count Herbert of Maine died in 1062, Duke William was able to seize the opportunity to expand his

9. The walls of le Mans, a mix of Roman, Merovingian and later work.

dominions without having to watch his back.

William of Poitiers explains that William's invasion of Maine was entirely in accordance with the laws of justice. Count Herbert, he says, had done homage to Duke William for the county because he had feared Count Geoffrey of Anjou and wanted a protector. He had also made William his heir should he die without offspring of his own. Whether or not this is true, the Manceaux had no intention of submitting to William, and instead offered the county to Count Walter of Mantes. William's response was to invade Maine, ravage the countryside and capture castles, so as to terrify the people into surrender and gain possession of the land. The city of Le Mans was left until the very end of the campaign. William saw that it would take a great deal of effort to capture it and that his energies could be better spent elsewhere. And so he gradually isolated the city until, when the expected help from Anjou failed to materialize, it surrendered.

Even then, Geoffrey of Mayenne, one of the rebel leaders, continued to hold out against the duke. He fled from Le Mans to his castle of Mayenne and fortified it against the Normans. William, unable to tolerate such defiance, came to the castle and attacked it. William of Poitiers reports:

> On one side this castle, which is washed by a swift and rocky river (for it
> is situated on a high rock jutting out above the river Mayenne), cannot be
> stormed by either force or cunning or any human device. On the other side,
> stone fortifications and an extremely difficult approach protect it. However, a
> siege is begun, our army is brought up as far as the difficulties of the approach
> permit, while all marvel at the confidence of the duke in the face of such a
> formidable enterprise. Almost all think that such great forces of mounted
> and foot will be worn out in vain; many complain; no hope rises in their
> breasts, except that, perhaps, in a year or more, the defenders may be starved
> into capitulation. Indeed with swords, lances, and missiles nothing can be
> done; there is no hope of achieving anything. Similarly, there is no place for
> the ram, the ballista or other instruments of war; for the site is completely
> unsuitable for siege engines.

Although the fortress was surrounded by a stone curtain wall which made
it unusually strong – most castles were still of timber in this period – the
buildings inside the wall were built of wood. So the duke, who remained
uninfected by the pessimism of his troops, ordered his archers to lob flaming
arrows over the wall, and the castle was set on fire. As the Normans stormed
in, taking all the booty that had been abandoned, the garrison fled to the
citadel. The castle was surrendered the next day.

William intended to legitimize his rule in Maine by marrying Herbert's
sister, Margaret, to his eldest son, Robert. The marriage could not go ahead
immediately, however, because both were too young. Margaret was thus
'guarded with honour in safe places' until the marriage could be celebrated.
Unfortunately, however, Margaret died before it could take place. Nonetheless, Robert retained his central role, as he had done homage to Count Geoffrey for Maine at Alençon shortly after the conquest had been achieved. This
is indicative of the fact that, although William had been made to fight for his
inheritance, once he had obtained it, he intended to rule within existing lines.
All the eleventh-century counts of Maine had done homage to the Count of
Anjou, and that is why Robert Curthose, the new count, had done homage
to him, too. The Manceaux lords, even Geoffrey of Mayenne, retained their
estates. There was no purge, and no influx of Normans. William merely
placed a garrison at Le Mans and strengthened the defences of the castle
there. And just as he would do in England after the Conquest, he allowed the
bishop of Le Mans to remain in his post until his death in 1065. Only then
did William ensure that a man of his own choosing, Arnold of Avranches,
was elected to the bishopric; and as Arnold was also a member of the clergy

serving the cathedral, he was acceptable to all parties.

Around this same time there was some fitful fighting in the Vexin, caused not by the machinations of King Henry but simply by the competition for power of rival lords. Orderic tells us, in particular, about the area around Neufmarché, as one of his abbey's dependent priories was established there. And so we know that the duke expelled Geoffrey, 'the natural heir of the castle of Neufmarché', from the castle and gave it instead to a succession of lords who could scarcely defend the castle year-on-year against the attacks of the men of Milli and Gerberoy and other frontier towns. Eventually Duke William gave custody of the castle to Hugh of Grandmesnil. He is described as 'a man of outstanding bravery and courtesy', perhaps because he was one of the founders of Orderic's own abbey. Within a year he had succeeded in capturing the two leading lords of the Beauvaisis, thereby pacifying the surrounding region.

Hugh of Grandmesnil did not always have things his own way, however, and nor did the men who fought under him. On one occasion he engaged Count Ralph of Mantes in battle, despite his inferior numbers, and was put to flight. In the course of the retreat, one of Hugh's knights, Richard of Heudicourt, was badly injured. Orderic tells us:

> It happened that when he was urging his horse through the ford of the river Epte in his mad flight he received a serious wound in the back from the lance of one of his pursuers. His comrades carried him at once to Neufmarché; and as he lay in fear of death he took the advice of Hugh, in whose household he had served as a knight, and determined from that time forward to fight under the monastic rule by the practice of virtue. Accordingly he sent for monks from Saint-Evroult and submitted himself to the government of Abbot Osbern. Afterwards ... Richard made a partial recovery and lived for nearly seven years as a zealous monk, doing much good for the church ... He himself, though his wound never healed properly and every day, as those who saw it relate, discharged as much matter as would fill a goose's egg, strove to follow the daily routine of the cloister and carry out speedily all the duties which befitted his standing in the community.

Count Ralph subsequently performed a 'U' turn and allied himself with Duke William, probably after he had succeeded to the county of the Vexin in 1063 or 1064. Ralph's friendship was perhaps cemented by a life-grant of the important border fortress at Gisors, although Ralph also handed over his son Simon into William's custody. Effectively a hostage, he was brought up in

William's household and the two men seem to have developed a close friend-ship.[15] By 1066, therefore, by a combination of military successes and the vagaries of inheritance, the eastern border of Normandy was at peace.

In 1064 trouble flared up in the west, an area that had remained quiet up to that point. In the preceding years William had attempted to build a network of alliances with the Bretons who lay across this frontier. Breton lords such as Maino of Fougères and Ruallon of Dol were given small estates within Normandy. The grant of these estates provides, as David Bates puts it, 'a splendid example of the extension of influence through the attraction of men's loyalty',[16] but it was not enough to pacify the Bretons completely. In 1064 or 1065 Conan fitz Alan threatened to raid across Normandy's western frontier and then attacked William's ally, Ruallon of Dol. This brought Duke William to Brittany. Taking his army past Mont-Saint-Michel, he attacked the castles at Dol, Rennes and Dinan and drove Conan out. Down but not out, Conan sought the help of Count Geoffrey of Anjou. A combined force marched against William. Poitiers explains that although William awaited his enemies in Brittany, supplying his troops at his own expense, they failed to meet him. This gave William a psychological victory, which, in the world of mind-games that was eleventh-century politics, was almost as important as a real one.

At the same time as William was fending off these threats from his neigh-bours and kinsmen, he was consolidating his authority within Normandy by establishing trusted supporters and close friends in key areas. William fitz Osbern was given a new castle at Breteuil in the mid-1050s, and he developed the town there and founded an abbey nearby at Lyre. Roger of Montgom-mery married the heiress of the lordship of Bellême in *c.* 1050 and so brought that region, which previously looked to the count of Anjou, into Normandy's orbit.[17] As has been noted, potential rivals such as the Giroie family were crushed – by fair means or foul. After 1071 Roger ruled Bellême himself in right of his wife. In the west, the count of Avranches, who had been nota-bly absent from William's side at Val-ès-Dunes, was exiled from Normandy. He was replaced by William's own half-brother who, by 1063 at the very latest, became Count Robert of Mortain.[18] The only near-contemporary comment on his personality comes from the pen of William of Malmesbury, who would not have known the count himself. He says simply that Count Robert was 'dense and slow-witted', which seems a little unlikely given his prominence in the duke's counsels. From 1048 the bishop of Coutances was

Geoffrey of Montbray. He constructed the cathedral, founded a school and became a lynchpin of William's rule in the Cotentin.[19] These men were key to William's power in Normandy. They and a few others formed a clique around him and were to give him unfailing service. They watched over the regions of Normandy for the duke and ensured that his will was obeyed in places where he was seldom present in person.

William was now firmly established in his duchy. His rule embraced the whole of Normandy. He was, as the monks of Marmoutier put it, 'ruler of his whole land, something which is scarcely found anywhere else'.[20] But he had not just extinguished internal rebellions; he had neutralized his enemies outside Normandy. The king of France was a minor, the counts of Anjou were bested, Brittany was subdued. And with Normandy secure, William could cast his gaze across the Channel to England, where his kinsman, Edward, was king, and to whose throne William now considered himself heir.

CHAPTER 3

WILLIAM THE CONQUEROR, 1066

D uke William of the Normans is best known to history for his victory at the battle of Hastings and his subsequent conquest of England. According to Sellar and Yeatman, authors of *1066 and All That*, 1066 is one of only two dates in English history (the other is 55 BC). It looms so large in the national consciousness that the inscription that was carved into the white stone memorial in the British cemetery at Bayeux, where the men who died during the D-Day landings of 1944 are buried, reads (in translation): 'We, conquered by William, have liberated the Conqueror's land.'

The origins of the Norman Conquest can be traced back beyond 1066, at least to 1016. In that year the English were defeated by a Danish army at Assandun, a place probably to be identified today as either Ashingdon or Ashdon, both in Essex. The Danish leader, Cnut, soon to become king of the Danes, reached an agreement with the reigning English king, Edmund Ironside, the son of Æthelred II the Unready, by which the country was divided between them. When Edmund died just a month later, Cnut was recognized as sole king by a council of the English leaders. The same Englishmen who declared Cnut to be the lawful king concluded that Æthelred's other sons had no claim to the throne.

Two of those sons, Edward and Alfred (who was to die in England in 1036), consequently spent the next decades in Normandy, under the protection of their uncle, Duke Richard II, and his successors. Their sister, Godgifu, went with them and was married to Count Drogo of the Vexin, probably in 1024. By permitting this marriage to go ahead, Edward and his brother repaid their host for his hospitality as it led to grants of land and privileges to the Norman abbeys of Saint-Ouen, Jumièges and Saint-Wandrille. This patronage, in turn, brought Edward to the attention of Norman monks such as his future bishop of London and archbishop of Canterbury, Robert Champart. It might also have encouraged Abbot John of Fécamp to seek gifts for his own house from Edward and, as these gifts would be all the greater if Edward were to gain the English throne, the same abbot might have come up with an idea of promoting Edward as a future king of the English who also had the ability to heal the sick — the *Life of King Edward* suggests that he had gained a reputation for such healing during his time in Normandy, and as only the rightful ruler would have had such a power it might have strengthened his cause. Such help from Abbot John would certainly explain why Edward was so generous to Fécamp after he became king.[1] And it does seem to have been the case that Edward was treated in Normandy as a king-in-waiting. Indeed in 1033 Duke Robert sponsored an expedition to set Edward on the English throne. In the event, this was blown off course and ended up landing in the west of Normandy, but it was an attempt, nonetheless, and it left its mark not only in the pages of William of Jumièges's *Deeds of the Dukes of the Normans* but also in a series of diplomas, all of which date from 1033, and two of which describe Edward as king of the English.[2]

It seems certain that by the time Edward returned to England in 1041, after 25 years in Normandy and France, he had acquired French habits. He even had a French chef, Thierry, at Winchester. He had definitely made Norman friends, and he took some of these men to England with him. The *Life of King Edward* says that,

> when King Edward of holy memory returned from Francia, quite a number of men of that nation, and they not base born, accompanied him. And these, since he was master of the whole kingdom, he kept with him, enriched them with many honours, and made them his privy counsellors and administrators of the royal palace.

Among these men were Robert Champart, abbot of Jumièges, who was made bishop of London and then, in 1051, archbishop of Canterbury; Robert fitz Wimarc, who was given Clavering (Hertfordshire), and was to survive the Conquest; and Richard fitz Scrob, who gave his name to Richard's Castle in Herefordshire. It is only to be expected that Edward has consequently been imagined as a Frenchman by modern historians, seldom to be seen without the Norman friends that he brought to England with him. As Chris Lewis has so marvellously put it:[3]

the image is redolent of the 1940s: a beret-wearing Edward and his confrère fitz Wimarc idly passing their days in the pavement cafés of Winchester over Gauloises and existential conversation, waiting for the curé Robert to pass by after Mass and join them in an absinthe.

But Edward did not have a policy of favouring Normans over the English. There was no attempt to 'Normanize' the administration. There was simply a Norman element at a cosmopolitan court, which attracted and rewarded men from the continent. Among them was Giso, a Lotharingian, who became bishop of Wells, and Ralph the Staller, who was a Breton. The French in England before the Conquest – and there were many – did not form some kind of fifth column preparing the ground for a Norman takeover.

Did Edward even intend a Norman takeover? According to William of Poitiers, King Edward, with the consent of his Witan, promised William that he should succeed him as king of the English. The story is found only in continental sources, all of them written after the battle of Hastings. Some modern historians, in particular Pauline Stafford, consequently doubt that the promise was ever made.[4] The state of the evidence is such that no conclusive answer will ever be reached, but the very fact that William risked all by invading England in 1066 suggests that he believed, indeed was certain, that he had been promised the throne at some point during Edward's reign.

The problem, however, was that while William and the Normans might have seen the promise as binding, Edward almost certainly did not. It was not binding because William was not put in possession of England before Edward's death. There was no coronation during Edward's lifetime. All that happened, according to the poem known as the *Song of the Battle of Hastings*, written by Bishop Guy of Amiens in 1067–68, was that William was given a ring and a sword as symbols of his right to succeed. This was not enough, and so Edward the Confessor was not bound by his promise. He clearly felt no compulsion to keep his word, as he seems to have made promises of the succession to others. King Swein of Denmark told the German chronicler Adam of Bremen, writing in the 1070s, that Edward had promised *him* the throne. Edward the Exile, a son of Edmund Ironside, had been recalled from Hungary by the Confessor in *c.* 1054, although he arrived in England only in 1057. The king's purpose was, it may be supposed, to appoint *him* as his successor, but as the Exile died in mysterious circumstances before he had seen the king, Edward's intentions will never be known. And at the very end of his life, even as he lay on his deathbed, Edward nominated Harold

Godwinson as his successor. To the English, or so William of Poitiers has it, a deathbed bequest was sacred.[5] It trumped the earlier, inchoate promise to William, and it was enough to ensure that Harold became king in January 1066.

Who was this Harold Godwinson?[6] He was the second son of Earl Godwin of Wessex, who rose high in the service of King Cnut. Godwin continued to serve the king's son, Harold Harefoot, after Cnut's death in 1035, blinding Æthelred's younger son, Alfred, when he came to England to claim the throne in 1036 – and doing it so badly that Alfred died. This was an unfortunate episode that would come back to haunt Harold Godwinson in 1066. In 1042 Godwin's support was important in securing the throne for Edward, and he was soon rewarded with grants of earldoms for two of his sons, Swein and Harold, the latter being given the earldom of East Anglia. In January 1045 the ascendancy of Godwin's family seemed to have been secured when Edward married Godwin's daughter Edith. But soon afterwards the relationship between Edward and his wife's family grew uneasy. Around the end of August 1051 there was an affray at Dover in which some men of Count Eustace of Boulogne were killed. Edward commanded Godwin to punish the men of Kent and Dover for this outrage. The earl refused and was consequently summoned to court at Gloucester at the beginning of September to answer for his contumacy. There was an armed stand-off, and the court was adjourned to London later in the same month so as to give tempers a chance to cool. In the meantime Godwin's support dissolved, and he and his children fled; Godwin, his wife, and three of his sons, including Tostig, fled to Flanders, while Harold and his brother Leofwine fled to Ireland. They returned in the summer of 1052. Godwin and Harold were reunited and then collected a fleet from the Kentish ports and sailed up the Thames to London. While the boats lay off the south bank of the river, an army of Godwin's supporters camped on the north shore. Faced by this threat, the king was forced to negotiate with his enemies, and Edward and Godwin were soon reconciled at Westminster. The Norman archbishop of Canterbury, Robert Champart, whose appointment had contributed to the bad feeling between the king and earl, fled and was deposed. He was replaced by Stigand, who continued to hold the bishopric of Winchester with his new archdiocese.

Godwin died on 15 April 1053 after suffering what appears to have been a stroke. Harold succeeded to his earldom of Wessex almost immediately. We have a description of Harold provided by the author of the *Life of King Edward*, who was writing for Harold's sister, Edith, and who would have known the earl at first-hand:

> Both [Harold and Tostig] had the advantage of distinctly handsome and graceful persons, similar in strength as we gather; and both were equally brave. But the elder, Harold, was the taller, well-practised in endless fatigues and doing without sleep and food, and endowed with mildness of temper and a more ready understanding. He could bear contradiction well ... The senior brother studied the character, policy and strength of the princes of Gaul, not only through his own servants but also personally; and adroitly and with natural cunning and at great length observed most intently what he could get from them if he needed them in the management of any business. And he acquired such an exhaustive knowledge of them by this scheme that he could not be deceived by any of their proposals.

These words were written before Harold's defeat in 1066, but even then we may doubt that Harold was able to read William of Normandy quite as well as the anonymous author of the *Life of King Edward* suggests.

Such doubts arise because when Harold visited Normandy in 1064 or 1065 he seems to have been manipulated into promising to support William's claim to the English throne. His reasons for going to Normandy have been a source of some debate. The *Anglo-Saxon Chronicle* omits all mention of his visit. Eadmer of Canterbury, writing at the beginning of the twelfth century, whose story is perhaps the most plausible, says that Harold went to the duchy to negotiate the release of the English hostages – Wulfnoth, his brother, or Hakon, his nephew – who had been given to Edward as hostages for his father's good behaviour in 1052. Edward, it seems, had later placed them in William's custody, presumably to have them kept more securely. William of Poitiers says that the hostages had been handed over as security for William's succession as king, and that Harold was sent to Normandy to confirm Edward's promise to William. But it is possible that Harold was not intending to visit Normandy at all. He may have been heading for Flanders – his brother Tostig was married to the count's daughter and he had already visited the count's court at Saint-Omer in 1056 – and was blown off course. Any of these stories could be reflected in the Bayeux Tapestry.

In any event, Harold was forced to land in the county of Ponthieu, and it was Duke William who extracted him from Count Guy's clutches. This is Eadmer's report:

10. Detail of the Bayeux Tapestry (eleventh century). Harold (with
the moustache) is captured by the men of Count Guy of Ponthieu.

But soon the sea grew stormy and those on board were terrified, as the ship
was tossed by the violence of the towering waves. At last she was driven with
all that she had on board into a river of Ponthieu which is called Maye. There,
in accordance with the local custom, she was adjudged captive by the lord of
the land and the men on board were put under strict arrest.

So Harold was held a prisoner. But he managed to bribe one of the common
people with a promise of reward and sent him secretly to the duke of
Normandy to report what had happened to him. The duke thereupon
promptly sent messengers to the lord of Ponthieu and told him that, if he
wished to have his friendship for the future as he had had it in the past, Harold
and his men must be sent to him as quickly as possible and that free of any
charge against them.

After Harold had been delivered to William, he explained to the duke why he
had come to Normandy. William indicated that he was not averse to the idea
of releasing the hostages, but made it clear that there was a price to be paid:

He said that King Edward, when years before he was detained with him in
Normandy … had promised him … that if he, Edward, should ever be king
of England, he would make over to William the right to succeed him on the
throne as his heir. William went on to say this: 'If you on your side undertake

to support me in this project and further promise that you will make me a stronghold at Dover with a well of water for my use and that you will at a time agreed between us send your sister to me that I may give her in marriage to one of my nobles and that you will take my daughter to be your wife, then I will let you have your nephew now at once, and your brother safe and sound when I come to England to be king. And, if ever I am with your support established there as king, I promise that everything you ask of me, which can be reasonably granted, you shall have.' Then Harold perceived that here was danger whatever way he turned. He could not see any way of escape without agreeing to all that William wished. So he agreed. Then William, to ensure that all should thenceforth stand firmly ratified, had relics of saints brought out and made Harold swear over them that he would indeed implement all that they had agreed between them.

William of Poitiers gives a similar story, saying that Harold swore an oath at Bonneville-sur-Touques that for as long as he lived he would be the vicar (agent) of William in England and strive to ensure that the duke succeeded to the English throne. He also promised to fortify Dover for William and his knights. And as King Edward was known to be near death, William confirmed Harold in all his lands in England in anticipation of his succession. The Bayeux Tapestry portrays Harold swearing the oath on these relics, but places the occasion at Bayeux — 'Where Harold made the oath to Duke William' says the legend above the scene. Orderic, who is later and probably less reliable as a result, puts the oath-swearing at Rouen. Eadmer does not name the venue.

Harold then joined William on his Breton campaign (although the Bayeux Tapestry reverses the order of events, showing the Breton campaign first and the oath second). William of Poitiers says that,

> because he knew Harold to be high-mettled and anxious for new renown, he provided him and the men who had accompanied him with knightly arms and the finest horses, and took them with him to the Breton war. He treated his guest and envoy as his companion in arms so as to make him by that honour more faithful and beholden to him.

The Tapestry shows Harold rescuing some Normans from the quicksands around Mont-Saint-Michel, and William presenting the Englishman with arms at the end of the campaign. The picture may have been intended to emphasize the fact that Harold had become William's man and so owed him his loyalty.

11. Detail of the Bayeux Tapestry (eleventh century).
'Where Harold made the oath to Duke William.'

Did William and Harold develop a friendship during these months? It was only William of Malmesbury, writing *c*. 1125, who saw such a relationship between the two men. He notes, in accordance with other sources, that the duke took Harold to Brittany. 'There, Harold, gaining approval both for his character and in the field, won the duke's affection, and ... [after swearing the oath and being promised one of the duke's daughters in marriage] ... was reckoned one of his intimates.' No other chronicler takes this line. In contrast, Poitiers shows William manipulating Harold so as to make him 'beholden' to him, and Eadmer suggests that Harold realized full well that he had been trapped – hardly conditions conducive to the development of friendly relations. There is no suggestion in their accounts that the two men became friends, and no hint that William was trying to create an affective relationship. He was concerned only to bind Harold to him by a mixture of subtle threats and faux generosity. And we may suppose from his later actions that Harold was not taken in, and did not consider his promises, made under duress, to be binding. It is certainly and famously the case that when Edward the Confessor died in January 1066, Harold broke his oath and took the throne for himself. For the Normans, this made Harold a perjurer.

When word reached William early in 1066 that Harold had been elected king and crowned, he was furious. So far as he was concerned he had been promised the succession to the kingdom and Harold had sworn on holy relics to support that claim. Harold's oath was not dissolved simply because Edward had nominated him as his successor on his deathbed – a claim which even William of Poitiers allows. And so Duke William summoned a council to Lillebonne, and there, before his assembled magnates, he set out his case. William of Poitiers tells us that many of the greatest men of Normandy counselled against the invasion, but that others agreed. Henry of Huntingdon, writing in the 1130s, suggests that consent was only obtained by a trick:

> William fitz Osbern, the duke's steward, was among those who came to advise the duke. He told them (the lords of Normandy) beforehand that an expedition to conquer England would be very difficult and the English nation was very strong, and he argued vehemently against the few who wished to go to England. Hearing this, the nobles were very glad, and gave him their word that they would all agree with what he was going to say. Then he went into the duke's presence ahead of them, and said: 'I am prepared to set out on this expedition with all my men.' Therefore all the Norman leaders were obliged to follow his word.

William prepared for the invasion in a variety of ways. First he collected troops and the ships that were necessary to transport them across the Channel. Some of these were constructed from scratch – the Bayeux Tapestry shows timber being felled and ships being built – but many would have been provided or requisitioned by his vassals. A document known as 'the ship list' purports to show the number of vessels provided by Count Robert of Mortain, Bishop Odo of Bayeux and Hugh of Avranches, amongst others, but the authenticity of this document remains open to doubt.[7] In addition, William sent an embassy to Pope Alexander II to seek his approval for the campaign. Alexander, whose relations had been taught by Lanfranc, even if it is now thought that he himself had not, was amenable and sent a papal banner to be carried at the head of William's army.[8] In June of 1066, in a further attempt to gain divine approval for the expedition, William and Matilda's abbey of the Holy Trinity in Caen was dedicated, and the duke and duchess gave their daughter, Cecilia, aged about seven, to the nuns.[9] William also prepared for the governance of Normandy during his absence. His wife Matilda, his son Robert, and his friends Roger of Montgommery and Roger of Beaumont were entrusted with the duchy while he was away. It was probably at this time that his son received the homage of the nobles of Normandy in case William failed to return.

The army, composed of knights, infantry and archers, not just from Normandy but from Poitou, Brittany, Picardy and elsewhere, is reckoned by modern historians to have comprised 6,000–10,000 men. Of this number perhaps 2,000–3,000 were mounted knights. All of them were assembled at Dives-sur-Mer, where they probably camped on a hill overlooking the broad estuary where the ships were gathered (which no longer exists). The army remained at Dives for a month and was provisioned by the duke at his expense. This saved the duchy from being plundered by hungry knights, so that Poitiers was able to praise the maintenance of order – the cattle remained grazing, the crops remained standing and 'a man who was weak or unarmed could ride singing on his horse wherever he wished'.

The logistics of this exercise have been examined by Bernard Bachrach, who has produced some remarkable statistics based on an army of 10,000 plus another 4,000 hangers-on – although these should be taken only as estimates rather than established figures.[10] For the month spent at Dives, Bachrach reckoned, the army would have needed a supply of 2,340 tons of grain (for men and horses), 1,500 tons of hay and around 155 tons of straw, all of which would have made up around 8,000 cart-loads of supplies. To cook, 420 tons of firewood would have been consumed, and more than 26,000 gallons of wine might have been drunk. How potentially disease-causing waste products were dealt with is not known, but it is estimated that the horses would have produced something like 700,000 gallons of urine and 5 million pounds of manure. All of this had to be removed from the camp, and the manure alone comprised another 5,000 cartloads. No doubt the fields around Dives bloomed for years to come. The figures are guesswork, and they have been challenged,[11] but we do not have to be completely convinced of their accuracy to be impressed by the effort required to keep William's army together, provisioned and healthy.

After a month waiting at Dives, the duke moved his army up the coast to Saint-Valéry-sur-Somme, which was in Ponthieu rather than Normandy. The move might have been made for a number of reasons. It is possible that supply issues were beginning to arise, necessitating a move to a new area. More likely, William wanted to take advantage of the shorter Channel crossing but had previously been unable to do so because of the threat posed by Harold's navy, stationed off the Isle of Wight. The move north was made four or five days after these ships were released. This is unlikely to be a coincidence. The 'C' version of the *Anglo-Saxon Chronicle* (which ends on the very eve of the battle of Hastings) says that Harold let his ships go because 'the men's provisions had run out and no one could keep them there any longer', but there may have been more to it than that. The short season for catching herring was about to begin – it ran from Michaelmas (29 September) to Martinmas (11 November). Herring was vital. At a time when meat could not be eaten on Fridays or feast days, preserved fish, chiefly herring, was an important source of food, and so the sailors needed to return to their home ports to make ready to go fishing.[12] An even more likely reason for the move is that William had sailed for England directly from Dives, but before his fleet had been able to make landfall it had been blown back to France and took refuge at Saint-Valéry.[13] William certainly lost some ships and men during this passage – he buried them in secret – and these losses could have occurred as the ships jostled for position in the estuary.[14] That would also explain why the bodies could be recovered rather than being lost at sea.

At Saint-Valéry, William had to wait for a favourable wind for a fortnight. The poem known as the *Song of the Battle of Hastings* describes the prayers

12. Saint-Valéry-sur-Somme – from where William sailed to England.

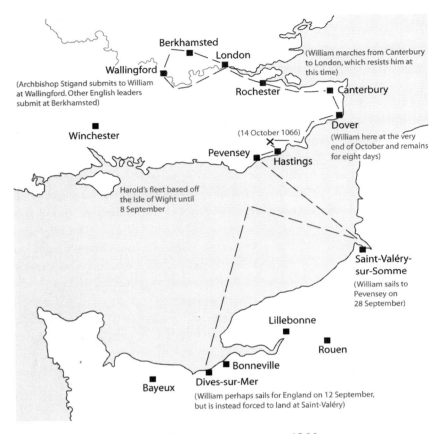

Map 4. The Hastings campaign, 1066.

and offerings that the duke made in the church of St Walaric, and how he would repeatedly glance up at the weathercock to see if his prayers had been answered and the wind had changed direction. Malmesbury, on the other hand, talks of the mutterings in the army:

> A man must be mad, they said, who wants us to take over land rightfully belonging to others; God is against us for He denies us a wind; his father had the same idea and was prevented in the same way; there is a curse on this family – it always conceives more than it can perform and finds God in opposition to it.

It was for this reason that the duke gave orders that the body of St Walaric, the patron of the town, should be brought out of the church and exposed under the skies to support the Norman prayers for a favourable wind. God had to be shown to be on William's side. At least he could show that the pope was, for William would by now have received the papal banner that showed that Christ's vicar approved of his plans and would protect him in battle.

Finally the grey skies cleared and the wind began to blow from the south. The signal to depart was given, trumpets sounded across the estuary, and men, horses and arms were loaded onto the boats. So long did this take, despite the duke haranguing all those who seemed to be dawdling, that it was already evening before the boats pulled out of the harbour. As the duke did not want his ships to lose each other in the night, nor to arrive in England before dawn, he commanded by way of a herald that the fleet should drop anchor in mid-Channel during the night, and that they should remain stationary until they saw a lantern lit at the top of his mast and a trumpet was sounded. All went to plan until the signal to move off was given. The duke's boat was so much speedier than the others that it left them behind, and when dawn came the duke found himself alone in the sea. Anchor was dropped again, and the duke, who wanted to keep up morale, spent the time eating a plentiful meal, with spiced wine.[15] Eventually the others ships were sighted, their masts like a forest on the sea.

The rest of the crossing passed without incident, and on the morning of 29 September 1066 (or so the majority of contemporary sources say), Duke William and his army landed at Pevensey – a place now a mile or so from the sea.[16] According to William of Malmesbury, the duke tripped while disembarking. This could have been taken as an ill-omen, but the knight closest to him cried out: 'You have England in your hand, duke, and shall be king.' As Suetonius tells us that the same thing had happened when Julius Caesar landed in Africa,[17] we may question whether William really did fall; it is perhaps more likely that Malmesbury is simply embroidering the story with a telling anecdote.

A castle was constructed within the old Roman fort above the beach, and the land round about was ravaged – the Bayeux Tapestry depicts soldiers burning down a house and carrying off livestock, while a woman and her son stand by helplessly. The army advanced to Hastings, and there another castle was constructed on the cliff, most of which has long since fallen into the sea. The army, meanwhile, continued to ravage the land to force Harold (in Yorkshire when William arrived) to give battle.

13. Detail of the Bayeux Tapestry (eleventh century).
The Norman fleet crossing the Channel.

14. The castle at Pevensey, seen from the original beach.

Two weeks after his arrival, on Saturday 14 October 1066, Duke William of Normandy found himself armed and mounted on the slope of Telham Hill. He had chosen this position on learning that King Harold was in his immediate vicinity, and now awaited the English army. According to the *Song of the Battle of Hastings,*

> suddenly the forest spewed out its cohorts; and columns of men stormed out of their hiding places in the woods. Near the forest was a hill and a valley and land too rough to be tilled. The English, as was their custom, advanced in mass formation and seized this position on which to fight. For that people, unskilled in the art of war, spurn the assistance of horses: trusting in their strength they stand fast on foot. And they consider it the greatest honour to die in battle to prevent their country falling under the yoke of another. To prepare for the encounter the king mounted the hill, defended his flanks with noblemen, planted his standard on the summit, and ordered all other banners to be joined to his. They all dismounted and left their horses in the rear. Once in position they had trumpets sound their calls to battle.

Harold's position was well chosen. The English had a higher position than the Normans, and the hill up which the Normans had to march or charge is quite steep – more so than it looks. The English were protected by marshy ground which prevented an attack on their flanks, while the trees from which they had emerged prevented an attack from the rear. At the front of the line, the English formed a shield wall, overlapping their shields to form an impenetrable barrier, and packed so close to each other that they were unable to fall when they were killed. To the rear, Harold stood below his personal banner – the fighting man – and the dragon standard of Wessex, surrounded by a well-armoured and well-disciplined group of warriors whom Harold retained in his household, known as housecarls.

Against these, William had archers, foot and cavalry. The most prestigious and well armed were the knights, who comprised about one-third of William's army. These men wore a conical iron helmet with a nose-guard, and knee-length coats of chain mail. Further protection was provided by a broad, kite-shaped shield, to protect the rider's left side. His right-hand side was protected by his weapons, either a lance or a sword. The Bayeux Tapestry shows knights holding their lances in a number of ways: thrusting overarm, or tucked under their arm (couched) to use the momentum of the charge against their enemy. These men had been trained in the art of fighting on horseback since childhood.[18] Their horses had been well schooled to prevent them (so far as possible) from shying or bolting when in battle. The average height of these horses has been estimated at about 12 hands, so they would be classed as ponies today, although some men preferred them to be even smaller. One Norman, Richard fitz Asclettin, who became prince of Capua in Italy, liked to ride a horse that was so short that his feet all but brushed the ground as he rode.[19]

The fighting began at about nine o'clock in the morning. William of Malmesbury says that the Normans sang the poem known as the *Song of Roland* as they advanced into battle, to build up their courage by recalling Roland's great battle with the Moors in Spain of 778. Their choice of song might have been due to Roland's association with Normandy, for according to Einhard, Charlemagne's biographer, he had been lord of the Breton Marches.[20] We get a sense of the noise and urgency of the first stages of the battle from a number of sources. According to Wace the Normans shouted their battle cry, 'God help!', while the English shouted 'Out, out!' back at them. The *Song of the Battle of Hastings* insists that 'Helmeted soldiers rush to crash shields against shields'. A juggler called Taillefer makes an appearance in a number of the sources.[21] He encouraged the Normans, throwing his sword high into the air and then catching it again. One Englishman ran down the hill to attack him, so Taillefer spurred his horse towards him and cut off his head, which he then brandished.

And so the battle raged. Wace captures the reality of the fighting:

> You would have seen many English falling, lying on the ground and kicking their legs; those unable to get up were trampled by the enemies' horses. You would have seen brains flying out in great number and bowels lying on the ground.

At some point in the battle – and Stephen Morillo believes that this happened before even an hour of fighting had passed – the footsoldiers and Bretons on the left of the army fell back, thinking that William had been killed.[22] Desperate to stem the flow, William rode up to them and, lifting up his helmet, showed them that he was not dead at all. He encouraged them to turn and attack their pursuers. This they did, cutting down the English before they could get back to the safety of their lines. Having fled and turned once, to such effect, the Normans and their allies feigned flight on a further two occasions.

The result of this is made explicit by the *Song*: 'The rustic folk rejoice, thinking that they have conquered, and pursue them with naked swords.

15. Detail of the Bayeux Tapestry (eleventh century). William shows himself to his men, thereby scotching the rumour that he has been killed.

With the removal of the able-bodied, the corpses fall, and the once-thick wood is thinned.'

The men who ran down the hill found themselves isolated and were easy prey for groups of cavalry which, after feigning flight, regrouped and turned on their pursuers. This thinned the English lines and opened up gaps in the shield wall. But still the Normans found it difficult to make progress. Poitiers says that 'up to now the enemy line had been bristling with weapons and most difficult to encircle. So a combat of an unusual kind began, with one side attacking in different ways and the other standing firmly as if fixed to the ground.'

During the afternoon, further infantry and cavalry attacks were launched. During one of these the duke was unhorsed. The *Song* claims that Harold's brother, Gyrth, was responsible. His success was shortlived. Gyrth was almost immediately killed by the duke, who is praised as having cloven many more while fighting on foot. Seeing a knight from Maine, William signalled that he should come over to him, but the knight refused to surrender his mount to the duke for fear that he would die as a result. 'But the duke, like a mindful knight, turned sharply towards him, and, infuriated, seized the nasal of his helmet, pulled him to the ground head over heels, and speedily mounted the horse thus presented to him.'

16. The battlefield at Hastings, looking down to the Norman position. Telham Hill, from where the Normans had advanced, is in the background.

Duke William was not to stay remounted for long. His Manceau horse was soon killed under him by a javelin. A third horse was then provided by Count Eustace of Boulogne, who in turn was given one by a member of his own household. According to the *Song of the Battle of Hastings*, William and Eustace then rode together to where the fighting was hardest and helped to clear the field. Duke William spied Harold on the hill and, with Count Eustace still in tow, went to that position. Harold was killed, still according to the *Song*, by four men including William and Eustace. Historians have been reluctant to accept this testimony, although establishing just how and when Harold died is no easy matter. Of all the early English or Norman sources for the battle, it is the Bayeux Tapestry alone that appears to show Harold being wounded by an arrow in the eye and then cut down by a passing, unnamed knight. The earliest chronicler to mention this famous injury was, unexpectedly, a monk at the abbey of Montecassino in the south of Italy, Amatus by name, who composed his *History of the Normans* in around 1080. Whatever the truth of the matter, this was the story that became accepted, and it thus provided the basis for later accounts of the battle. Malmesbury says that Harold's brain was pierced by the arrow and thus he fell, while Wace, following the Tapestry more closely, says that Harold, dazed by the pain of his destroyed eye, was knocked to the ground and then, as he was struggling to rise, attacked by a knight who cut his thigh open to the bone. He was eventually killed by the advancing Normans.

Even after Harold was dead the resistance continued. A remnant of the English army retreated to a strong position, protected by a concealed ditch. The Normans, unaware of the obstacle, launched a charge and fell victim to the trench, their horses tumbling to the ground, taking their riders with them. Some of the noblest Normans fell attacking this last stand of the English army, although we only know the name of one of them, Engenulf of L'Aigle. But this *ad hoc* fortification could not and did not withstand the Normans indefinitely. Once the Normans had pushed through, the English fled. By this time it was perhaps nine o'clock in the evening. Hastings was one of the longest battles of the Middle Ages, and for all but the last hour the result had been in the balance.

Like Caesar after the battle at Pharsalus, William spent the night on the battlefield among the dead.[23] The next morning he commanded that the fallen Normans should be buried, but left the English where they were. Wace thinks that their relatives came looking for them, and this may be right. Who came for Harold? The sources differ on this point. Poitiers says that Harold's mother asked for her son's body but was refused. Instead William commanded that Harold's body be buried on the cliff so that it might command the defence of the shore – something he had failed to do when he was alive. The *Waltham Chronicle*, however, claims that clergy from that church, which had been founded by Harold, asked for the body and that William gave it to them, declaring that although Harold had neglected his good faith he still deserved Christian burial.[24] The clerks offered to pay ten gold marks for it, but William refused their offer. An obstacle arose, in that no one could identify the body, and so Edith Swan-Neck, Harold's wife, had to be brought to the battlefield. (Some sources maintain she was actually his mistress, but it is generally believed that the marriage was made *more danico*, according to the custom of the Danes; in other words, that they had entered into a recognized marriage but that the union had not been blessed by the Church.) She identified the mutilated body by certain 'secret marks' known only to her.

Contemporaries as well as modern historians have all asked the same question: why did the English lose at Hastings? The 'D' version of the *Anglo-*

Saxon Chronicle opines that the French won because the English had lost God's support as a result of their sins.[25] William of Malmesbury says much the same, although at greater length:

> Zeal both for learning and for religion cooled as time went on, not many years before the coming of the Normans. The clergy, content with a mere smattering of knowledge, scarce mumbled the words of the sacraments; a man who knew any grammar was a marvel and a portent to his colleagues. Monks, with their finely-woven garments and their undiscriminating diet, made nonsense of their Rule. The nobles, abandoned to gluttony and lechery, never went to church of a morning, as a Christian should, but in his chamber, in his wife's embrace, a man would lend a careless ear to some priest galloping through the solemn words of matins and the mass ... Drinking in company was a universal practice, and in this passion they made no distinction between day and night ... There followed the vices that keep company with drunkenness, and sap the virility of a man's spirit. As a result, there was more rashness and headlong fury than military skill in their conflict with William, so that in one battle – and a very easy one – they abandoned themselves and their country to servitude.

William of Poitiers thought that Harold lost because he was an oath-breaker, a tyrant and a fratricide (holding him responsible for Tostig's death at the battle of Stamford Bridge, near York, where Harold had defeated Harald Hardrada, king of Norway, on 25 September 1066). William of Jumièges blamed it on Godwin's murder of Edward the Confessor's brother, Alfred, in 1036 – it was a case of the sins of the father being visited on the son. Orderic echoed all of this, but added to Harold's sins that of perjury for ignoring the oath that he had taken to William in 1064 or 1065.

Twentieth-century historians, less willing to see divine intervention deciding the outcome, have been more concerned with the generalship of Harold and William, and with the composition of the forces at their disposal.

William was not an experienced commander in 1066. He had not led the army at Val-ès-Dunes in 1047, when overall command had lain with King Henry of the French. He had not fought at Mortemer in 1054. Varaville had seen the fortuitous destruction of the French rearguard. And so Hastings was the first time that William had taken command in a pitched battle. He had taken up a reasonable position, apparently in a hurry, but he had to fight uphill. He led his men from the front, rushing headlong into the fighting, but although this might demonstrate his confidence and sense of righteous-ness, and provided an inspiring model for his men to follow, it also put him in harm's way. Two horses were killed from under him. It is no wonder that he had to scotch a rumour that he had been killed, and his success in calming the Bretons needs to be qualified by the fact that it was his own actions that had caused the problem in the first place. The feigned flights that were to win William the day were apparently only suggested by the fortunate success that had followed the genuine rout of the Bretons. They were not William's own idea, as such, although at least he saw how such tactics could be repeated to help him gain the victory.

Harold has been criticized for giving battle with only a third of his army. But his unwillingness to wait for the rest of his men might not have been crucial. The hilltop on which his army formed up was only just large enough for the troops he had with him. John of Worcester says that some of Harold's army deserted when they saw how constricted their position was. Harold, then, already had too many troops for the position that he occupied on Senlac Ridge. And what he had, he used well. His infantry were required only to withstand wave after wave of cavalry charges and infantry advances – and this they were quite capable of doing. And it should be remembered that Harold did not need to win. A draw was enough so far as he was concerned.

The decisive moment in the battle came with the flight of the Breton wing, which caused sections of the English line to leave the shield wall and chase their enemy down the hill, only to be cut down when the knights wheeled round and re-formed. Two subsequent feigned flights reduced the English numbers still further, thinning the line and perhaps bringing the flanks closer to the centre, allowing the Norman knights to get behind the English lines. These fundamental mistakes, however, seem to have been spontaneous responses to what appeared to be favourable moments in the battle rather than disciplined advances commanded by Harold and his lieutenants. But planned or not, the actions, and subsequent loss of troops, lost Harold the battle. That at least was William of Malmesbury's view:

> By this stratagem the close battle order of the English was broken up, in hopes of cutting down the enemy from behind as they fled at random, and thereby they hastened their own doom ... So they were undone by a trick and earned a glorious death in avenging their country.

The feigned flights worked because William's cavalry was so much more mobile than the English infantry, and this is another important reason for William's victory. The knights provided a highly mobile body that could feign flight, regroup and then charge the English who had chased them down the hill. This had the effect of thinning and opening gaps in the English ranks, making them vulnerable to direct attack from the Norman knights. William's archers also gave him an advantage towards the end of the day when they began to lob arrows down on the thinning English army. Harold's troops, on the other hand, were composed almost entirely of infantry, with perhaps just a very few archers. If he had waited for his archers to arrive, then perhaps the outcome would have been different. Perhaps the Norman horses would have been shot down as they charged the English line. Or perhaps the outcome would have been the same.

The Normans, then, had the advantage, but only just. It took around 12 hours for them to make this advantage count, and all the way the final result was in the balance. To misquote the duke of Wellington, the battle of Hastings was a damn close-run thing (and the battle was considered by J.H. Round to be Waterloo without the Prussians). Casualties were high on both sides. Many of William's army were killed in the fighting, so many that Eadmer of Canterbury was convinced that God alone had decided the outcome. Luck thus played an important part. And John Gillingham makes a salient point when he suggests that William the Bastard should really be known to posterity as 'William the Lucky Bastard'.[26]

After the battle William stayed in the area around Hastings for a few days, perhaps waiting in vain for the English officially to admit defeat.[27] He then left a garrison at the castle and took the remainder of his army to Romney. The villagers were punished for slaughtering those of his men who had landed there by mistake on the morning of 29 September. He then marched to Dover and invested the fortification that Harold had constructed on the clifftop. The English garrison swiftly decided to surrender, but Norman men-at-arms, greedy for gain, set fire to some buildings and much was destroyed in the conflagration. The duke regretted the harm inflicted on men on the point of surrender, and gave them ample compensation, paying for the repair of the buildings. He stayed at Dover for eight days, strengthening the castle. He then led his army on a great loop through Kent, marching up to Canterbury, which surrendered, and then along Watling Street through Rochester to London. However, the 'D' version of the *Anglo-Saxon Chronicle* says that,

> Archbishop Ealdred and the citizens of London wished to have Prince Edgar for king, as was indeed his right by birth, and Edwin and Morcar promised that they would fight for him, but always when some initiative should have

been shown there was delay from day to day until matters went from bad to worse, as everything did in the end.

London, then, resisted William at this time, and so he continued his march around the city, following the south bank of the Thames. As he moved west, he allowed his men to ravage the countryside. John of Worcester says that he laid waste Sussex, Kent, Hampshire, Middlesex and Hertfordshire, and Domesday Book reveals that the effects of this harrying of the south were still in evidence 20 years later. A small force, possibly under William fitz Osbern, was dispatched to take control of Winchester, while the main body of the army crossed the Thames at Wallingford. It was there that Archbishop Stigand of Canterbury submitted to William. He then moved through the Chilterns to Berkhamsted. It was there, or so the 'D' version of the *Anglo-Saxon Chronicle* states,

> he was met by Bishop Ealdred, Prince Edgar, Earl Edwin, Earl Morcar, and all the best men of London, who submitted from force of circumstances, but only when the depredation was complete. It was great folly that they had not done so sooner when God would not remedy matters because of our sins. They gave him hostages, and swore oaths of fealty, and he promised to be a gracious lord to them.

Poitiers says that before agreeing to become king of the English, William consulted with his men. He desired, he told them, the peace of the kingdom rather than the crown, but was persuaded to agree to become king by Aimery of Thouars, a Poitevin. We do not have to believe this. Indeed it seems barely credible that William had not intended to take the crown from the very outset, given that the cause of the invasion in the first place was Harold's seizure of the crown despite the oath that he had sworn to William. So why is the passage there at all? Poitiers might have hoped that it deflected claims of ambition levelled against William. He had sought the consent of his men, even the ordinary knights, before taking up the kingship. He might also have been explaining why William had himself crowned so quickly, and it might have needed explaining, because the coronation oath prevented William and his men from stamping hard on English resistance in the months that followed.

✝

CHAPTER 4

I SEE GOD!
RITUAL AND GOVERNMENT

How did William rule his duchy and his new kingdom? How did he put his will into effect? In an age in which men and news moved no more quickly than a galloping horse, in dominions studded with castles, when every man of substance was armed and had a small band of warriors at his disposal, how did William maintain order and ensure that his subjects obeyed his commands? These are the concerns of this chapter.

First, we must consider how it was that William was in a position to rule Normandy and England. To become duke of the Normans,[1] William had to be a blood relation of earlier dukes. But he also had to go through a simple but important ceremony. The Norman magnates placed their hands in his and promised to do him service in war and in peace. They then swore an oath on relics, to the same effect.[2] The one was a symbolic act, the other a binding one. Although the assembly at which the oaths were sworn is likely to have been a large and impressive one, no further details about the ceremony are on record. Our sources do not mention the role of the archbishop of Rouen or other clergy, although the presence of relics suggests that the Church was involved; we hear nothing of liturgy, choirs or even of feasting. The whole affair seems, at this distance, to have been very simple, to the point of austerity.

William had become king of the English as lawful successor to Edward the Confessor, a right demonstrated by his victory at Hastings. The coronation that followed was an altogether more elaborate affair than the ceremony that had made him duke, as we have seen. But the coronation was not the only time that William wore his crown. According to the 'E' version of the *Anglo-Saxon Chronicle*, he wore his royal crown three times a year as often as he was in England: at Easter at Winchester; at Whitsuntide at Westminster; at Christmas at Gloucester. On these occasions, all the great men of England were assembled about him: archbishops, bishops, abbots, earls, thegns, and knights.[3]

In fact William's actual location at these feasts varied – the circuit laid down in the *Chronicle* seems only to have been accurate for the last three or four years of the reign. Nonetheless, although the places might differ, it does seem that William wore his crown during the three great feasts of the Church when he was in England. There was, then, a regular calendar of magnificent occasions at which William could emphasize his authority and power by a display of his wealth and magnificence.[4] This power was also reflected in part by the number of people that William could compel or influence to attend. These occasions, known by modern historians as crown-wearings, seem to have been unknown in England before 1066. As William could not shake off his kingship the moment that he crossed the Channel (and although he continued to rule Normandy as duke rather than king, Norman diplomas and Orderic's *Ecclesiastical History* do talk about William's royal power extending over his subjects in the duchy) his court in Normandy probably became much more splendid after 1066.[5] There is even a chance that he wore his crown in the duchy after the Conquest – certainly his authority would have gained from such a display. Nonetheless, it cannot be assumed that what happened in England also happened in Normandy, and the silence of William of Poitiers here is disturbing, for he of all people would be expected to crow about the king-duke's magnificence at his great courts and, with the exception of that of 1067, he does not do so.

This magnificence in dress, in food and in men was important: it symbolized power. William of Malmesbury talks about the great feasts that characterized the crown-wearings:

> The dinners in which he took part on the major festivals were costly and splendid ... all great men of whatever walk of life were summoned to them by royal edict, so that envoys from other nations might admire the large and brilliant company, and the splendid luxury of the feast. Nor was he at any other season so courteous or so ready to oblige, so that foreign visitors might carry a lively report to every country of the generosity that matched his wealth.

King William knew he was playing a game, and played it well. This was recognized by William's jester, as can be seen from the following story in

Milo Crispin's *Life of Lanfranc*. The incident happened while King William was at one of these feasts, sitting next to his archbishop of Canterbury, Lanfranc:

> It was one of those three great festivals on which the king, wearing his crown, is accustomed to hold his court. On the day of the festival, when the king was seated at table adorned in crown and royal robes, and Lanfranc beside him, a certain jester, seeing the king resplendent in gold and jewels, cried out in the hall in great tones of adulation: 'Behold I see God! Behold I see God!' Lanfranc turned to the king and said, 'Don't allow such things to be said of you. These things are not for man but for God. Order that fellow to be severely flogged so that he won't ever dare to say such things again.'[6]

The king, who had clearly not been offended himself, did as he was commanded.

We know very little about how William appeared during the services that saw the crown replaced on his head by the archbishop of Canterbury. The Bayeux Tapestry shows both King Edward and Duke William at court in a number of scenes. They sit on cushions on carved, backless seats, with their feet on a footstool. They were thus raised above their subjects, even when seated. As duke, William is dressed in clothes that are not clearly differentiated from those of the people around him, unlike Edward's, which are rather more elaborate. Both wear cloaks, but whereas William holds a sword to symbolize his power, Edward is crowned and holds a sceptre. Whether or not this is how they looked in reality is unknown, and this is because the images in the Tapestry are derived from the ruler portraits of the Ottonian (German), Carolingian (French) and English traditions – although they were probably an innovation in Normandy, as no such images appear to exist from before the Conquest.[7]

William is not depicted as magnificently dressed before he became king, but Orderic suggests that he was already aware of the importance of appearances before 1066: 'William duke of Normandy was growing in power and influence, and surpassing all his neighbours in the magnificence and display of his way of life.'

After the Conquest his magnificence increased. William of Poitiers, for example, remarks that when William returned to Normandy in 1067, and displayed the spoils of his victory, his magnates 'recognized that far more distinguished and memorable than these things was the splendour of the king himself'. It may even be the case that the lost final panels of the Bayeux Tapestry represented William sitting crowned on a throne and dressed in much

17. Detail of the Bayeux Tapestry (eleventh century). William sitting in majesty in his palace (shown to his left), holding a sword that symbolizes his temporal power and seated on a clawed throne.

more elaborate costume, to make the point that his conquest had brought him undreamed-of riches.

William of Malmesbury tells a tale which, although it concerns the Conqueror's son and successor, William Rufus, reveals how expensive clothes reflected royal dignity:

> The cost of his clothes he liked to be immensely inflated, and spurned them if anyone reduced it. For instance, one morning when he was putting on some new shoes, he asked his valet what they had cost. 'Three shillings,' the man replied, at which the king flew into a rage. 'You son of a whore!' he cried, 'since when has a king worn such trumpery shoes? Go and get me some that cost a mark of silver (about four times as much).' The servant went off and returned with a much cheaper pair, pretending they had been bought at the price specified. 'Why,' said the king, 'these are a good fit for the royal majesty.'

William's person was thus an important part of his kingship. He had to look the part, as well as act it. And if he did not always quite fit the part, that might have been the result of his magnificent feasting. William of Malmesbury says that, 'He had great dignity both seated and standing, although his prominent corpulence gave him an unshapely and unkingly figure.'

But although William's person was of great importance, he could not rule alone or act on his every whim. Dukes and kings were required to listen to the views of their greatest men and to act with regard to their counsel, and this counsel was taken at the crown-wearings and at other assemblies, great and small.[8] Sometimes William had to fight to get his way. In 1066, for example, many of the Norman lords were initially reluctant to risk their lives in pursuing William's claim to the English throne. As we have seen, Henry of Huntingdon goes so far as to claim that they were tricked into agreement.

The men who gave William counsel were the greatest in the land. Poitiers says that 'Normandy had in its counsels' not only the bishops and abbots but also laymen – 'shining luminaries' is how Poitiers describes them – such as Count Robert of Mortain, Count Robert of Eu, Count Richard of Evreux, Roger of Beaumont, Roger of Montgommery and William fitz Osbern. These were the men whom William had promoted to positions of power in his duchy, and who had been close to him from his earliest days.

William, as both duke and king, did not have to take advice from everyone, however. The views of mere knights were seldom canvassed. When William asked the knights who were with him at Berkhamsted whether he should accept the offer of the English throne, William of Poitiers makes the Poitevin Aimery of Thouars speak out in wonder: 'Rarely or never have knights been admitted to a debate such as this.' Aimery was most probably right, especially as Poitiers seems to have added this passage to ensure that William should appear to have complied with the conditions necessary for the making of a legitimate king (among other things). For a king who was not chosen by his people was nothing but a tyrant.

A king or duke or count might, however, ignore the counsel given to him if he thought that it was badly thought through. For example, in around 1086, Roger, the great count of Sicily, was offered the assistance of a Latin army if he would lead an expedition to Africa against the sultan of Mahdia (in Tunisia). The Arab historian Ibn al-Athir says:

> Roger assembled his men and consulted them about this. They said, 'By the truth of the Gospel, this is excellent for us and them. The lands will become Christian lands.' Roger raised his leg and gave a loud fart. 'By the truth of my religion,' he said, 'there is more use in that than in what you have to say!' 'How so?' they asked. 'If they come to me,' he replied, 'I shall require vast expenditure and ships to convey them to Africa and troops of mine also. If they take the territory it will be theirs and resources from Sicily will go to them. I shall be deprived of the money that comes in every year from

agricultural revenues. If they do not succeed, they will return to my lands and I shall suffer from them. [The sultan] will say 'You have betrayed me and broken the agreement I have [with you].'[9]

Roger's view prevailed. But he had still taken the counsel of his subjects, even if he did not act on it.

The same shining luminaries of Normandy, on whom William depended for the maintenance of his rule, were also to achieve positions of responsibility and authority in England. William fitz Osbern, lord of Breteuil, was made earl over part of Wessex.[10] Roger of Montgommery, so important in the south of the duchy, was given the Sussex rapes of Chichester and Arundel and, a little later, was made earl of Shrewsbury.[11] Bishop Odo was made earl of Kent and Geoffrey of Montbray was given vast estates, centred on the south-west of the country.[12] These men enforced William's will in the regions, and were tied to the duke by bonds of faith and friendship that had been tempered by the longevity of their association. They were all more or less of an age with their duke and they formed a tight-knit clique at the very centre of government.

William's victory at Hastings in 1066 meant that he would no longer be always resident in Normandy. Equally his continuing rule over Normandy meant that he would also be an absent king. For the rest of his life, William was to cross and recross the Channel, spending no more than 18 months in either part of his dominions at any one time. Of course William was personally absent from most of his dominions all of the time. That was why a variety of officials were appointed who represented him in the regions of England and Normandy, and who collected and accounted for the revenues produced by his lands and rights. These officials continued to do their job, no matter where William was residing, and had done so since before 1066. Equally it was always possible for determined individuals to track William down, no matter where he was. Monks might, and did, cross the sea to find the king if they wanted him to do something for them badly enough. And, indeed, there were some things that only William could agree to, or command. It seems, for example, that lawsuits could only be heard in Normandy with William's permission (the situation may have been different in England). Bishops and abbots, too, could only be elected on William's say so.

Nonetheless, there was still a need for someone to be appointed to protect England and Normandy when William was not there, to preside over his court and to receive the messages and embassies that might arrive in the king's absence.[13] William of Poitiers notes that William had made arrangements for the security of his duchy before invading England in 1066:

> For its government had been carried on smoothly by our lady Matilda, already commonly known by the title of queen, though as yet uncrowned. Men of great experience had added their counsel to her wisdom; among them the first in dignity was Roger of Beaumont (son of the illustrious Humfrey), who on account of his mature age was more suitable for home affairs, and had handed over military duties to his more youthful son ... But in truth the fact that neighbours had not dared to make any attack though they knew the land to be almost emptied of knights, must, we think, be attributed primarily to the king himself, whose return they feared.

Matilda was assisted, too, by Roger of Montgommery and by her son Robert Curthose, and in 1071, when Matilda was again acting as William's deputy, William fitz Osbern was sent to support her. Their role in Normandy is not clear, but it was certainly limited. Matilda and her associates should not be thought of as regents or viceroys. They had no independence of action. The same is true of the men whom William left in charge of England when he was in Normandy. William fitz Osbern and Odo of Bayeux were given that responsibility when William returned to the duchy in 1067, and provoked trouble by their oppression of the people. In 1075 it was apparently Archbishop Lanfranc who presided over William's government, while between 1077 and 1080 Odo again took up the reins. At the time of William's death in Normandy, Eadmer implies that Lanfranc was once more in control of England. Of all of these, only Odo seems to have had the power to act without direct instructions from William – one example of this independence will appear later in this chapter – and it is the bishop alone who could be described as having been put 'in my place in my kingdom' by King William.[14]

As has been mentioned, day-to-day government continued no matter where William was and no matter who had been appointed to protect his dominions. That government was carried out by a variety of officials, the greatest of whom held the equivalent positions of sheriff (in England) and *vicomte* (in Normandy). These two offices are first evidenced in both England and ducal Normandy in the tenth century, and by the eleventh century (and possibly before) their holders performed more or less the same functions on both sides of the Channel. The *vicomte*, or sheriff, managed the ducal or royal estates in their county. They collected and accounted for the revenues produced by the land and the people who lived on it, whether in the form of rents or tolls (the latter were paid for using bridges or on sales and purchases made at markets). They administered law and order, apprehending offenders, enforcing judgements and supervising the collection of fines, although the *vicomte* at least seems not to have presided over court cases. The two officials may both have had a role in maintaining order in their counties, but they were not military leaders as such and did not necessarily have the right to hold the royal castles located in their regions. Where they did hold such castles, however, their power was greatly increased.[15]

Some sheriffs took the opportunities offered by their office to enrich themselves at the expense of the men or churches in their counties. As a result, in 1077 William was obliged to issue a writ commanding that any property that had been appropriated from the Church should be restored:

> Summon my sheriffs by my order and tell them from me that they must return to my bishoprics and abbeys all the demesne and all the demesne land which my bishops and abbots, either through carelessness or fear or greed, have given them out of the demesne of my bishoprics and abbeys, which they have consented to hold or which they have seized by violence. And unless they return those things belonging to the demesne of my churches which they have up to now wrongfully held, you are to compel them to make restitution.[16]

One particularly notorious offender was Picot, who served as sheriff of Cambridge from around 1071 until the end of William's reign. Picot acquired lands for himself in the shire by means both fair and foul. Something of his activities can be seen in the complaints made against him at the beginning of the Domesday account of Cambridgeshire:

> Before 1066 the burgesses (of Cambridge) lent their ploughs to the sheriff three times a year. Now they are demanded on nine occasions. Before 1066 they found neither cartage nor carts; they now do so through an imposed due. They also claim back for themselves from Picot the sheriff the common pasture taken away through him and by him. Picot himself has made three mills there which diminish the pasture and have destroyed many houses ... Picot also had £8, a riding horse, and arms for one man at arms from the heriot (a payment that was made in order to inherit land) of the lawmen. When he was sheriff Ælfric Godricson had 20s. as the heriot of one of them.

Although Normans were appointed as sheriffs from as early as 1067 and 1068, a number of Englishmen did remain in office. Thus Thurkil of

Warwick was sheriff of Staffordshire for at least the first two years of the reign, and possibly until the 1070s;[17] Tofi was sheriff of Somerset, possibly until 1080 or 1081; and Swawold held office in Oxfordshire in 1067 and possibly until 1070. More remarkable, perhaps, is the fact that the Englishman, Earnwig, was made sheriff of Nottinghamshire in *c.* 1070, replacing the previous Norman incumbent. Indeed Englishmen were still acting as sheriffs in William Rufus's reign, although they are increasingly difficult to identify, as the adoption of Norman names by Englishmen means that they no longer stand out in the surviving records.[18]

When William wanted things done in the regions of Normandy and England, he would send a command to these officials. In England this would be done by means of a writ. The writ had developed before 1066, but in William's time it usually took the form of a short document written in Latin to which was appended the king's seal. Writs were succinct and to the point. They told the recipient what he was expected to do or not to do. This is the key thing with a writ: they required the recipient to take, or desist from, some action.[19]

In addition, King William might send documents known by historians as writ-charters to the bishop, sheriff and men of the shire. These notified the shire court of a transaction. So, for example, King William granted the abbey of Abingdon to a Norman monk called Adelelm, and gave him the following writ-charter:

> William king of the English to Archbishop Lanfranc, Robert of Ouilly, and Roger of Pîtres and all his other faithful men of the whole realm of England, greeting. Know that I have granted to St Mary of Abingdon and to Adelelm, abbot of that monastery, all the customs of their lands which belong to the said church wherever it has them, in borough or out of borough, as the aforementioned Abbot Adelelm can show by writ or charter that the church of St Mary of Abingdon and his predecessor had these customs by gift of King Edward.

It may be supposed that the newly appointed abbot had asked the king for such a document, and been prepared to pay for it, because of the tribulations that were afflicting his abbey. That is certainly the tenor of the abbey chronicle, which also reveals what was done with this act after Abbot Adelelm had brought it back from the king's court:

The reading of these letters in the shire court of Berkshire very greatly profited both this abbot and the church. For in those days royal officials were causing great harm to people living on various of the church's possessions. They made them suffer now some, now other very heavy customs. But when these imperial orders were produced, publicizing in that shire court the church's rights by charter of King Edward and the witness of the shire, the royal officials suffered a reverse.

These documents, then, were used to make public the transaction that had taken place. They were filed away in the abbey archives, but only after they had been read out to the shire community. And the public nature of a transfer of property was not limited to land or office. Even the sale and purchase of valuable chattels had to be done in the public gaze. The *Laws of William the Conqueror*, which despite their name probably date from the twelfth century, state: 'We forbid also that any live cattle shall be bought or sold for money except within cities, and this shall be done before three faithful witnesses.' [20]

Writs and writ-charters were produced by the king's writing office, which would develop later into the chancery. The writing office was staffed by scribes who might also have served William as chaplains. It was presided over by the chancellor. It seems virtually certain that both the writing office and the office of chancellor had existed under Edward the Confessor.[21] Nor did the Conquest create a break. Regenbald was William's first chancellor, and had acted as such for both Edward the Confessor and Harold. Equally documents continued to be written in Old English perhaps almost until the end of William's reign, although the use of English decreased markedly from 1070. The wording employed in William's writs, whether written in Old English or Latin, remained close to that found in documents issued before the Conquest. All of this indicates institutional (if the writing office could be called an institution at this time) continuity.

In contrast, there was no writing office or chancellor in Normandy before 1066,[22] and the concept of using writs to convey orders to officials does not seem to have been known there before that date. After the Conquest there is some evidence that the use of writing to convey orders became more usual, but it is unlikely that it ever became routine in William's reign.

In the absence of writing, William must have summoned men to his court to give them his orders directly, or used messengers to convey his will by word of mouth. That he did so is indicated by the record of a dispute which concerned the abbey of Marmoutier (dedicated to St Martin) on one side and the duke's *vicomte*, Robert Bertram, on the other. While he was still but duke of the Normans, William had given Marmoutier all the customs arising from the land that the abbey held at Héauville in the Cotentin:

> And this St Martin had well until Robert Bertram took the office of *vicomte*, who took this gift from St Martin, saying that he had no knowledge that the king had done this thing. Then Gauzelin the monk ... for this thing crossed the sea, and made a claim to the king, who angrily sent back the said monk with his chaplain Bernard fitz Ospac to the queen, commanding her to do justice to St Martin about Bertram, and restore the said gift. And the queen, obedient to the king, compelled Robert to restore whatever he had taken of the possessions of St Martin, in the feast of St John, during Christmas, in the house at Cherbourg.[23]

Robert Bertram was only doing his job. He had no knowledge of William's grant, and so he refused to allow the monks of Marmoutier to alienate his duke's property. The abbey was not able to produce any viable evidence of the grant – it would have been mentioned in the record if they had any – and so had nothing they could use to back up their claim. Consequently, one of the monks had to go to England to remind William of his gift. As a mnemonic, the monks had noted that William had wanted to hit Hugh the forester with the shoulder blade of a pig, as he had spoken against the gift when it was first made. This may – and was certainly intended to – have jogged William's memory. And so William sent back one of his chaplains, a man who would be familiar to Queen Matilda and therefore trustworthy, to convey his instructions to her. This was apparently done by word of mouth alone. No mention is made of any document or of a seal.

Although writing seems to have become more commonly used to give orders in Normandy during William's reign, there are few surviving examples of such executive documents. Only one of them could be properly described as a writ, however, and this was issued for the monks of the king's own foundation at Montebourg after *c.* 1080. It was written by a scribe working in the king's writing office according to a loose formula, as all royal writs already were in England and would be shortly in Normandy. The other two, in contrast, were drafted by the beneficiary: the monks of the abbey of Marmoutier outside Tours. One exempted the monks from tolls in Normandy when transporting fish and other commodities for the monks' own use, and although phrased as a grant was actually a command, as it would have to be presented to royal officials when the monks wanted to benefit from it.

The other, more clearly an executive letter, dates from between 1068, when Matilda was crowned, and 1083, when she died. It reads:

> William by the grace of God king of the English to Queen Matilda his dear wife, perpetual greeting. I make it known to you that I have granted the church of St Mary of Les Pieux, and the alod that pertains to the same church, quit from all custom, to St Martin of Marmoutier, just as Hilgot the priest held it on the day he died. I also command you that you make all the land of St Martin that is within Normandy absolved and quit from all collectors of *gravarium* (a tax) and foresters, as is right. And specifically you shall command Hugolin of Cherbourg not to interfere further therein.

The monks would have come to the court with their letter already written, and would have handed it over to William so that he could either attach his seal or make the sign of the cross to authenticate it. Then it was given to a trusted messenger to take to Matilda. Matilda, acting in William's place, was to put its contents into effect. How she would do this is unclear – she had to command Hugolin not to interfere with the abbey's estates, but she could do this in a number of ways: face-to-face, by messenger, by a new document, or by the same document.[24]

That writing was becoming increasingly important in Norman government is also revealed by a letter written by Abbot Anselm of Le Bec around 1078. In it he professed himself reluctant to accept at face value the word of a messenger sent by a certain Abbot Henry. His reasons were that 'since I see neither your letter nor your seal, which is a reliable witness to a document, I do not entirely trust your messenger'.[25] Clearly Anselm was not sufficiently familiar with Abbot Henry and his household to recognize the man he had sent. And by 1078 he expected to see some additional proofs of the veracity of the message – a seal or a letter. As further evidence that written orders were becoming more common, there is a letter sent by Roger of Montgommery to his son, Robert of Bellême, commanding him to confirm a gift made to St Martin of Sées. That Roger was happy to allow a document in this form to be issued in his name is a further indication that Normans in general, and Roger in particular, were becoming more familiar with such things. This was no doubt as a result of their exposure to the English writ after the Conquest and the needs of cross-Channel government.[26]

It is worth pausing briefly to note Anselm's words more carefully. He did not trust Abbot Henry's messenger because he had seen neither a letter nor a seal. The two are treated as separate indicators of authenticity. And this is important in a Norman context, for although the seal was always appended to documents drawn up in the English writing office, it was much more rarely seen in Normandy.

Most of the Norman acts of Duke William's reign, both before and after 1066, take a form that historians call a diploma. Diplomas usually begin with an invocation of the Holy Trinity rather than an address, and are customarily signed rather than sealed. They were always drafted by the beneficiary and then taken to the duke for authentication. The whole process is succinctly described by Orderic Vitalis, who in this extract describes the diploma as a charter (*carta*). After setting out the various donations made to the new abbey of Saint-Evroult in *c*. 1050, he says:

> These are the gifts which William and Robert and their nephews Hugh and Robert and other relatives gave to the church of St Evroult; which they recorded in a charter and took to William, duke of Normandy, for his confirmation. He readily granted their petition and graciously confirmed their gifts to the abbey. He also favoured the church of St Evroult with a ducal privilege, exempting it for all time from subjection to any other authority ... Finally, the duke inserted this clause at the end of the record and confirmed it with these words: 'I William, count of the Normans, have caused this charter of donation to be written and have handed it to the archbishop of Rouen and the bishops, abbots, and lords whose names and subscriptions follow for confirmation, with the intention that it should remain ratified and inviolate henceforth for ever, so that if anyone presumes to infringe its provisions or seeks to diminish them in any way ... he is warned that by the will of God and all the saints he will be excommunicated throughout Christendom and utterly damned.' Uttering these words, Duke William signed the charter with the sign of the cross.

After the duke had made the sign of a cross at the foot of the sheet, a scribe would have added his name, and those of any others who signed, in the appropriate place. This sign was, therefore, equivalent to the seal, for both of them served the same purpose of showing that the duke wanted the act to be recognized and enforced.

As to the seal, William does not seem to have had one until after the conquest of England. When it first appeared, William's seal must have seemed rather impressive, because seals were still confined to the very highest ranks of the nobility. The first non-royal figure in France to have one seems to have been Count Geoffrey Martel of Anjou, who first used his in around 1060. The second nobleman to use a seal was the count of Flanders, who adopted one in

1065. The third was King William, who was certainly using a seal by 1069 and had probably used it since his coronation.[27]

King William's seal was, like that of Edward the Confessor, double-sided. However, while Edward's had depicted the king on his throne on both sides, William's showed him enthroned as king on just one. On the other side – actually the obverse – he was depicted as a mounted knight carrying a gonfanon. Around the edge of the seal there is a legend which begins on the equestrian side and reads: 'With this [seal] recognize William the advocate of the Normans or / with this acknowledge him as king of the English.'

As duke and king, William's most important functions were to keep the peace and do justice.[28] To do this he should make laws and enforce them. And this is what William did. William of Poitiers was not the only one to think so, but these are his words on the subject:

> By his strict discipline and by his laws robbers, murderers and evil-doers have been driven out of Normandy. The oath of peace which is called the Truce has been most scrupulously observed in Normandy, whereas in other regions it is frequently violated through unbridled wickedness. He listened to the cause of widows, orphans, and the poor, acting with mercy and judging most justly. Since his fairmindedness restrained greed, no one, however powerful or close to him, dared to move the boundary of a weaker neighbour's field or take anything from him. Villages, fortified places, and towns had stable and good laws through him.

The 'oath of peace which is called the Truce', mentioned in this passage, was imposed on his subjects by Duke William in the immediate aftermath of his victory at Val-ès-Dunes. The oath was made at a great assembly at Caen, in the presence of holy relics that had been brought to the spot from across Normandy. The occasion was, of course, intended to celebrate William's victory and to demonstrate his power. Kings and other secular rulers often made laws after a time of crisis; it was a way of re-establishing their authority in a very public manner. As to the Truce itself, it limited violence by prohibiting the waging of disruptive, and damaging 'private' war between Wednesday evening and Monday morning, as well as during Advent, Lent, Easter and Pentecost.[29]

Not all of William's enactments were made for the general good, however. 'Murdrum' had been the term applied to any secret killing in England before the Conquest, but now William limited its application to the secret killing of Frenchmen. Frenchmen were defined as those who had come to England with

18. The reverse of William's seal, showing the king in majesty, seated on a throne, wearing a crown, and holding a sword and the orb, all of them symbols of his rule.

William. Richard fitz Nigel, writing in the 1170s, explains the concept to a figurative pupil in his *Dialogue of the Exchequer*:

> Now, in the primitive state of the kingdom, after the Conquest, the remnant of the conquered English secretly laid ambushes for the Normans whom they distrusted and hated, and … when opportunity presented itself, they slew them in secret. When, to avenge their deaths, the monarchs and their ministers had for some years taken violent measures against the English … and yet the latter had not altogether ceased their attacks, at length the following plan was devised, namely that the hundred in which a Norman was found slain in this way – no evidence being found as to the identity of the slayer – should be condemned to pay into the treasury a large sum of tested silver … It is said that this was done so that the imposition of a general penalty might make it safe for wayfarers, and each man might hasten to punish so great a crime and hand over to justice the man by whose fault such an enormous indemnity was imposed on the whole neighbourhood.

The hundred was a subdivision of the shire, so that, as Richard fitz Nigel makes clear, the community was punished for the death if the murderer was not identified. The fine was usually 46 marks of silver, although Richard fitz Nigel says that it could be as high as £44 'according to the different localities and the frequency of homicide'. This was indeed a vast sum of money – more than the annual revenue that the king received from Guildford in 1086 (£32) and only a little less than the revenues from Oxford or Gloucester (£60).

If an individual broke the laws or transgressed the customs of England or Normandy, they would face trial. First of all, they had to be accused. This would usually be done by the individual or family that had suffered harm, but the community was responsible for policing itself and might also accuse those who were believed to have committed an offence. Offenders might be heard in one of a number of courts, but the offences of William's greatest subjects would be tried in his own court, although not always in his presence.

There are few examples of serious criminal cases being heard before William, but one is found in Orderic's *Ecclesiastical History*. Mabel of Bellême, the wife of Roger of Montgommery, was murdered, while she was relaxing in her bed after a bath, by Hugh Bunel, probably in 1077. Not long afterwards, William Pantulf, whose castle at Peray had been seized by Mabel, returned to Normandy from Italy. He found himself implicated in the murder:

> So a suspicion arose that she had perished by his scheming, especially as Hugh and William were close friends ... Consequently Earl Roger and his sons took possession of all his lands and demanded his death. But William with his wife and sons fled to Saint-Evroult and remained there for a long time ... under the protection of the monks. The knight steadfastly denied the charge against him; but while no one could produce certain proof of his guilt, none would accept his denial of the crime and his offer to purge himself by due process of law. At length by judgment of many of the greatest lords it was decreed in the king's court that the accused man should be given an opportunity of clearing himself of the shocking crime by undergoing the ordeal of hot iron at Rouen in the presence of the clergy. This was duly carried out. He carried the glowing iron in his bare hand, and by the will of God remained unscorched ... His enemies, eager for his blood, stood looking on ready armed, so that if the accused were found guilty by the ordeal of fire they might forthwith punish him by cutting off his guilty head.

William thus cleared his name through ordeal by hot iron (see Chapter 6). Had he been found guilty, he would have been executed – in this instance by members of the victim's family as a result of the subsequent feud.[30] Where the death penalty was avoided, either because of the judges' leniency or because the crime did not warrant it, a convicted person might suffer a lesser form of corporal punishment.

Mutilation, particularly the cutting off of hands, as well as blinding and castration, were punishments that were frequently handed down to rebels and criminals alike. Some, such as Luke of La Barre, who rebelled against Henry I in 1123–24, preferred to kill themselves rather than face blinding. Luke smashed his head against a wall until he split his skull open.[31] Others had to live with the punishment inflicted upon them. Some of these may have equipped themselves with prosthetic limbs to replace those they had lost. This happened in the following case, reported by Orderic and apparently dating from between 1113 and 1124, which concerns the death of the eldest son of Earl David, the future David I of Scotland (king 1124–53). The story might be fantasy, but it does nonetheless suggest what might be done when offenders were mutilated:

> David's wife bore him a son called Henry, and two daughters, Clarice and Hodierna. They had another boy, their first-born child, who was cruelly murdered by the iron fingers of a certain wretched clerk. This man was punished for an appalling crime, which he had committed in Norway, by having his eyes put out and his hands and feet cut off ... Afterwards, Earl David took him into his care in England for the love of God, and provided him and his small daughter with food and clothing. Using the iron fingers with which he was fitted, being maimed, he cruelly stabbed his benefactor's two-year-old son while pretending to caress him, and so at the prompting of the devil he suddenly tore out the bowels of the suckling in his nurse's arms. In this way David's first-born son was killed. The murderer was bound to the tails of four wild horses and torn to pieces by them, as a terrible warning to evil doers.

In some political cases a rebel, or potential rebel, might be exiled. But William had a reputation as a man who imprisoned his enemies. Guibert, abbot of Nogent from 1104 until *c.* 1121, wrote:

> in the days of King Henry the French were locked in a bitter combat with the Normans, and with their count, William, the one who was later to conquer the English and the Scots. In the course of an armed encounter between the two peoples my father was taken prisoner. It was a habit with the count in question never to hold his prisoners for ransom but to put them in prison for the rest of their lives.

Guibert was not quite right. In his case, his father died after eight months as William's prisoner, so when or if he would have been liberated is not known. Some of William's prisoners certainly were released. Count Guy of Ponthieu provides one example. He spent two years as William's captive, but was then set free. However, some were kept in prison for many years. Grimoult of Le Plessis-Grimoult was kept in chains for 30 years. Eventually 'he died in the king's prison at Rouen and was buried ... still having his legs in iron fetters as a sign of the treachery of which he was accused by the same king'.[32] Roger of Hereford remained in prison from 1075 until at least 1087. Odo of Bayeux was incarcerated from 1082 or 1083 until 1087. But William was not the only ruler to hold prisoners, and Guibert probably complains because of his personal circumstances.

Our knowledge of the prosecution of crime in William's day is limited. We know more, although still not enough, about what would today be classed as civil claims. In particular there is a relatively large amount of information about disputes over property. To take just one example, at some time between 1077 and 1082, a dispute arose between Bishop Gundulf of Rochester and Picot, the sheriff of Cambridgeshire, about land in Gisleham (Suffolk). Picot had granted the land to one of the king's men. He said that he could do this because the land in question belonged to the king. The bishop, however, declared that Picot had acted unlawfully, as the land belonged to the church of Rochester. And so the bishop and the sheriff came before the king and set out their cases. The king then ordered a meeting of the shire court to deal with the matter. At the shire court, the men of the county declared that the land belonged to the king. The report of the lawsuit, written by the monks of Rochester, says that in doing so they perjured themselves because they were afraid of the sheriff. But if the bishop was not satisfied with this verdict, then neither was Bishop Odo of Bayeux, who was presiding over the shire court. He demanded that if the jurors were sure what they said was true, they should select 12 of their number to swear an oath to that effect. The 12 men chosen withdrew to consider the matter. While they were working out their plan of action, they received a message from the sheriff. As they were 'struck with terror' by it, we may suppose that it contained threats. So when they returned to the court, they swore that what they had said before was true, even though they knew it was not. And so the land was judged to belong to the king and Rochester's claim was dismissed.

But this was not the end of the matter. Some time later a monk called Grim came before the bishop of Rochester. He had heard what had happened in the shire court and was amazed, for he knew that Gisleham belonged to Rochester. Still more to the point, Grim knew that at least one of the jurors knew that the land belonged to Rochester too. The bishop got tremendously excited at the news and went to the bishop of Bayeux to tell him what he had heard. Odo, wanting to hear the story from Grim in person, summoned him to court and had it out of him again. Then he summoned the juror whom Grim had named. He, in full knowledge that the deception had been uncovered, threw himself at the bishop's feet and acknowledged that he had lied.

It was now very clear that justice had not been done in Suffolk, and so Odo commanded that all the other men who had sworn the oath in the shire court should be sent to London. He also commanded that another 12 men of the shire should be sent with them, so that they might confirm on oath what the first 12 had already sworn to. He then summoned many of the greater men of England to the court – apparently without an order from the king – for a judgement would be needed and Odo wanted to make sure that it was pronounced by men of high standing. The judges declared that all the men of Suffolk were perjured, and the land was returned to the bishop of Rochester. The second batch of jurors, however, asserted that they did not agree with the statement of the perjured 12, in an attempt to avoid liability. Odo commanded that they should prove their innocence by ordeal of iron. They failed, and so became liable to pay a fine of £300 to the king.[33]

In England, pleas over land such as this one were generally heard in the shire or hundred courts – first, to keep the number of cases coming before the king in person down to a manageable level, second so that pleas might proceed in accordance with the custom of the shire, which might differ from county to county, and third because it was usually only the shire or hundred community that was able to say who held what land and who owed what services to whom.[34] The shire had this communal memory, of course, because all transfers of property were publicized there. It was the suitors of the shire or hundred courts who found the judgement, and it may be supposed that there were usually enough men of stature in these courts to ensure a fair result. Here, though, Picot's overbearing power, and the fact that the bishop was an absentee, meant that the sheriff could use threats to 'nobble' the judges.

In Normandy there seems not to have been any equivalent, in terms of a forum for justice, to the shire or hundred courts. Lawsuits would therefore be heard either by the lords of the duchy (when they had a jurisdiction), or before the duke or his appointed deputies. Where pleas came before William, both in Normandy and in England, he might listen to the plea, but he would not usually judge the case himself. He would instead appoint a number of judges from among the greatest men in attendance. The judges reached their decision on the basis of the arguments and the evidence presented to them. There might be witnesses, or there might be some documentary evidence. There might also be some bars to pleading. If a claimant took a long time to make his claim, for example, the defendant would use that as evidence to support his own case.[35] These procedures are much closer to the second part of this case, which dealt with the jurors' perjury. And it could be closer to Norman procedures because the question was no longer about the right to the land, so that the shire memory was no longer relevant.

William was renowned as a just ruler, and this was recognized and celebrated. 'We must not forget the good order he kept in the land,' says the 'E' version of the *Anglo-Saxon Chronicle*, 'so that a man of any substance could travel unmolested throughout the country with his bosom full of gold.' It is a sentiment echoed by William of Poitiers for Normandy: 'A man who was weak or unarmed could ride singing on his horse wherever he wished, without trembling at the sight of squadrons of knights.' William's subjects obeyed the laws because they knew that if they did not they would be severely punished. But, despite Poitiers's words, strong judges and severe penalties were not enough to keep his subjects in check. To maintain order and his position, William needed not only to be stern but also strong. How, then, did he raise the knights and soldiers that he needed to put down rebellions or to fight his external enemies?

In 1133 Henry I ordered that an inquisition be held into the possessions of the bishop of Bayeux. The inquest is, in essence, a list of the names of the men who held land from the bishop and the service that they owed for it. The inquest reports, for example, that Ranulf, *vicomte* of the Bessin, owed the bishop the service of seven-and-a-half knights for the lands that he held, while Robert of Gloucester owed 25 knights to the bishop. This is the classic picture of the 'feudal system' – men held their lands in return for a set quota of knights – but the extent to which it provides an accurate picture for the Normandy and England of William the Conqueror's day is not clear, and has been much debated.

There were certainly knights in Normandy before 1066, and it is also clear that they performed military service for their lords, including castle-guard.[36] The earliest surviving evidence from Normandy that mentions property held in return for a fixed number of knights, however, is an act for the abbey of Saint-Amand in Rouen, dating from between 1066 and 1087.[37] Nonetheless, it is likely that once the principle had been accepted, the number of knights required from each lord was quickly established. It is likely that the duke had an idea of the number of knights he expected from each man, and would negotiate with them on an *ad hoc* basis before each campaign. If a particular lord agreed to provide a particular number of knights on one occasion, it seems unlikely that he would be able to offer a smaller number on a subsequent occasion, without good reason. Thus quotas of knights were established. That the number demanded from each lord could become fixed so quickly is indicated by Wace. The lords of Normandy were concerned that the number of knights they offered Duke William in 1066 – double the usual figure according to this later source – might become customary. They were reassured that this would not be the case, but Wace's story shows that just one occasion could produce an expectation of identical service on subsequent occasions.

The Normans, then, arrived in England with a developing concept that land should be held in return for military service. But this was not unique to them. It was an idea that had also taken root in England before 1066. By then it had become established that those who possessed book-land (land held by a written charter in heredity) as well as those who held loan-land (land given to a man in return for his service, usually for life) were expected to provide military service to their lords. The number of men owed might have been based on a general concept of one man for every five hides of land, although this is only expressly set out in the entry in Domesday Book for Berkshire.[38] (A hide was a notional unit of land, adequate to support one family. It might vary dramatically in size depending on the quality of the land.) In any event, it seems clear that English lords were expected to bring a certain number of men with them to serve in the king's army well before 1066.

The Norman Conquest, therefore, did not bring about a seismic change in the way that land was held in England. There was already a sense that the number of warriors owed was related to the amount of land held. This relationship might have provided the basis for the imposition of quotas after 1066 – or it might not. There is insufficient evidence on this point to reach conclusions either way. Nor do we know when such quotas were imposed. Historians used to point to a writ of 1072, addressed to the abbot of Evesham, which required the abbot to come to serve William with 'those five knights which you owe me from your abbey'. However, the most recent editor of the Conqueror's acts, David Bates, has suggested that it is not an authentic document and that it perhaps dates from the thirteenth century.[39] Even without the evidence necessary to reach a conclusion on this point, it still seems unlikely that quotas were a truly novel or outrageous idea in England. The only real innovation of the Conquest here, then, was that the service due should be performed by a mounted knight rather than an armoured infantryman.

Aside from his ability to raise an army, William's rule depended on castles, especially on his construction and control of them. The point is most famously made by Orderic Vitalis:

> the king rode to all the remote parts of his kingdom and fortified strategic
> sites against enemy attacks. For the fortifications called castles by the
> Normans were scarcely known in the English provinces, and so the English
> – in spite of their courage and love of fighting – could put up only a weak
> resistance to their enemies.

Castles are extremely difficult to define as a group, although easy to recognize on a case-by-case basis. But because there are no surviving intact Anglo-Saxon fortifications, historians have for years been fascinated with what the difference might have been between an English burh, a fortified residence, and a Norman castle. Ann Williams has looked at the requirement, laid down in the eleventh-century tract called *The Rights and Ranks of People*, that a thegn possess a 'burh gate'.[40] The word 'burh', she argues, was used to mean a private residence as well as a town or communal defence. Her argument has been supported by the excavations carried out at Sulgrave (Northamptonshire) and at Goltho (Lincolnshire). At Goltho, archaeologists found a tenth-century fortified house which was rebuilt and redesigned over time, until by *c.* 1080 it had become a motte-and-bailey castle. In the late ninth or tenth century the hall and ancillary buildings were surrounded by an earth bank and by a ditch up to seven feet deep and 18 feet wide. The Norman castle, however, was 'considerably stronger'.[41]

The extent to which English Goltho looked different to a Norman ringwork is not clear from the excavations. And as there have been so few excavations, we are thrown back on documentary and narrative sources. These suggest that the chief difference lay in the respective functions of the burh and castle. It is not clear that private burhs like Goltho were truly defensible. They were surrounded by a hedge or a simple fence, which might have provided a sturdy barrier against anyone seeking to force entry, but which could provide only a passive form of defence. A castle, on the other hand, was usually protected by a palisade which had a wall-walk behind it, perhaps crenellations to provide cover for archers and other defenders, and perhaps towers along the perimeter of the wall.[42] Norman castles thus allowed their garrisons to shoot at their enemies from the top of the wall or towers, or to hurl objects down on them. These features would also have meant that they looked very different from the burhs. Secondly, burhs may not have been garrisoned. As such, they could not have fulfilled the castle's function as a strongpoint in time of attack or rebellion. Williams notes that burhs were not used by rebels to defy the king. Whereas Normans fortified their castles when they rebelled, English thegns took to their ships and raided instead. The castle, then, kept its alien garrison safe and posed a palpable threat to those in its shadow in a way that the burh did not. Thirdly, many castles were constructed, as Orderic notes, at strategic sites: at river crossings, on main roads and inside towns. Burhs do not seem to have been constructed with strategic considerations in mind, although that did not prevent the conversion of Goltho from burh to castle.

These questions, although interesting, are diversions. No matter how modern historians define a castle, and no matter precisely how it was different to the English burh, it is clear that the English saw the castle as an unwelcome innovation. It is equally clear that the Normans constructed them across the country in large numbers. The 'D' version of the *Anglo-Saxon Chronicle* states that in 1067, when William returned to Normandy, 'Bishop Odo and Earl William were left behind here and they built castles far and wide throughout the land, oppressing the unhappy people.' It may be supposed that the people were unhappy in part because they were coerced into providing the labour with which to construct these fortifications, as well as because the fruit of their labours prevented them from resisting further demands for tribute or service. Domesday Book, compiled at the very end of the reign, mentions just under 50 castles, but there were certainly more. Exactly how many more is not known, but somewhere around 500 is not unlikely.

Castles provided a threat not just to the English but also to William himself. In the hands of a discontented lord, such as Count William of Arques in 1052 or Earl Ralph of East Anglia in 1075, they might be held against him, necessitating the trouble and expense of a siege. As a result of this clear danger, William sought to control castle building in Normandy – this was, of course, impossible in England after the Conquest. He also demanded the right to garrison his subjects' castles at will, thereby taking away their ability to use them against him. A list of William's rights as duke, drawn up in 1091 or 1096, states that,

> no one in Normandy might dig a fosse in the open country of more than one shovel's throw in depth, nor set there more than one line of palisading, and that without battlements or allures. And no one might make a fortification on a rock or in an island, and no one might raise a castle in Normandy, and no one in Normandy might withhold the strength of his castle from the lord of Normandy, if he wished to take it into his own hand.[43]

19. The Warenne castle at Castle Acre (Norfolk). Athough of typical motte-and-
bailey form from *c.* 1130, the motte was originally lower and contained a
'country house' that was only later reconstructed as a keep.

And William did indeed take castles into his hands, as can be seen from the
following passage from Orderic's *Ecclesiastical History*. It is a passage that not
only makes William's control over his subjects' castles clear, but also reveals
the wisdom of his policy:

> Robert of Bellême was hastening to the king's court to speak with him on
> important matters when, coming to the gates of Brionne, he heard that the
> king was dead. Instantly, wheeling round his horse, he galloped to Alençon,
> caught the king's men off their guard, and drove them out of the stronghold.
> He did the same at Bellême and in all his other castles ... In like manner
> William, count of Evreux, drove the king's watchmen out of the keep [of
> Evreux], and William of Breteuil, Ralph of Conches and others gained control
> of all the castles in their domains ... So the magnates of Normandy expelled
> the king's garrisons from their castles and, plundering each other's lands
> with their own men at arms, they stripped the rich country of its wealth.

J.O. Prestwich has said that 'the whole history of the development of the
Anglo-Norman administration is intelligible only in terms of the scale and the
pressing needs of war finance'.[44] This might be an overstatement, but it does

indicate how war and finance and, for that matter, success were all linked. William financed his rule and his wars using a variety of means, some of them well established and others rather more opportunistic.

In Normandy and, after 1066, in England, William was able to draw on the revenues produced by the lands that he had inherited or retained in his own hands. He did not oversee these estates himself; instead they were 'farmed'. This means that the lands and any associated rights and dues were leased out for one year to a man, usually the *vicomte*, or sheriff, who would pay a set rent for them. This money was paid into the treasury each year. The farmer would, of course, hope to make a profit on the deal. William, however, is said by the 'E' version of the *Anglo-Saxon Chronicle* to have farmed his land for the highest possible price, with dire consequences for the farmers and the population as a whole:

> The king granted his land on the hardest terms and at the highest possible price. If another buyer came and offered more than the first had given, the king would let it go to the man who offered him more. If a third came and offered still more, the king would make it over to the man who offered him most of all. He did not care at all how very wrongfully the reeves got possession of it from wretched men, nor how many illegal acts they did ... Unjust tolls were levied and many other unlawful acts were committed which are distressing to relate.

The men had offered too much for the land, and so resorted to extortion to recover their costs.

We have no figures for the income from Normandy until the end of the twelfth century, but at that time the farms brought in something like £5,000 sterling every year. For England, Domesday Book reveals that the royal manors and rights brought the king an income of almost £14,000. Aside from money, the king also received a variety of payments in kind, such as honey, herrings, hawks and, from Norwich, 'one bear and six dogs for the bear'.

William also charged for his justice and for the writs and diplomas issued in his name. An idea of the relative importance of these various categories of income is provided by the pipe roll of 1130. The pipe rolls were produced at an annual audit at Westminster, held around 29 September, and they recorded the revenue that the king received or was owed. The roll for 1130 is the earliest that survives. In that year, according to the figures compiled by Judith Green, the king's estates brought in £11,700 out of a total of £23,000. 'Pleas', the financial penalties arising from lawsuits, produced £2,396. Murdrum fines accounted for £122. And Danegeld brought in £2,400.[45]

Danegeld (which had been called 'heregeld' before 1066) was the most important tax in England. It had first been levied in 1012 and was then raised as occasion demanded by Æthelred II, Cnut and Edward the Confessor.[46] William seems to have levied gelds annually, although the 'D' and 'E' versions of the *Anglo-Saxon Chronicle* only complain about the taxes demanded in 1066, 1067, 1083 (actually 1084) and 1086. In 1086, for example, it laments that William 'did as he was wont, he levied very heavy taxes on his subjects, upon any pretext, whether justly or unjustly'. Domesday Book reports that the burgesses of Norwich had been 'utterly devastated', partly because of Earl Ralph's rebellion in 1075, partly because of fires, and 'partly because of the king's tax'.

The geld of 1084 was levied at an unusually heavy rate of 6s. on the hide, which would account for the 'E' chronicler's complaint for that year. Normally the rate was 2s. on the hide. But no matter how high the rate, the money was always forthcoming, because if someone could not pay the geld assessed on their land within a set time, then anybody who was able and willing to produce the money due could take that land from them. Worcester's cathedral lost five estates in Warwickshire in Cnut's time because of this.[47]

Apart from having these formal means of raising money, William was also opportunistic. After Hastings the English were allowed to buy back their land, thereby swelling William's coffers. The campaigns in Maine in 1063 and in England between 1068 and 1072 saw William gaining wealth through plunder. In 1070 William appropriated the money that rich Englishmen had deposited in the abbeys for safekeeping, apparently at the suggestion of William fitz Osbern. The collectors did not, it seems, always distinguish between the deposited property and the church's own possessions. Hence the complaint of the 'D' and 'E' versions of the *Anglo-Saxon Chronicle* that 'in the spring of the same year the king had all the monasteries in England plundered'.

Plunder might be taken in the form of plate and jewels. Some renders might be made in kind. But both England and Normandy at the end of the eleventh century were money economies. And in both England and Normandy, William had a monopoly on the minting of coins. In Normandy there were two mints, one at Rouen and one at Bayeux. In England, which was of course much larger, there were mints in 60 or 70 towns, employing around 200 moneyers. These men hammered out coins using dies that had been produced

20. Silver penny of the two stars type, struck by Oswald at the Lewes mint.

centrally by Otto the Goldsmith, and then distributed to the mints. It seems likely that Otto used a standard set of punches to build up the design, rather than engraving each set by hand.[48]

William's English coins carry his portrait, often with some symbolic accoutrement. Thus the issue of William I's coinage known as the 'bonnet type' shows him wearing an imperial crown in the style of a Byzantine emperor; the 'sword type' reflects the conventional ruler portrait, and shows William holding a sword as a symbol of his temporal power; while the 'profile/cross and trefoils type' shows William in profile, like a Roman emperor. William's name is found around the edge of the obverse. In the centre of the reverse of the coin there was a cross, and the moneyer's name and his mint were embossed around the edge. With their high silver content and their symbolism, these coins could be said both to present an image of royal power and to reflect it. No wonder that Henry I acted to protect the coinage when it was threatened. In 1124, according to Robert of Torigny,

> while the king was ... engaged in warfare in Normandy, almost all the moneyers of the English kingdom produced, I do not know by what wicked perversity, money out of tin containing scarcely one-third of silver, whereas it should have consisted of pure silver. It happened that some of the false money, having been taken to Normandy, was used to pay the king's soldiers.

The soldiers complained to the king, and the result was that all the moneyers in England, with one exception, lost their right hands and were castrated.

The Norman coins, in contrast, did not depict the ruler; they did not even bear his name. Indeed after 1027 the legend was composed not even of real letters but simply of dots and linear patterns. It was only at the very end of William's reign that there was a slight improvement; a legible legend returned to the reverse of the coin. This read 'Rouen'. At around the same time a new group of coins appears, with the inscription 'Norman Dux' or 'Normannia' on the reverse. There is a great variety of design among these coins, although almost all of them have a triangle surmounted by a cross on the obverse. Some also have the word 'PAX', which might have been brought to Normandy from England. This type continued into Henry I's reign.[49]

The English and Norman coinages thus remained distinct, and this reflects a broader trend. The Norman Conquest did not see the wholesale importation of Norman ideas and procedures into England, or English ones into Normandy. Both parts of William's dominions continued to operate more or less as they had before 1066. But they did begin to affect each other. Ideas crossed the Channel in both directions, causing assimilation in some areas and evolution and innovation in others. But this took time to bear fruit, and it was only in Henry I's reign that the changes wrought by the Conquest became clear.

CHAPTER 5

STERN BEYOND MEASURE, 1066–76

Three months after his coronation as king of the English, in March 1067, William recrossed the Channel to Normandy to celebrate his victory. He took with him Archbishop Stigand, Edgar Ætheling, the brothers Earl Edwin of Mercia and Earl Morcar of Northumbria, Earl Waltheof and others. They were taken to Normandy to ensure that there would be no rebellion in England during his absence, not only because he had with him all those around whom such a rebellion might coalesce but also because these men were now effectively hostages for the good behaviour of their countrymen. They were also chosen so that William could show them off to the prelates and lords who celebrated his triumph at courts at Rouen and Fécamp. Orderic says how French as well as Norman nobles attended these courts and how they were,

> eyeing curiously the long-haired denizens of England, wondering at the splendid garments, interwoven and encrusted with gold, worn by the king and his court, and praising the gold and silver vessels, and horns of wild oxen decorated with gold at both ends.

At those same triumphant courts William distributed rich gifts to the churches of his duchy, many of them looted from churches in England. William's gifts to his own abbey of Saint-Etienne in Caen are especially singled out by William of Poitiers. The abbeys of Saint-Pierre-sur-Dives and Jumièges would also have benefited when William visited them to celebrate the consecration of their churches. Jumièges might even have been given Hayling Island (Hampshire) at this time – a gift that was to bring it into conflict with Winchester Cathedral which claimed prior ownership. William of Malmesbury says that William devoted much attention to almsgiving, 'lavishly bestowing much English property on churches overseas'. Domesday Book reveals just how much English property had been transferred to the hands of Norman abbeys and churches by 1086.

William crossed to and from England to Normandy for the rest of his reign. The table below gives an idea of the times William spent on each side of the Channel, although it is not possible to provide a definite itinerary.[1] For example, it is just possible that William made a flying visit to Normandy in 1069, although on balance it seems unlikely. Equally we do not know whether William crossed back to Normandy in late 1072 or early 1073. The following then is no more than a guide, based on an interpretation – and not the only possible one – of the existing evidence.

Normandy	England
March 1067–December 1067	
	December 1067–late 1068
late 1068–early 1069	
	early 1069–autumn 1070
autumn 1070–early1071	
	early 1071–late 1071
late 1071–spring 1072	
	spring 1072–spring 1073
spring 1073–late 1073	
	late 1073–early 1074
early 1074–autumn 1075	
	autumn 1075–after May 1076
after May 1076–autumn 1080	

Table 1. William's Channel crossings, 1066–76.

For the first few years after the conquest all was quiet in Normandy. The king travelled around the duchy, hearing lawsuits and reforming his administration. But although Normandy itself remained at peace, trouble was to flare up on its borders in 1069 when the city of Le Mans revolted against Norman rule. William was in England at the time, dealing with an uprising there. He was consequently unable to take action, as Azzo, an Italian lord who had married Gersendis, the sister of the late Count Hugh, gathered support and led a revolt that saw William's steward killed, the Norman garrison expelled from Le Mans and the flight of Bishop Arnold to William in England. Once Azzo believed that he had ousted the Normans and gained control of Maine for his wife, he returned to Italy. Gersendis and Azzo's young son, Hugh, were left in charge. But once Azzo had gone, Geoffrey of Mayenne took Gersendis as a mistress and seized control of the county. His rule provoked a further rebellion in Le Mans, but he was able to suppress this successfully.

King William must have been concerned about the situation. Norman control of Maine had collapsed. If it were not re-established quickly, then some other power, most likely Anjou or France, would intervene. But before William could address the issue, yet more bad news arrived. On 16 July 1070 Count Baldwin VI of Flanders, William's brother-in-law, died. His lands were divided between his two sons, Arnulf and Baldwin, but as they were still young, government devolved to their mother, Richildis. Her rule was opposed in Flanders by Robert the Frisian, a younger son of Baldwin V and thus another of William's brothers-in-law. Richildis appealed to King Philip of France for help. She also approached William fitz Osbern, King William's right-hand man, who had been sent to Normandy to keep an eye on events in Maine. Indeed Richildis offered to marry William fitz Osbern and placed her son, Arnulf, in his wardship. William fitz Osbern then hastened to Flanders, with only ten knights, 'as if to a game'.[2] On 20 or 22 February 1071 a battle was fought at Cassel.[3] On one side was Robert the Frisian and his supporters. On the other were King Philip and William fitz Osbern. King Philip lost, William fitz Osbern was killed, Richildis was overthrown and the victorious Robert the Frisian became count of Flanders.

King William returned to Normandy towards the end of 1071. His actions are unclear, but he must have taken stock of the situation in both Flanders and Maine, garrisoned his castles along what were now exposed borders and perhaps even visited the grave of his friend, William fitz Osbern, at Cormeilles. And then, as soon as William had satisfied himself that the duchy was not in imminent danger of attack, he crossed back to England to lead a campaign against the king of Scots.

It was only in 1073 that William was able finally to deal with Maine, where the situation was worsening. By now Count Fulk of Anjou had become involved. The citizens of Le Mans had asked for his help against the tyranny of Geoffrey of Mayenne, and had delivered up the castle to him. It was time for

King William to deal with the situation, and so he assembled an army – made up of Norman *and* English soldiers – and descended 'like a scourge' on the county of Maine. William of Malmesbury says that he threatened to turn it into a desert. The chronicle known as *The Acts of the Bishops of Le Mans Residing in the City* is a little more measured:

> During the same time, William, king of the English, gathered an innumerable army and came into the county of Maine. He besieged the castle of Fresnay-sur-Sarthe and devastated with fire and sword all the fields and vines in the vicinity of the castle. And when the castellans of Fresnay found themselves unable to sustain his assault, they made peace with him as best they were able. After the castle had been reconquered and the king had installed his own garrison in its donjon, William travelled to Le Mans and set up fortifications at Mantula, which is near the city and the Sarthe river. The leading men of the city came out of Le Mans to Mantula where they held a peace conference with the king. The citizens accepted oaths from William: he promised them freedom from treachery and promised to uphold the ancient customs and justice of their city. In turn the citizens gave themselves and all their things completely into his power and authority.

William had seen off Fulk of Anjou, but his activity in Maine was a warning that Anjou was once again a power to be reckoned with. At the same time, Robert the Frisian was hostile to Normandy, and King Philip of France, now 20 years old, was able to see the possibilities for gain in uniting Flanders and Anjou against Normandy. The years of easy success, brought about by a young king of France and a weak Anjou, were coming to an end. The future would see much more trouble in William's continental dominions.

But let us now return to England. Almost the first thing that William did after London submitted to him in 1066 was to begin the construction of three castles there. The most important of these stood in the south-eastern corner of the city. Around 1075 work began on a new stone tower within the enclosure. This was the White Tower of the Tower of London, which still stands as a memorial to William. From London William travelled around the south of England, building castles. His itinerary is not clear, but he certainly visited Winchester, which he put into the custody of William fitz Osbern, who seems to have been appointed the successor to part of Harold Godwinson's earldom of Wessex. He was to exercise power not only in Hampshire but also at various times before his death in 1071 in Herefordshire, Somerset, Gloucestershire and possibly Wiltshire, in each case in a manner which

21. The White Tower of the Tower of London, begun *c.* 1075.

might suggest that he was acting like an English earl.[4] Odo of Bayeux was likewise left in charge of the castle at Dover. The lands of other Englishmen who had fought or fallen at Hastings were redistributed among a selection of William's Normans, although this was an ongoing process. This explains the comment in the 'E' version of the *Anglo-Saxon Chronicle* that William 'gave away every man's land' after he returned from Normandy at the end of 1067. Indeed William sent a writ to the abbot of Bury St Edmunds demanding that the lands of those who had been killed at the battle should be identified and surrendered to him. Some Englishmen, unable or unwilling to come to terms with the new order, left the country, and their lands, too, were taken into the king's hands as the possessions of fugitives. Some of them ended up in Constantinople where they took service with the emperor and fought, with more success, against the Normans of southern Italy. Some Englishmen, however, reconciled themselves to the new regime and were allowed to buy back their lands. Abbot Brand of Peterborough, for example, paid £240 to redeem the property that he and his brothers had given the abbey.[5]

William of Poitiers is keen to point out that 'nothing was given to any Frenchman which had been taken unjustly from any Englishman'. This looks like a response to the complaint of the 'E' version of the *Anglo-Saxon Chronicle* that William 'gave away every man's land'. Indeed there is a great deal in Poitiers's work that looks like a response to criticisms of the Conquest. He praises William's choice of custodians, explicitly criticized in the *Chronicle*, and he declares that William's enrichment of the Norman Church was not the despoliation of the English Church. As David Bates has remarked, 'many aspects of his work make best sense as attempts to rebut criticism' and the whole should be seen as intending to legitimize William's succession.[6]

William of Poitiers was certainly in a good position to hear this criticism. He was a Norman from Préaux, and he clearly came from a good family because his sister was made abbess of the abbey of Saint-Léger. Orderic tells us that,

> we call him 'of Poitiers' because he drank deeply of the fountain of learning there. When he returned home he was conspicuous for his learning in his native parts, and as archdeacon helped the bishops of Lisieux, Hugh and Gilbert, in the administration of their diocese. He had been a brave soldier before entering the Church, and had fought with warlike weapons for his earthly prince, so that he was all the better able to describe the battles he had seen through having himself some experience of the dire perils of war. In his old age he gave himself up to silence and prayer, and spent more time in composing narratives and verse than in discourse.

He had served as one of William's chaplains and was therefore close to his subject – perhaps too close. He wrote his *Deeds of William* between 1071 and 1077, probably after he had left the court and become archdeacon of Lisieux. His aim was to glorify William's deeds, to portray him as a good ruler by providing him with the necessary attributes, and to rebut the criticisms of his actions as king. At one point he even pleads with the English to give William the opportunity to show his greatness. The work's obvious sympathy for its subject has been a problem almost from the time it was written. Orderic, who used it extensively, simply refused to include any passages praising William's mercy to the conquered English in his *Ecclesiastical History*. Modern historians have been even less kind. John Gillingham has described the *Deeds of William* as 'nauseatingly sycophantic'.[7] Poitiers's work, however, is enormously valuable, if also full of pitfalls for the unwary reader.

William returned to Normandy in March 1067. He left Bishop Odo and William fitz Osbern behind and they, perhaps because they were concerned about an English backlash, ruled with a firm hand, building castles and oppressing the people. As noted above, William had taken all the obvious potential leaders of a national rebellion – Edgar Ætheling, Archbishop Stigand and the earls – with him to Normandy, and this tactic might be supposed to have worked, because there was no widespread uprising against Norman rule in his absence. But there were a number of small and isolated revolts. Perhaps the first happened at Dover. It was fomented by Count Eustace of Boulogne, who is described by Poitiers as 'working against the king' at this time. The count, who had played a central role at Hastings, seems to have felt that he had not received his due. His claim to the English lands that had been held by his relatives was passed over. He might, in particular, have coveted lands in Kent which would increase the profits of his ports at Boulogne and Wissant. Without outside support Eustace could have done nothing about this, but he was encouraged to invade by the English of Kent. And so, in the words of William of Jumièges:

> Eustace, count of Boulogne ... dared to prepare an invasion of the stronghold of Dover. In the middle of the night he crossed the sea and at the crack of dawn besieged the fortress with his entire army ... But the garrison ... to whom the defence of the fortress had been entrusted ... with great courage they opened the gates and all burst out together unexpectedly, joined battle, and put the besiegers to flight in shame. Eustace with some of his men turned about to the sea and fled by ship in disgrace. Others fled to the slope of the cliff that hangs over the sea with very sharp rocks and crags, panic-stricken by God all threw themselves into the water and met justice for their crime.[8]

Count Eustace lost all his English property as a result of this piece of foolishness. It took several years, perhaps a full decade, before he and King William were reconciled and his English lands were returned to him.

Meanwhile, in the west, Eadric the Wild called on the kings of the Welsh for aid, and laid waste Herefordshire up to the River Lugg. This, so John of Worcester tells us, was because the Hereford garrison, as well as Richard fitz Scrob of Richard's Castle, had razed his own lands at every opportunity, because he had refused to surrender them to the king. He now vented his anger and frustration on his enemies with considerable success.

In the north the Yorkshireman Copsi, who had been made earl of Bamburgh by William in 1067,[9] was murdered by his rival Earl Osulf 'in the fifth week after he received the earldom'. Copsi was feasting at Newburn (now a suburb of Newcastle) when Earl Osulf and his men attacked. Copsi fled to the nearby church, which was set on fire. As he emerged from the burning building,

Osulf cut off his head. Ann Williams has suggested that this murder had nothing to do with English dislike of Norman rule. It simply reflected the fact
that all rule from the south, whether West Saxon or Norman, was resented.
The Northumbrians did not care to have an earl sent to them from the south
when they had their own house of Bamburgh.[10] King William realized that
he had made a mistake and seems to have borne the Northumbrians little
rancour – perhaps because Copsi had been English rather than Norman. He
allowed Gospatrick, Osulf's cousin (Osulf himself had by now been killed by
a robber), to purchase the earldom of Bamburgh from him. And so peace was
restored north of the Tyne – for the time being.

Even as William extinguished the flames in one part of the country, so the
fire of rebellion broke out somewhere else. The men of Exeter rebelled early
in 1068, perhaps as a result of a combination of the high geld demanded by
the king, and the presence in the city of Harold's mother, Gytha. The king
marched to the west. Some of his troops were Englishmen who were now
called up to serve under him for the first time. Initially the citizens were
prepared to cooperate with him, going so far as to provide hostages. But they
treated William's demands for submission as the basis for negotiation, and
the talks broke down. The king brought up his army to the walls and had
one of the hostages blinded to encourage the citizens to surrender, but it just
made them more determined to stand firm. The city was besieged for 18
days. William of Malmesbury tells us that during this time one of the defenders bared his bottom at the Normans below and farted loudly to show his
contempt for them. The king refused to believe that God would side with
men who behaved in such a manner, and when part of the city wall collapsed
shortly afterwards he ascribed it to divine disgust. The collapse of the wall,
or the increasing hunger suffered by those inside, or their realization that
they could not win, led to the surrender of the city. A delegation was sent
to the king and they threw themselves on his mercy. William graciously
accepted their submission and forgave the citizens. Gytha fled to Flatholme in
the Severn Estuary and then, in 1069, to Flanders.[11] William was, it seems,
still prepared to try to win English hearts and minds. But the citizens did
not escape entirely scot-free. A castle was constructed in the corner of the
city where 48 houses had previously stood. William took the opportunity to
march further west into Cornwall, apparently just to show his face and assert
his authority by his presence, before retiring to Winchester for Easter.

22. (above) Bamburgh Castle. The keep dates from the reign of Henry II, although it has been much altered, but the site had been associated with the kings of Northumbria from the seventh century.

23. (left) The gate-tower at Exeter, which seems to betray English workmanship in the triangular-headed openings.

There is no sense of a national English resistance in all of this. Gytha's supporters in Exeter might have tried to rally support elsewhere in the country, but these were all separate, small-scale revolts, caused by William's offence to local self-interests. But if there was no connection, and no unifying purpose, behind these risings, there were many more of them than the chroniclers report in detail. William of Jumièges says that 'throughout the country bandits conspired with the intention of slaying the soldiers whom the king had everywhere left behind to defend the kingdom'. Similarly the *History of the Church of Abingdon* reports that,

> many plots began to be hatched in the English kingdom. At such plots worked away those now compelled to bear the lordship of men from overseas, to which they had not hitherto been accustomed. Some hid themselves away in woods, some in islands, living by plunder like pirates, slaughtering those who came their way.

No wonder that William was compelled to impose the murdrum fine.

But King William does seem to have attempted to settle the grievances that caused these risings. His leniency to the Northumbrians has been mentioned. In addition, Orderic says that, at least before the rebellion at Exeter, the king was gracious to everyone, that he gave them the kiss of peace and smiled on them all, granted the favours that they sought and listened to them. In this way he hoped to appease them. He certainly thought that the country was adequately pacified by the spring of 1068 to summon Matilda from Normandy. She arrived shortly after the Easter court at Winchester and was taken to London for her coronation. She was crowned queen on Whit Sunday (11 May) by Archbishop Ealdred of York.

William was to be disappointed, however. England was still to be disturbed by rebellion and invasion. Later, in 1068, Earls Edwin and Morcar rebelled. Orderic Vitalis says that they were provoked to rebellion by the king's failure to agree to set a date for the marriage of one of his daughters to Earl Edwin, as he had promised. The brothers were joined by King Bleddyn of north Wales, their brother-in-law. Meanwhile, in the far north, appeals were made to Malcolm Canmore, king of Scots, to invade. Orderic tells us that the king built a castle at Warwick and that 'after this, Edwin, Morcar and their men, unwilling to face the doubtful issue of a battle, and wisely preferring peace to war, sought the king's pardon and obtained it at least in outward appearance'. Hearing this, York surrendered and William built a castle there too.[12] Other castles were constructed at this same time at Nottingham, Lincoln, Hunting-don and Cambridge.

The castle at Shrewsbury was also probably erected during this spate of building. It certainly seems to be the case that Earl Edwin was now deprived of his position in the shire, as Chris Lewis has all but proven that Roger of Montgommery was made earl of Shrewsbury in 1068.[13] The appointment was no doubt intended to send Edwin a stern warning as to his future pros-pects should he continue to rebel, while at the same time it stopped short of provoking him to further rebellion. A second bird was also killed with this one stone. Eadric the Wild, who had raided south into Herefordshire, was one of the greatest of Shropshire landholders. The creation of Montgommery as earl would rein him in too.[14]

From the very beginning of 1069 the troubles continued. Robert of Commines, earl of Durham, was killed on 28 or 31 January 1069, during his very first night in the city. Rather like Copsi, Robert was apparently seen as an unwelcome outsider, so that the people of Durham had conspired to murder him before he had even arrived there. The king sent an army north to avenge his death, but, as the chronicler Simeon of Durham relates, a dark mist arose which entirely obscured their path. As the halted Normans were deciding what to do, someone remarked that Durham was protected by St Cuthbert, who would revenge himself on anyone who attacked the city. At this, the army returned to their homes. (Cuthbert, whose remains are still buried in the cathedral, might well have pulled off a similar feat in April 1942, when a thick white mist hid the city and cathedral from German bombers.)

Immediately after the Durham incident, Edgar Ætheling attacked York and its castle.[15] William Malet, the constable, sent word to King William that he would be compelled to surrender to the English unless he was speed-ily relieved. The king did not disappoint him. So quickly did King William advance that he caught the rebels entirely off guard. He fell on the besiegers and spared no man. He stayed in York for eight days, and while he was there commanded that a second castle should be built outside the city – this is Baile Hill which stands across the River Ouse from Clifford's Tower. No less a personage than William fitz Osbern was left there as constable. This done, the king returned south and held his Easter court at Winchester. The English tried one more attack on York but could not defeat William fitz Osbern.

And then, in August, the rebels were reinforced and the rebellion stepped up a gear. Harold and Cnut, the sons of King Swein of Denmark, arrived off the coast of England in command of 240 ships.[16] They first appeared off Dover and then sailed north along the coast to Sandwich, Ipswich, Norwich and on to the Humber. William, then in the Forest of Dean, heard of their arrival and sent a warning to York, which he must have guessed was the force's ultimate destination, telling his lieutenants to prepare for an attack and to send for him if they were hard pressed. They replied that they could hold out for a year without help. John of Worcester says that on Saturday 19 September, the garrison, in preparation for the attack, set fire to the houses nearest the castle to stop them from being dismantled and used to fill in the ditch. The fire spread out of control, destroying many buildings, including the cathedral of St Peter.

When the Danes reached the smouldering ruins of York the next Monday, they were joined by Waltheof and Edgar Ætheling. The surviving citizens of York, seeing that liberation was at hand, rose to a man. Earl Waltheof and other leading figures entered the city as an advance guard, and the garrison sallied out to attack them. This was an error. They were hugely outnumbered by the English and were all slain or taken prisoner. William of Malmesbury adds the detail that Waltheof had beheaded Normans one-by-one as they came through the gate: 'He had great strength of arm, powerful chest muscles, his whole frame tough and tall.' The castles that had been built in the city were destroyed.

Hearing that the king was coming, the Danes left the city with untold spoils – even these allies of the English took the opportunity to plunder the remains of the city – and crossed into Lincolnshire. King William dispatched Count Robert of Mortain and Count Robert of Eu to Lincolnshire to deal with the Danes who were still there. The two counts inflicted some casualties on them, but the rest fled back to York. In the meantime William himself marched south-west to Stafford to quell a rebellion there, and then moved back to Nottingham. Further south, the castle at Montacute was attacked, a revolt that was dealt with by Geoffrey of Montbray, and Exeter was besieged by the sons of King Harold, who had returned, for the second time, from Ireland. They were dealt with by William fitz Osbern and Count Brian of Brittany. These two short-lived revolts, again the result of local circumstances rather than part of a national rebellion, were the last to be staged in the south of England. All open resistance there was now ended.

While William was at Nottingham, news came that the Danes, who had escaped from the counts of Mortain and Eu, were preparing to re-occupy

York. William consequently moved north once again, although he was delayed at Pontefract for three weeks by the flooded River Aire. By the time he arrived at York, the Danes had fled – or had been bribed to depart – but that did not prevent William from venting his fury on the countryside and the population at large. A number of chroniclers, writing some decades after the events in question, and at a time, perhaps, when the tale had grown in the telling, describe William's campaign in near-apocalyptic terms. Thus Orderic Vitalis, in an emotional passage, says that,

> he cut down many in his vengeance; destroyed the lairs of others; harried the land and burned homes to ashes. Nowhere else had William shown such cruelty ... In his anger he commanded that all crops and herds, chattels and food of every kind should be brought together and burned to ashes with consuming fire, so that the whole region north of the Humber might be stripped of all means of sustenance. In consequence so serious a scarcity was felt in England, and so terrible a famine fell upon the humble and defenceless populace, that more than 100,000 Christian folk of both sexes, young and old alike, perished of hunger.

John of Worcester notes the destruction, and says that 'famine so prevailed that men ate the flesh of horses, dogs, cats, and human beings'. The northern author of the *History of the Kings* says that,

> it was horrific to behold human corpses decaying in the houses, the streets, and the roads, swarming with worms, while they were consuming in corruption with an abominable stench. For no one was left to bury them in the earth, all being cut off by either sword or famine, or having left the country on account of the famine.

Some fled south. A train of refugees passed through Evesham, where they received help from the abbey. For some, however, it was already too late, as the later *History of the Abbey of Evesham* explains:

> King William had some shires in these regions of England laid waste because of the exiles and outlaws who were hiding in the woods everywhere ... the counties affected were Yorkshire, Cheshire, Shropshire, Staffordshire and Derbyshire, and from these regions a large number of young and old, of women and children, came fleeing to Evesham in great distress from the misery of famine. In his concern for them all Æthelwig [the abbot] gave them all the sustenance he could. Many who had long been oppressed by severe hunger died through eating the food too ravenously. Throughout the whole

vill wretches lay languishing either in the houses or in the streets, even in the cemetery itself, being exhausted by hunger before they got there, and therefore when they tasted food for the body most of them died. For this reason there was high mortality among such people, so almost every day five or six people, sometimes more, perished miserably and were buried by the prior of this place.

In the middle of this desolation, William called for his crown and regalia to be brought from Winchester and celebrated Christmas in state at York. In January 1070 he led his army still further north and, at the Tees, Waltheof and Gospatrick submitted to him. Both were pardoned, Waltheof to the extent that he was given the king's niece, Judith, in marriage. William then swung west across the Pennines, through rain and hail, and, with his troops complaining loudly all the time, went on to Chester. Another castle was constructed in the town and given to a Fleming called Gerbod. This is likely to have irritated Earl Edwin a great deal. A second castle was built in Stafford, which had been shown to be vulnerable earlier in the year. Finally William marched south to Salisbury where he disbanded his army – although, to teach them a lesson, those who had complained were kept on for an additional 40 days after their more stoic companions had left.

William's campaign in the north of England, generally known as 'the harrying of the north', has provoked controversy and some strong reactions. But some accounts, including those of John of Worcester and Orderic, need to be treated with some circumspection, as they were written a long time after 1070. Those written much closer to events, the *Anglo-Saxon Chronicle* and the *Deeds of the Dukes of the Normans*, do not use such apocalyptic terms, although the *Anglo-Saxon Chronicle* does say that William 'completely devastated' Yorkshire. Domesday Book should provide a useful control, a cold statistical account, to be put alongside the narrative sources. Unfortunately, however, there is uncertainty over precisely what Domesday Book tells us. The survey lists many manors in Yorkshire as 'waste', but it is not clear what 'waste' means. In the twelfth century, Richard fitz Nigel said that if a person standing by a felled tree in a wood could see another five or more felled trees, then that land was 'waste'. Did the same definition apply in 1086? Was it used merely as an accounting device?[17] There are also questions about the collection and compilation of the information that comprises the Yorkshire entry in Domesday Book, which have a bearing on the thoroughness and accuracy of the survey. But even if we assume that 'waste' means 'ravaged in 1069' – and

24. Detail of the Bayeux Tapestry (eleventh century). Ravaging the land and
burning down buildings was typical of warfare in the eleventh century.
Here Normans burn down a house in Sussex to force Harold to battle,
leaving a woman and her son alive but homeless.

this seems likely – then it is still the case that by no means the whole of Yorkshire (to mention no other counties) was affected. Maps based on the Domesday record reveal that the damage was mostly confined to a wide strip of land
that ran along the route that we may suppose was taken by the army, which
then seems to have fanned out to attack the valleys leading up to the Pennines
and also headed east to the coast.[18] Domesday reveals the same sort of pattern
in the south-east of England, which had been harried in similar fashion four
years earlier.[19]

The real extent of William's actions in the north thus eludes us. But how
did people react to it? William of Jumièges and the men who wrote the 'D'
and 'E' versions of the *Anglo-Saxon Chronicle* noted but passed no judgement on
William's campaign. The Evesham chronicler makes no comment, despite his
description of the starving hordes who made their way to his town. William
of Malmesbury mentions the near destruction of York and the death of both
English and Normans in the fighting, but does not criticize William. Hugh the
Chanter, a member of the cathedral community at York during the first half
of the twelfth century, blamed the destruction, which he does not condemn,

on the disloyalty of the English. The *History of the Kings*, a chronicle written in the north, perhaps by Simeon of Durham, makes only the most subtle
criticisms of William's actions, but also speaks of Malcolm Canmore's activities in the north in 1070 in far worse terms; the Scots ran old men and women
through with pikes and hurled babies up in the air, catching them on the
points of their lances. William is not described as having acted with such
cruelty. Contemporary writers, then, did not judge William's actions, and
among the great twelfth-century historians, Orderic alone condemned them:
'My narrative has frequently had occasion to praise William but for this act
which condemned the guilty and innocent to die by slow starvation I cannot
commend him.'

Contemporaries did not pass judgement on William because his methods
were entirely in keeping with the way that war was waged in his time. Ravaging territory, particularly enemy territory, was not at all unusual. The Roman
writer Vegetius, whose work still provided the basis for military thinking
in the eleventh century, said that 'the main and principal point in war is to
secure plenty of provisions for oneself, and to destroy the enemy by famine'.[20]
Hardly surprising, then, that the destruction of the enemy's resources was the
aim of Caesar during the Gallic wars, of Charlemagne when fighting against
the Saxons, of William the Conqueror in Maine and in both the north and
south of England, and of the English in France during the Hundred Years'
War. Nor is it clear that the harrying of the north represents an unusually
extensive and intensive example of such destruction. The war fought between
Anjou and Blois over the Vendômois in the eleventh century left the area
ravaged and desolate. A diploma states that as a result of these wars,

> many people sold their patrimonies in order to eat, and many were reduced
> from considerable means to such mendacity that they would not dwell in
> their own homes, where they might have prepared the necessary food and
> sustenance. It happened that many from the Vendômois, the Blésois, and
> the Dunois abandoned their native soil and took themselves to other places
> where they might better be able to support their poverty.

This, then, was not a form of war that William aimed only against the north.
It was not genocide, as some have claimed.[21] And although William might
have been, in the words of the *Anglo-Saxon Chronicle*, 'stern beyond measure
to those who opposed his will', he was no 'war criminal'.[22] We should not
impose our own standards of morality on William, or on any other medieval
person, for our standards were not theirs, and what William did was not in

contravention of the standards of his own day. He can only be understood and judged – if we must judge him – against those rules.

From Salisbury William moved to Winchester for Easter. And there he held an important Church council, at which William was crowned for a second time, on this occasion by papal legates. One of them, Ermenfrid, imposed penances on the king and his army for the death and destruction they had caused at Hastings and during the aftermath of the battle. There too, under the eye of the legates and the king, the reorganization of the English Church was begun. So far as John of Worcester was concerned, the council saw,

> the king striving to deprive so many Englishmen of their offices. In their place he would appoint men of his own race and strengthen his position in the newly acquired kingdom. He stripped of their offices many bishops and abbots who had not been condemned for any obvious cause, whether of conciliar or secular law. He kept them in prison for life simply on suspicion ... of being opposed to the new kingdom.

But John of Worcester, and those later historians who have followed him, have gone too far here. It is not the case that many bishops and abbots were deposed for no offence. The council hardly saw a purge of the bench. So who was deposed? Archbishop Stigand was the highest-profile casualty. He was removed for three reasons: he unlawfully held the bishopric of Winchester together with the archbishopric (bishops were only allowed to hold one bishopric at a time); he had driven Archbishop Robert from Canterbury and had for some time used his pallium to perform the mass (an archbishop had to get his own pallium from Rome before he could exercise his office); and he had afterwards received his own pallium from an unlawful pope, Benedict. His deposition was in accordance with the canons, and was overseen by the legates. The second head to roll was that of Stigand's brother, Æthelmaer, bishop of Elmham. He too was deposed with the backing of the legates.

At a second council, at Whitsun, Bishop Æthelric of Chichester was deposed. The reasons for this are not clear, but seem to have been uncanonical, for the pope subsequently ordered that he should be reinstated. His orders were ignored. In 1071 Leofwine, bishop of Lichfield and Coventry, surrendered his see to the king. He had disqualified himself for office on account of his sexual incontinence, which was evidenced by the existence of a wife and children. He then returned to the monastery where he had been brought up, abandoning his family in order to expiate his sins.[23] Bishop Æthelwine of

HIC RE SIDET: HAROLD
REX: AN GLORVM:
STIGANT
ARCHI EPS

25. (above) Detail of the Bayeux
Tapestry (eleventh century).
Archbishop Stigand, as depicted
at Harold's coronation in the
Bayeux Tapestry.

26. (right) Archbishop Lanfranc
from Oxford, Bodleian Library,
MS Bodley 569, a manuscript of
c. 1100 containing Lanfranc's
treatise *On the Body and Blood of
the Lord*.

Durham was replaced in this same year. He had been outlawed in 1068 or 1069 because he had refused to punish some laymen who had been delivered to him by the king, and seems to have intended to resign his see anyway.[24]

In the period 1070–71, then, four bishops were deposed and one resigned his see. The deposition of four bishops, three of them for very good reasons, is hardly evidence of a purge of English ecclesiastics. Bishops and abbots did become increasingly Norman (or at least French) over the course of the reign, but these men were appointed only as and when Englishmen died and posts became vacant. Thus in 1087 one Englishman, Wulfstan, was still bishop of Worcester and the Lotharingian, Giso, who had been appointed in 1061, was still bishop of Bath and Wells. Equally, according to David Knowles, there were still English abbots in a dozen of the 'twenty-odd' monasteries for which we have complete records in 1073, eight in 1083, and three in 1087 – these at Bath, St Benet of Hulme and Ramsey.[25] John of Worcester thus overplays the change of personnel in 1070. But he was right in saying that William put his own men into important positions as soon as he had the chance to do so. He needed to be certain of the Church's support, and so he needed his own men in the cathedrals and abbeys. It was this same need that caused the English to attempt to forbid the appointment of Irishmen to the bishoprics of Ireland in the thirteenth century.[26]

The Viking army that had fled York in 1069 returned to England the next year, and this time King Swein was with it. From the Humber, at least some of the Vikings sailed down to the Wash and entrenched themselves on the Isle of Ely. There they were joined by a Lincolnshire thegn named Hereward, and a miscellaneous band of malcontent Englishmen.

Their first move, at the beginning of June, was to attack the abbey at Peterborough. Abbot Brand, an Englishman and one-time supporter of King Harold, had died, and a new Norman abbot named Turold had been appointed. The monks got wind of the planned attack, and sent a messenger to Abbot Turold, who had not yet arrived at Peterborough, to warn him. The 'E' version of the *Anglo-Saxon Chronicle*, which was written at Peterborough, provides a detailed account of what happened next:

> Then in the morning … all the outlaws came with many boats, determined to get into the monastery, but the monks resisted them so that they could not force an entrance. Then they set it on fire and burned down all the monastic buildings and the entire town, except for one house. By fire they forced an entrance at Bolhithe Gate. The monks came to meet them and begged to be

spared, but they took no heed and entered the monastery. They climbed up to the holy cross and took the diadem, all of pure gold, from our Lord's head, then took the foot support made entirely of red gold which was underneath His feet. They climbed up to the tower, and brought down the altar frontal, made entirely of gold and silver, that was hidden there. They seized there two golden and nine silver shrines, and fifteen great crosses made of both gold and silver ... Then they returned to their ships and went to Ely, and there handed over all those treasures.

They handed them over to the Danes, and the Danes took them away with them shortly afterwards when they were bribed to leave England by King William.

The king did not, however, immediately concern himself with Hereward. He must have thought that, now the Danes had departed, the English rebellion would collapse. Instead Hereward was joined by Edwin and Morcar, who had heard that the king intended to make them his prisoners. Edwin soon decided that they were not making progress, and left Hereward and his brother in the Fens and moved north to join King Malcolm of Scots. On the way, he was ambushed and slain – it seems that three brothers who numbered among his following gave him away to the Normans. Many mourned him, we are told, French and English alike, grieving 'as though he had been a close friend or kinsman' – one is reminded of the public grief following the death of Princess Diana in 1997.[27] He had been a handsome man, 'that few could compare to him', and a generous friend to the clergy and the poor. Even King William was saddened by his death, and exiled the three brothers when they came before him to claim a reward.

William now advanced against Ely in person. He built a causeway across the marshes, and the rebels, seeing that their position was now hopeless and that their fortification constructed of peat blocks would not be able to withstand such a force, surrendered.[28] They were led away into captivity. Earl Morcar was to remain a prisoner for the rest of the Conqueror's reign, and is found in the company of his gaoler, Roger of Beaumont, at Vatteville in Normandy in 1086.[29] Others were allowed to go free, but only after the king had cut off their hands or gouged out their eyes. Only Hereward escaped, and while he himself now disappears from history, his deeds passed into legend.

With Edwin gone, the earldom of Mercia, which had already been reduced in both extent and prestige, was swept away entirely. Edwin's estates were divided between a number of Norman lords, and new castles, perhaps including Tutbury, Peveril and Leicester, were constructed.[30] Without an earl to oversee justice across Mercia, Abbot Æthelwig of Evesham was given a role similar to that of sheriff in Worcestershire, Gloucestershire, Oxfordshire, Warwickshire, Herefordshire, Staffordshire and Shropshire. 'Hence, the councils of all the men of this region and the judgements depended almost entirely on him.' So says the Evesham chronicler. Yorkshire, too, previously held by Morcar, was now subject to Norman settlement. By 1086 nearly all the Englishmen living there had been reduced to the level of sub-tenants, holding their lands from Norman lords.

Some historians have seen what happened in 1070–71 as comprising a real change in William's policy in England. The English were everywhere swept away. Writs were now produced in Latin rather than Old English. But this is perhaps not quite right. Writs might still have been drafted in Old English at the very end of William's reign. There are just fewer than for the period before 1070.[31] As noted above, there were still English bishops and abbots in 1080. Waltheof was still earl in Northumbria until 1075. William was still trying to work with the English even at this stage. His main problem in this regard was that there were fewer Englishmen to work with than before. The English earls had been removed because they had proved to be untrustworthy – a point made by William of Malmesbury. The English bishops and abbots were slowly being replaced by Normans or other foreigners. The year 1070 saw not a change of policy, but a tipping point, where the number of Englishmen in office was reduced to the extent that there was less demand for writs in Old English and where there was no longer any possibility of maintaining the old order.

King Malcolm of Scots had played a role in all the rebellions that disturbed the north of England. He had also harboured Edgar Ætheling. William probably reasoned that he was unlikely to have peace in the north so long as Malcolm continued to act as a refuge for his enemies and as a potential supporter of further revolt. And so in August 1072 he launched an invasion of Scotland. Accompanied by Eadric the Wild, who had submitted to William, presumably in return for being allowed to keep his lands, he invaded Scotland by both land and sea. His army advanced as far as Abernethy in Fife, and there, according to John of Worcester, Malcolm came to make submission 'and became his man'.[32] By November William was back at Durham.

For the next two years there was peace in England. The threat to security provided by the king of Scots had been nullified. The Danes did not return to stir up trouble. Almost all of the native nobility had now been removed from office because of their involvement in earlier uprisings. As a result of all this, when yet another rebellion brewed up in 1075 it was qualitatively different from those that had gone before. This was not an English uprising. It was led by a Breton, Earl Ralph of Norwich, and a Norman, Earl Roger of Hereford, both of whom were discontented with the king's treatment of them. William of Malmesbury says that,

> Ralph ... was by the king's gift earl of Norfolk and Suffolk, a Breton on his father's side, and a man of warped mind as regards every good action. Betrothed as he was to a kinswoman of the king, a daughter of William fitz Osbern, he conceived ambitions beyond what was right, and planned to usurp the throne. And so, precisely on his wedding day, a feast was held on the most lavish scale (for English luxury had now influenced Norman appetites); and when the guests were intoxicated and flown with wine, he laid his plans before them in a lengthy speech. In the minds of his audience all reason had been darkened by drink, and they received his remarks with prolonged applause.

Earl Roger of Hereford, in contrast, seems to have rebelled because he had not been accorded the same power enjoyed by his father, William fitz Osbern – and so there are echoes here of the actions of Nigel II of the Cotentin in 1046–47. Royal sheriffs impinged on his rights in Herefordshire, while Abbot Æthelwig of Evesham had been entrusted with the care of at least some of the counties that comprised his earldom.[33] This had not been the case in the days of his father and it was not something that Earl Roger was prepared to tolerate.

The two earls consequently fortified their castles and sent messengers everywhere to raise support. They claimed, according to Orderic Vitalis, that William was unworthy to be king because he was a bastard. They also attacked William's political methods and the ingratitude that he had shown to many of those who had helped him to obtain the kingdom. Even when he did grant land to his supporters, it was nothing but a worthless waste-land, devastated by his armies; and as soon as the land had been made fertile again, the king demanded it back. The two earls seem to have made a particular attempt to encourage Earl Waltheof to join the rebellion, pointing out that it would give him the opportunity to recover his position and to save his people (presumably the English as a whole). They may have done this because Waltheof's support might have given their revolt a popular dimension. Waltheof, however, refused to get involved and betray a king to whom he had sworn allegiance. All that the conspirators could elicit from him was a solemn oath not to reveal the conspiracy to the king.[34]

When the rebellion finally broke out, the king's regents raised an army and fought against Earl Ralph at Fagaduna – possibly Fawdon in Whaddon (Cambridgeshire).[35] The king's men won, and cut off the right foot of every prisoner, no matter what their status. They then pursued Earl Ralph to his castle at Norwich and besieged him there for three months. Ralph entrusted the castle to a garrison made up of loyal men and slipped away to Denmark, were he hoped to recruit the Danes to his cause. In his absence, Norwich surrendered. Earl Ralph, with nowhere in England to take refuge, returned to Brittany – where the king could not touch him – to live on his patrimony. Archbishop Lanfranc wrote a triumphant letter to the king, telling him of their victory:

> Glory be to God on high, by whose mercy your kingdom has been purged of its Breton dung. Norwich castle has been surrendered and those Bretons in it who held lands in England have been granted their lives and spared mutilation; they have sworn for their part to leave your kingdom within forty days and never to enter it again without your permission. The landless mercenaries who served Ralph the traitor and his associates begged for and were granted the same terms within the limit of one month ... By God's mercy all the clamour of warfare has fallen silent in the land of England.

But what of Earl Roger of Hereford? His army was opposed by the combined forces of Bishop Wulfstan of Worcester, Abbot Æthelwig of Evesham, Urse of Abbetot, sheriff of Worcestershire, and Walter of Lacy, a local baron, who had determined to prevent Roger from crossing the Severn. News dripped through to Lanfranc at Westminster, and we have four of the archbishop's letters which provide something of how news of the unfolding events came to him, and how he received it. At first Lanfranc had no inkling that Roger was one of the rebels. When news of his involvement reached him he could hardly believe it. And when Roger remained obdurate, Lanfranc hardened his tone. Reading these letters is rather like listening to someone on the telephone; we have only one side of the conversation, but something of what is being said down the line comes through. They suggest that, as time went on, Roger realized that he had made a serious mistake:

Our lord the king of the English greets you and all of us as his faithful subjects
... commanding us to do all in our power to prevent his castles from being
handed over to his enemies ... I urge you then ... to be so scrupulous in this
matter and in all your duty as a vassal of our lord the king that you may have
the praise of God and the king and all good men. Never forget your father's
distinguished career: the faithful service he gave his lord, his zeal in winning
great possessions and how honourably he held what he had won. On another
point, the king has ordered his sheriffs not to hold any courts within your
lands until he himself returns to England and can hear personally the matters
in dispute between you and those sheriffs. I wish that I could speak to you in
person. If that is your desire too, let me know where we can meet and discuss
both your affairs and the interests of the king.

I grieve more than I can say at the unwelcome news I hear of you. It would
not be right that a son of Earl William – a man whose sagacity and integrity
and loyalty to his lord and all his friends is renowned in many lands – should
be called faithless and be exposed to the slur of perjury or any kind of deceit
... I therefore beg you, as a son whom I cherish and the dearest of friends ...
if you are guilty of such conduct to return to your senses; and if you are not,
to demonstrate this by the clearest possible evidence. In either case, come
to see me.

I grieve for you inexpressibly, for God knows I loved you and desired with
all my heart to love and serve you. But because the devil's prompting and
the advice of evil men have led you into an enterprise which under no
circumstances should you have attempted, necessity has forced me to change
my attitude and turn my affection not so much into hate as into bitterness
and the severity of justice. I have sent messengers, I have sent letters not once
but for a second time inviting you to come to me ... and ... to abandon the
foolish undertaking which you had planned. You would not do so. Therefore I
have cursed and excommunicated you and all your adherents by my authority
as archbishop ... I can free you from this bond of anathema only if you seek
my lord the king's mercy and if you render satisfaction to him and the other
men whose property you have unjustly seized.

You sent word that you wished to come and see me. Personally I should agree
to this most willingly, did I not fear to incur the king's anger by so doing.
But I shall inform him by both messenger and letter of your repentance and
humble prayers for mercy, and I shall give you all the help that is compatible
with my allegiance to him. For the moment I strongly advise you to lie low:
take no initiative that may bring down his anger upon you more fiercely still.

Perhaps because he was encouraged by these words, when Earl Roger was summoned to court, he went. Hauled up before the king, Roger could not deny his involvement in the rebellion. He was condemned to imprisonment and remained a prisoner for the rest of his life.[36] He may have considered himself unfairly treated. He certainly remained defiant. One Easter, the king sent honourable servants with a store of valuable garments to him. Roger commanded that a huge pyre should be made and the finery – a cloak and silken tunic and mantle of ermine skins from distant parts – was burned. It availed him nothing. So far as we know he remained in prison even after the king's death, but he did at least have the satisfaction of knowing that William knew just how much he despised him.

Earl Waltheof did not escape the fallout of the rebellion. He too was summoned before the king and accused, on the testimony of his wife, Judith, of being a party to the conspiracy. He admitted that he had learned of the rebels' intentions, but said that he had refused to support them. A judgement was demanded, but the judges could not agree on his guilt. While the question of what to do with the earl remained undecided, Waltheof was kept in prison at Winchester. Eventually, so Orderic says, a powerful group of his enemies judged him worthy of death:

> Without delay, the Normans, who coveted the wealth and wide fields of Waltheof ... led him out of the town of Winchester early in the morning whilst the people slept, and took him up the hill where the church of St Giles ... now stands. There he piously divided among the clergy and poor who happened to be present the rich garments which he wore as an earl, and prostrating himself on the ground gave himself up for a long time to prayer with weeping and lamentation. But since the executioners feared that the citizens would wake and prevent them carrying out the royal will ... they addressed the prostrate earl in these words: 'Get up,' they said, 'so that we may carry out our lord's orders.' To this he replied, 'Wait a little longer, for the love of almighty God, at least until I have said the Lord's Prayer on your behalf and mine.' As they agreed he rose, and kneeling with his eyes raised to heaven and his hands stretched out he began to say aloud, 'Our Father, who art in Heaven'. But when he reached the last sentence and said, 'And lead us not into temptation', such tears and lamentations broke from him that he could not finish his prayer. The executioner refused to wait any longer, but straightaway drawing his sword struck off the earl's head with a mighty blow. Then the severed head was heard by all present to say in a clear voice, 'but deliver us from evil. Amen.'

This happened on the morning of 31 May 1076. Two weeks later the body was taken to Crowland Abbey in the Fens and interred there.[37] A minor cult developed. Miracles are recorded from 1112. The fate of Waltheof was clearly controversial, and it divided later historians. Orderic Vitalis is sympathetic to the English earl, perhaps because he had visited Crowland at the time these miracles were performed. He argued that the bad luck that plagued William's reign after 1076 was the result of the way that he had dealt with the earl. William of Malmesbury, on the other hand, says that Waltheof had rebelled because he was 'unable to control his natural perversity'. No doubt this is how King William would have seen it too.

27. The view over Winchester from St Giles Hill,
where Waltheof was executed in 1076.

✝

CHAPTER 6

WILLIAM AND THE CHURCH

In the eleventh century the Church mattered. It mattered a great deal, and it mattered for a number of different reasons. For everyone living in Normandy and England, from the highest to the lowest, the Church, in the words of Frank Barlow, 'interceded with God for humanity at large and benefactors in particular. It offered through its sacraments the only road to salvation. It provided beautiful places for corporate worship, a satisfying ritual, and a comforting message.'[1] For aristocratic families, the Church provided job opportunities. Younger sons, whose presence in the world might lead to the fragmentation and diminution of family estates, might carve out their own careers as priests, perhaps even bishops. For counts, dukes and kings, however, the Church might be a rival: the bishops, a group of men almost out of their control, who answered to a pope in Rome over whom the duke or king could exercise only a little influence.

William I's relationship with the Church consequently had tensions. His aim, however, was clear: to lead the Church in Normandy and in England, and to refuse to countenance any rival to his power. That this was William's intention is made abundantly clear by Eadmer of Canterbury, writing at the beginning of the twelfth century. He says that William,

> would not, for instance, allow anyone in all his dominion, except on his instructions, to recognize the established pontiff of the city of Rome as pope, or under any circumstances to accept any letter from him, if it had not first been submitted to the king himself. Also he would not let the primate of his kingdom, by which I mean the archbishop of Canterbury ... if he were presiding over a general council of bishops, lay down any ordinance or prohibition unless these were agreeable to the king's wishes and had first been settled by him. Then again he would not allow any one of his bishops, except on his express instructions, to proceed against or excommunicate any one of his barons or officers for incest or adultery or any other cardinal

offence, even when notoriously guilty, or to lay upon him any punishment of ecclesiastical discipline.

We can begin this discussion of William's relationship with the Church with his dealings with the popes, and those who appealed to their authority.

William's relationship with the popes was, on the whole, good. It is possible that papal authority had not been recognized in Normandy before William's reign. It is certainly the case that no legate had entered Normandy since the creation of the duchy in 911. This all changed with William, and examples of the duke and the popes working together are common. So, for example, William deposed Archbishop Malger of Rouen in 1054 with the support of the papacy, and secured the election of Maurilius in his place. Maurilius was himself succeeded by John, bishop of Avranches, who was transferred to Rouen in 1067 with papal blessing – indeed, Pope Alexander II conceded openly that the choice of archbishop lay with William.[2] In 1070 Archbishop Stigand of Canterbury was deposed, again with papal consent, and replaced by Lanfranc, then abbot of Caen. And Pope Alexander II had supported William's plan to invade England in 1066, sending him a banner to carry into battle.

There was, though, a difficult period in William's relationship with the pope from 1079 to 1081. Alexander's successor, Pope Gregory VII (1073–85), had spent much of his reign fighting the emperor, Henry IV, over the right to elect and to invest bishops with their bishoprics.[3] Now he turned his attentions to Normandy. With William weaker in 1079 than at any time since 1047, Gregory launched a three-pronged attack on William's position *vis-à-vis* the church. He sought to enforce the regular attendance at Rome of Anglo-Norman bishops; he tried to diminish the authority of the archbishop of Rouen; and he tried to claim that William owed him fealty for the kingdom of England.

Gregory's attacks had no teeth, however, and he was forced to backtrack in the face of resistance from Lanfranc and King William. The king's approach is best summed up in his response to Gregory's demand for fealty for England. William replied in the summer of 1080 as follows:

> Your legate Hubert, who came to me, holy father, has on your behalf directed me to do fealty to you and your successors and to reconsider the money payment which my predecessors used to send to the Roman Church. The one proposition I have accepted, the other I have not. I have never desired to do fealty, nor do I desire it now; for I neither promised on my own behalf

nor can I discover that my predecessors ever performed it to yours. As to the money, for almost three years it has been collected without due care, while I was engaged in France. But now that by God's mercy I have returned to my kingdom, the sum already collected is being sent to you by the above-named legate and the balance will be conveyed when the opportunity arises by the legates of our faithful servant, Archbishop Lanfranc.

In the words of Sir Frank Stenton, 'no statesman has ever settled a major issue in fewer words or more conclusively'.[4] William would not do fealty, and that was that. His answer reveals, however, that he was content to allow the pope those things that he claimed of right where he was justified in doing so.

It is likely that Gregory's ongoing dispute with Emperor Henry IV would have prevented him from taking an uncompromising stance against William. He would not have wanted another enemy, especially as he was relying on the Normans of south Italy for support. But confrontation was also avoided because William promoted and protected the Church in his dominions. Gregory himself admitted this in a letter of 1081. He wrote:

> The king of England, who to be sure does not in certain respects conduct himself as scrupulously as we desire, nevertheless in that he does not destroy or sell the churches of God, and takes steps to provide peace and righteousness among his subjects, and because when asked by certain enemies of the cross of Christ to enter into an agreement against the apostolic see he would not consent, and he compels even by an oath priests to abandon the wives and laymen the tithes that they are holding, shows himself a good deal worthier of approval and more to be honoured than other kings.[5]

And so William continued to choose his bishops without receiving censure or opprobrium from the pope. And when Gregory died in 1085 William and Lanfranc simply chose not to recognize either of the successors to the papacy. The Church in Normandy and England governed itself, with ecclesiastical questions being heard before the archbishop of Rouen or before the archbishop of Canterbury, primate of England, as and when the need arose.[6]

The cathedrals and the abbeys were the main centres of religious life in Normandy and England. There were seven bishoprics in Normandy, which together comprised the province of Rouen. All of the Norman bishoprics had been established in the distant past. What became the archbishopric of Rouen was established in the third or fourth century AD, while the rest date from the fifth or sixth centuries. However, the Viking invasions of the ninth and tenth centuries had proved highly disruptive, so that the continuity of each of the Norman bishoprics, with the sole exception of Rouen, seems to have been broken at that period.[7] They were slowly restored following the creation of the duchy of Normandy in 911, although the bishopric of Coutances was still in the process of recovery when William became duke. It had been only around ten years earlier, at most, that work had begun on the cathedral in the city. Until that point it had been abandoned by the titular bishop, who had lived instead at Rouen and then at Saint-Lô. That work was still in progress throughout William's minority, and it was only completed during the episcopate of Geoffrey of Montbray, bishop of Coutances from 1048 to 1093.

Geoffrey, whose bishopric was purchased for him, in breach of canon law, headed to Italy with the intention of extracting funds from the Normans there, the leaders of whom were from the Cotentin. In this he was successful. A narrative written at Coutances just after Geoffrey's death reports that he returned to Normandy with a vast quantity of gold, silver, gems and precious cloth. With this haul, and perhaps with the money generated by pilgrims following a number of miracles performed by the Virgin Mary during his pontificate, he enriched the church of Coutances within and without. His new cathedral was dedicated on 8 December 1056. He established a body of 14 canons to serve it, and attempted to make Coutances a centre of learning, maintaining grammarians, dialecticians and organists at his own expense. He also built himself a palace with stables. And he constructed a stone bridge across the River Vire at Saint-Lô which so increased the volume of traffic passing through the town that the amount of money brought in by the tolls charged rose from 15 to 220 *livres*.[8]

If Coutances were not fully restored until the 1050s, then the bishopric of Sées was fully functional but remained out of the control of the duke of the Normans until the 1050s when the activities of Roger of Montgommery and Duke William's successful campaign against Geoffrey of Anjou brought it under Norman influence. William made his first appointment to the see when Bishop Ivo of Bellême died in 1071. Sées was the last of the Norman bishoprics to come under William's control, and when it did, his mastery of the Church in Normandy was complete.

In England the eleventh century saw the removal of bishoprics from small or out-of-the-way locations into the greater cities of the kingdom. This reorganization had begun during Edward the Confessor's reign when Bishop Leofric had moved his see from Crediton to Exeter. It continued after William became king but it took until 1095 for the English Church finally to finish

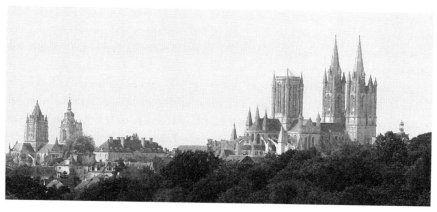

28. Coutances, with the cathedral. Although the present cathedral dates from the thirteenth century, some of Bishop Geoffrey's work is concealed in the nave.

relocating its cathedrals, and even then new bishoprics were founded at Ely in 1109 and Carlisle in 1133.

The bishops of England and Normandy led the Christian life of their dioceses from their cathedrals, many of them newly constructed at this time, and lived in palaces and castles built across their estates. And the bishops and also the abbots and the monasteries did hold a lot of land. In England Domesday Book shows that the Church held between one quarter and one fifth of those parts of England covered by the survey. There is no equivalent record for Normandy, but it is clear that enormous amounts of land were held by the bishops and abbots of the duchy. By the end of the eleventh century, for example, Marbod of Rennes, a poet who had benefited from the patronage of Bishop Odo of Bayeux, could declare that Odo's diocese would support three bishops, and the survey of the bishopric made in 1133 reveals that the bishop could command the service of 120 knights.[9]

The resources of the Church, then, were such that no ruler could afford to lose its support. But the bishops were also part and parcel of the local administration by which the Anglo-Saxon kings and Norman dukes ensured that their commands were put into operation in the localities.

Both before the Conquest and after, hundreds of documents issued by the king's writing office in England were addressed to the bishop, and either the earl or sheriff of a particular shire. These men were the presiding officers of the shire court, because they were the two great powers in the shire. One represented the king, and the other God. According to the author of the *Laws of King Henry I*, the bishops were obliged to attend the shire court, and the first business there was ecclesiastical, followed by the pleas of the crown and then private cases.[10]

Ecclesiastical business covered a variety of sins, as well as some serious crimes. The bishops had a monopoly on carrying out judicial ordeals, unrestricted disciplinary rights over their clergy, extensive rights of punishing the sins of the laity, such as adultery, and jurisdiction over matrimonial cases and questions of bastardy. The Church also heard cases of homicide, where the killing had taken place in a church, and in Normandy the bishops heard cases concerning murder or injury during the period covered by the Truce of God (see p 122).

The Church was therefore central to the administration of justice in Normandy and England, especially with regard to the holding of 'ordeals', a method of proof which had the widest application. As the ordeal represented the judgement of God, it is not surprising that by the eleventh century it was preceded by religious ceremonial. The accused person was taken to church for Vespers on a Tuesday dressed in penitential garb, and was kept there, fasting, for three days. On the Saturday the accused attended mass, was instructed by the priest not to take communion unless innocent, and was prepared for the ordeal. What happened next depended on whether the accused were going to undergo ordeal by cold water or hot iron. If it were the ordeal by cold water, the accused would be stripped of their clothes after mass and led in procession to the pit. This had to be 12 feet deep, 20 feet in diameter and filled with water to the brim. There was a platform over the pit, supported on poles and strong enough to bear the weight of the accused, the priest, the judges and the men who would immerse the accused in the water. The priest then blessed the water and prayed that it would accept the accused if innocent and reject him if guilty. The accused was then tied up with cords and lowered smoothly and gently into the water. On the rope was a knot, a long hair's length from the point of attachment, and the accused had to sink as far as the knot in order to succeed. If successful, they were pulled out quickly before they could drown. If the accused did not sink to the required depth, then they were guilty.

For ordeal by hot iron, there was again a mass during which the iron bar, which weighed one pound, was heated in the fire. Once mass was over, all would process to the fire, where the iron was blessed, and prayers were said that it should be cold to the innocent and burning hot to the evil-doer. It was then taken from the fire using tongs and placed on a log. The priest read the gospel, sprinkled the bar with holy water and made the sign of the cross. The accused then picked it up in one hand and carried it for nine feet. The hand was then bandaged and examined after three days. If the iron had corrupted the hand, in other words if it were not healing cleanly, then the accused was guilty. The ordeal was used when there were no witnesses to a crime or transaction. In the absence of evidence, the only alternative was to turn to God, and ask Him to do justice through the ordeal.[11]

It was important, then, that William should retain control of appointments to the bishoprics in both England and Normandy, and this he succeeded in doing. Pope Alexander went so far as to recognize William's right to make these elections. There are no recorded instances of monks or canons daring to elect a bishop who had not first been nominated by William, and so no occasion was given for him to vent the fury that this would no doubt have caused. In contrast, the canons of Sées took it upon themselves to elect a new bishop, Gerard, without reference to Geoffrey of Anjou, *de facto* duke of the Normans, in 1144. The result was brutal. William fitz Stephen says that:

> Geoffrey count of Anjou, who also subjected Normandy to himself by force, had eunuchs made of Gerard, elect of Sées and many of his clerks, and had the genitals of the castrated men brought before him in a basin because without the duke's consent to his election to the church of Sées he behaved as if he had got assent and acted as if elected.[12]

Orderic Vitalis finds no fault with William's choice of bishops and abbots:

> For when a bishop or abbot had come to the end of his life and died, and God's widowed church was mourning the loss of its head, this pious prince sent competent officials to the bereaved house and had all the church property inventoried to prevent its dilapidation by sacrilegious keepers. Then he summoned his bishops and abbots and other prudent counsellors, and with their advice tried to find the man most capable of governing the house of God in both spiritual and secular matters ... The heresy of simony was detestable to him, and so in appointing abbots or bishops he gave less weight to wealth and power than to wisdom and good life. He appointed abbots of known virtue to the English monasteries, so that by their zeal and discipline, monasticism, which had for a time been lax and faltering, revived and was restored to its former strength.

William may have been personally pious, but he appointed men with a talent for administration to the bishoprics that became vacant during his reign, although he did nominate holy monks to his abbeys. Many of his later bishops were chosen from among his own chaplains, and thus well known to him, rather than unworldly, spiritual men. The heresy of simony (paying for ecclesiastical office) was certainly not as detestable to him as Orderic makes out, as one of Geoffrey of Montbray's relatives purchased the bishopric of Coutances for him in 1048. Hauled before the council of Reims in 1049 for this offence, Geoffrey was able to excuse himself by claiming that this was done without his knowledge – and although this was sufficient excuse for the council, it does not absolve William from guilt. William indulged in simony a second time with regard to the appointment of Remigius to Dorchester. The case eventually came before Pope Alexander II. The charges, so Eadmer tells us, were that,

> having made a bargain with William, before he became king, he had in effect bought his bishopric from him by the service which he had rendered him by the outlay of much effort and of lavish expenditure on his behalf when he was setting out to subdue England.

It is a shame that Eadmer is not a little more explicit, but he does at least make it clear that Remigius was unable to excuse his actions and resigned his see to the pope – only to be almost immediately reinstated as a result of the intervention of Lanfranc.

William was also guilty of another abuse, nepotism (giving ecclesiastical office to relatives), when in 1049 or 1050 he appointed his half-brother, Odo, to the bishopric of Bayeux.[13] At the time Odo was well under the canonical age to receive such office – he should have been at least 30 years old but was somewhere between 15 and 20. William no doubt felt it worthwhile to break the rules to get the right men into office. But he did so rarely, and if Gregory VII thought well of William regarding Church appointments, then perhaps we should too.

In all, William made 15 appointments to bishoprics in Normandy between 1035 and 1087. Most were members of the duke's own family, or representatives of other important families. For example, John of Ivry, bishop of Avranches and then archbishop of Rouen, was a son of Count Ralph of Ivry, and a nephew of Duke Richard I; Hugh, bishop of Lisieux, was the son of Count William of Eu and a grandson of Richard I (making him William's second cousin); and Archbishop Malger of Rouen was a son of Duke Richard

II. David Bates has said that 'often his bishops were clerks who had served as ducal chaplains',[14] but this seems not to be the case in Normandy. Only three of them were chaplains – that is, they had served in William's own household. Among them was Gilbert Maminot, bishop of Lisieux, who was remembered as able but lazy, an inspiring teacher and priest but a gambler and huntsman.

In England lesser men tended to be appointed to the bishoprics. William appointed 16 English bishops, and 11 of them were royal chaplains. Among them was Herfast, who was made bishop of Elmham. He had been William's chancellor before his promotion, and was not well suited to a bishop's vocation. Archbishop Lanfranc of Canterbury sent him a letter at some point in the period 1070–81, rebuking him for his behaviour:

> Abbot Baldwin's clerk and servant Berard brought you our letter about his affairs. As he himself affirmed to me later, you made a coarse joke about it; you uttered cheap and unworthy remarks about me in the hearing of many; and you declared with many an oath that you would give me no assistance in that matter. There will be another time and another place to speak of these things ... Give up the dicing (to mention nothing worse) and the world's amusements in which you are said to idle away the entire day ... Banish the monk Hermann, whose life is notorious for its many faults, from your society and your household completely. It is my wish that he live according to a rule in an observant monastery or – if he refuses to do this – that he depart from the kingdom of the English.

Lanfranc himself was one of William's greatest appointments.[15] He had grown up at Pavia in Italy, and had come to Normandy after studying at Tours and Chartres. In Normandy he set up a school at Avranches where he taught the liberal arts. While he was there his devotion and desire for a religious life increased, and so, in around 1042, he left the city in search of a place where there were no *litterati* to honour and revere him. According to one story, he was robbed and abducted while travelling towards Rouen. Abandoned by his attackers, he sought out the poorest monastery in the area. He arrived at the recently founded abbey of Le Bec to discover the abbot, Herluin, constructing an oven with his own hands. He sought and gained entry to the community. According to Orderic,

> he chose the tiny monastery of Le Bec in Normandy, because of its remoteness and poverty; and then enriched it by his wisdom and painstaking administration, raising it to a condition of perfect order, ruling the community of brethren with a discipline that was both strict and merciful,

and humbly proffering sound counsel to the holy abbot, Herluin ... It was from this master that the Normans first learned the liberal arts, so that scholars well versed in both sacred and secular learning emerged from the school of Le Bec. For at an earlier period under the six dukes of Normandy, scarcely any Norman spent his time in liberal studies, and no man of learning was to be found there until all-provident God sent Lanfranc to the borders of Normandy.

In *c.* 1045 he was made prior of Le Bec and in 1063 he was appointed abbot of William's newly founded abbey of Saint-Etienne in Caen. As this promotion indicates, Lanfranc was by this point a close confidant of the duke. William of Poitiers says that Duke William,

> admitted to his closest circles a certain Lanfranc, of whom it was disputed whether he deserved respect and glory more for his remarkable knowledge of secular and divine learning or for his outstanding observance of the monastic rule. William venerated him as a father, respected him as a teacher, and loved him like a brother or son.

This being the case, it is hardly surprising that when Archbishop Stigand of Canterbury was deposed at Easter 1070, King William summoned Lanfranc, already between about 55 and 60 years old, to England and gave him the archbishopric in his place. Lanfranc was initially reluctant, but was persuaded to accept by the papal legates, who convened for the purpose a council of all the Norman clergy. He subsequently presided over the reorganization of the English Church, held a number of Church councils and sent letters to colleagues, monks and laymen, encouraging or rebuking them as necessary. He also succeeded in gaining the primacy for Canterbury in 1072, defeating York's claims for parity, although only for his rival's lifetime. This was essential if Lanfranc was to reform the English Church as he wished. And he proved his loyalty to William on many occasions.

If William appointed the bishops and abbots of his dominions, then he might, on occasion, also depose them. In some cases, as with Archbishop Malger of Rouen and Archbishop Stigand of Canterbury, this was done with papal blessing. In other instances it was not. For example, in around 1060 Robert of Grandmesnil, abbot of the monastery at Saint-Evroult, was exiled from Normandy. We are told by Orderic Vitalis that he had made scurrilous remarks about the duke to his prior (and thus committed *lèse majesté*), that the prior had informed the duke and that William had taken offence. Robert was deposed and a new abbot installed at the duke's command. Robert, hearing all of this, travelled to Rome to set his complaint before the pope, and received a favourable hearing. He then returned to Normandy with papal letters and with two papal legates, and set out for the duke's court which was meeting at Lillebonne.

> When the duke heard that Abbot Robert was approaching in the company of papal legates to claim the abbacy of Saint-Evroult and charge the duke's candidate, Osbern, with usurpation of his rights, he flew into a violent rage, declaring that he was ready to receive legates of the pope, their common father, in matters touching the Christian faith, but that if any monk from his duchy dared to bring a plea against him he would ignore his cloth and hang him by his cowl from the top of the highest oak tree in the wood nearby.

Abbot Robert was advised by his friends at court to beat a hasty retreat, and he did so.

During William's reign, Archbishop Lanfranc, as well as the archbishops of Rouen, held councils in their provinces so as to direct the religious life of the duchy and the kingdom. The earliest of these councils, held at Rouen at some point between 1037 and 1046, was not well attended, and did little that was of any practical use. But the very fact that it was held at all is remarkable – it denounced simony even before the reforming Pope Leo IX had done so at the council of Reims. All of these councils addressed the reform of the clergy, but the council of Winchester of 1072 also created legislation that shows how the Church could support William's rule. The council declared that every priest in England was to say three masses for the king's health and that anyone who committed treason should be excommunicated.[16]

These councils were, as both Eadmer and William of Poitiers inform us, supervised by the king. How interested William was in the business that was transacted is not clear. It may be that he was concerned to watch over these councils to protect his own rights. By 1100, however, the presence of the dukes or king at such councils would have been considered unusual, and so a justification was provided in the writings of the so-called Norman Anonymous. First, the Anonymous argues that kings have authority to rule over priests, basing his arguments on the authority of the Old and New Testaments. He goes on to argue that it is not improper for a king to call and preside over Church councils, or to give the bishops the ring and staff that symbolized their rule. Indeed, he argues, the exclusion of the king from the government of the Church would lead to division, desolation and lack of protection.[17]

And the Church did need William's protection and help. Thus, for example, in 1080, the Church council held at Lillebonne ruled that:

> All who refuse to observe [the Truce of God] or break it in any way shall receive just sentence from the bishops according to the ordinance already established. If anyone then disobeys his bishop, the bishop shall make them known to the lord on whose land he lives, and the lord shall compel him to submit to episcopal justice. But if the lord refuses to do this, the king's *vicomte*, on being requested by the bishop, shall act without prevarication.[18]

Similarly in England William issued a mandate that commanded that a man who had been summoned to answer in the bishops' courts on three occasions but who refused to come should be compelled to attend by the king or the sheriff. William thus provided the coercive force required to make the recalcitrant do what the Church could only ask them to do. He also took churches into his protection, shielding their clergy and possessions from rapacious lords, and he brought to justice anyone who damaged the Church, its personnel or its property.

The final point made by Eadmer was that churchmen were not allowed to excommunicate royal officials without the king's express permission. Excommunication was one of a very few weapons in the Church's arsenal. It meant that the target was ritually cut off from the body of the Church – that is the Church in its broadest sense of the body of all Christians. He or she was to be ostracized and shunned by everyone, and was forbidden to enter a church or hear divine service, until they repented of their error, made restitution and sought forgiveness. It could be an effective weapon, but it made it impossible for royal officials to do their job, and undermined their position as well as that of the king or duke.

If excommunication was no longer available to churchmen in the case of royal officials, then how might they protect their property and possessions from these men? One alternative was cursing, which seems not to have suffered from the same ban as excommunication. Archbishop Ealdred of York, for example, famously cursed Urse of Abbetot, sheriff of Worcestershire, when his construction of the castle at Worcester encroached on the cathedral's property. With a very Anglo-Saxon penchant for rhyme, he is said to have declared: 'Hattest thu Urs, have thu Godes kurs'. In this case it had no effect. The castle was finished, and Urse lived on for many years to come, although William of Malmesbury saw his son's rebellion and forfeiture as the belated fulfilment of this malediction.

The abbey of Fécamp in Normandy had a formula for cursing its enemies that dated from the end of the tenth or early eleventh century.[19] The authorities invoked at the commencement of the solemn pronouncement of this curse comprise the Trinity, the Holy Catholic Church of God, St Mary, St Michael and the nine orders of angels, St Peter, the other 11 apostles, the four evangelists, St Stephen and all the other martyrs, St Romain and St Ouen (who were early evangelists of Normandy and archbishops of Rouen), all the confessors, all the virgins, and 144,000 innocents. Once this wide-ranging body of intercessionaries had been invoked, the monks continued:

> We curse them and separate them from the company of the holy mother church and of all faithful Christians, unless they change their ways and give back what they unjustly took away. But if they will not do that, may there come over them those curses by which Almighty God cursed those (the wicked in Job 21:14) who said to the Lord God, 'stay away from us, we do not wish to know of your ways', and those (Psalm 82:13) who said 'let us take possession for ourselves of the sanctuary of God'.

A number of different forms of death are then called down upon the object of the curse, and it is also hoped that they should spend eternity in the flames of hell in the company of such reviled figures as Judas, Pilate, Nero, Herod, Julian, Valerian, Simon Magus and the Devil. After this comes a litany of curses:

> May their bodies be cursed. May they be cursed in the head and in the brain. May they be cursed in their eyes and their foreheads. May they be cursed in their ears and their noses. May they be cursed in fields and in pastures. May they be cursed in the mouth and the throat, cursed in the chest and the heart, cursed in the stomach, cursed in the blood, cursed in the hands and feet and in each of their members. May they be cursed going in and coming out. May they be cursed in towns and in castles. May they be cursed in streets and in squares. May they be cursed when sleeping and when awake, when going out and returning, when eating and drinking, when speaking and being silent. May they be cursed in all places and at all times.

The final flourish asks that the sky over them be made of brass and the ground beneath of iron, so that their souls will not be able to rise to heaven and their bodies will not be buried. The ceremony ended with the candles in the church being solemnly extinguished.

Human intervention might not be needed at all, however. The saints whose relics were housed in the abbeys and cathedrals might themselves act

29. The surviving Romanesque work at Fécamp, built around 1085.

so as to protect their community or their reputations. Royal officials could not be excommunicated but they might find themselves the target of saintly vengeance. Gervase, who administered Cambridgeshire on behalf of its sheriff, Picot, was one who was punished this way. He oppressed the abbey of Ely with exaction after exaction until, finally, Ely's patron saint, St Æthelthryth, and her sisters took action against him. They appeared before him in a vision, attacked him with their staves, and thus killed him.[20]

In some cases, instead of a political miracle in which a saint revenged him or herself on their enemies, God might intervene directly. On one occasion,

Orderic Vitalis saw God acting to shock men, too easily intoxicated with good fortune, out of their complacency:

> While Duke William was puffed up with worldly pride, and the people of Normandy were wallowing shamefully in every kind of luxury, giving no thought to the expiation of their countless sins, a terrible crash of thunder resounded in the chancel of the basilica of Lisieux, and a fatal thunderbolt struck down the people standing in the cathedral church. It happened on a Sunday morning in summer, during the celebration of Mass; a priest named Herbert was standing before the altar wearing his chasuble when suddenly there was a blinding flash of lightning, followed immediately by a terrifying crash and the fall of a thunderbolt. It struck the cross on the top of the tower and shattered it; then crashing into the church itself it struck the rood, breaking off a hand and foot of Christ and tearing the nails from the cross in an amazing way. Black smoke half-blinded the trembling populace and flickers of lightning flashed through the church, killing eight men and one woman. It burned the beards and pubic and other hair on the bodies of men and women, suffocating the crowd with the foul stench. One woman, named Mary, remained standing, petrified with fright in the corner of the church, and trembling saw the whole congregation stretched out as if dead on the stone floor of the church.

It was important not to anger God. William himself seems to have been personally, if conventionally, pious, and that no doubt moderated his behaviour towards the Church. And placating God was necessary not only for the salvation of an individual but also for the country at large.

Alfred the Great, plagued by the Vikings, had seen the evils that befell his country as the result of God's anger at the lack of religion there.[21] He had taken steps to appease Him by making reforms. As has been discussed, William presided over Church councils which were designed to reform the lifestyle of the clergy and to provide a good example to laymen; he appointed bishops to bishoprics whenever they fell vacant; he gave the pope his due; and he protected the Church. But William, and others, also founded monasteries. Why? The reasons are set out by Orderic when writing of the foundation of the abbey at Shrewsbury in 1083, a foundation that was urged on Roger of Montgommery by Orderic's own father, Odelerius of Orléans:

> Consider now what duties are performed in monasteries obedient to a rule by those trained in the service of God. Countless benefits are obtained there every day, and Christ's garrisons struggle manfully against the Devil. Assuredly, the harder the struggle of the spiritual warrior the more glorious

will be his victory, and the more precious his trophies in the courts of Heaven. Who can tell all the vigils of monks, their hymns and psalms, their prayers and alms, and their daily offerings of masses with copious tears? The followers of Christ devote themselves wholly to this, sacrificing themselves to be found truly acceptable to God ... Their lot is a harsh life, wretched clothing, scanty food and drink, and renunciation of their own wills for the love of the Lord Jesus ... And so I believe that their prayers, for whomsoever among the faithful they are offered up, rise immediately to the throne of God, and that whatever they ask of the King of Hosts they surely receive.

Despite its hardships, the religious life proved attractive to many living in the rough and tumble of eleventh-century Normandy and England. The Benedictines certainly seem to have had no problem in recruiting new blood into their ranks. Men, and boys too, might become monks for a number of reasons. In William's lifetime, small children might be given as child oblates. Orderic Vitalis was himself one. He tells us his story at the very end of his *Ecclesiastical History*. He notes, first, that kinsmen might prove to be a distraction to God's servants, and then continues:

And so, O glorious God, who did command Abraham to depart from his country and from his kindred and from his father's house, you did inspire my father, Odelerius, to renounce me utterly, and submit me in all things to your governance. So, weeping, he gave me, a weeping child, into the care of the monk Reginald, and sent me away into exile for love of you and never saw me again. And I, a mere boy, did not presume to oppose my father's wishes, but obeyed him willingly in all things, for he promised me in your name that if I became a monk I should taste the joys of Paradise with the Innocents after my death ... And so, a boy of ten, I crossed the English Channel and came into Normandy as an exile ... Like Joseph in Egypt I heard a language that I did not understand. But you allowed me through your grace to find nothing but kindness and friendship among strangers. I was received as an oblate monk in the abbey of Saint-Evroult by the venerable Abbot Mainer in the eleventh year of my age, and was tonsured as a clerk on Sunday 21 September. In place of my English name, which sounded harsh to the Normans, the name Vitalis was given to me, after one of the companions of St Maurice the Martyr, whose feast was being celebrated at that time.

Around 1120 Orderic was commanded by the abbot of the day, Roger of Le Sap, to write a history of the abbey. Orderic's commission was limited to a history of the founders, donors, abbots and property of the house – and Books 5 and 6 are very much focused on these topics – but he soon found himself looking at a broader picture. Book 3, the very first to be written, might have begun by recording the foundation of the abbey, but it was soon discoursing on Duke William's conquests of Maine and England, based in large part on William of Poitiers's *Deeds of William*. Orderic was encouraged to maintain this broader scope by Abbot Warin (1123–37), and so it was under his rule that the *Ecclesiastical History* took shape and grew. Orderic was, he said, concerned only with the truth. He was not interested in taking sides between English and Normans, and he did not write for reward or acclaim (which is fortunate, because the work seems not to have been popular, perhaps because of its length). His *Ecclesiastical History* does have its problems. Orderic wrote without much regard for chronology or structure, and his account of William's reign incorporates stories that had grown up in the 50 years since the Conqueror's death. Nonetheless, his work offers a real flavour of Normandy in the eleventh and twelfth centuries. It is full of stories of phantom hunts, demonic visions, miracles, lightning strikes, accounts of the deeds of the swashbuckling knights of Orderic's day, and his views on the good and bad rulers and lords of England, Normandy and elsewhere. All of this is communicated with the flair of the true raconteur. It is a marvellous work, and without the *Ecclesiastical History* historians of the Anglo-Norman period would be inestimably the poorer.

Some, such as Orderic, might become monks as children. Others became monks in adult life as the result of a number of different circumstances. Robert of Grandmesnil, for example, became a monk at the abbey he had jointly founded at Saint-Evroult in 1050 – the year of its foundation. He had previously been a knight, trained in the household of Duke William himself:

> But having regard to mortal frailty he chose rather to be a servant in the house of the Lord than for a little while to flourish like grass in the tents of wickedness. He often called to mind the perils of earthly warfare endured by his father and many like him who had met the death they had intended for others while bravely attacking their enemies. For on one occasion his father Robert fought with Roger of Tosny against Roger of Beaumont, and in that conflict ... Robert received a mortal wound in his bowels ... Deeply moved by this tragedy, Robert set his mind on fighting in better warfare.

Robert of Grandmesnil became a monk because, having witnessed his father's painful and protracted death from wounds sustained in battle, he no longer had the stomach for fighting. And so he turned to the Church. But was Orderic right to suggest that Robert became a monk solely because his mind

30. The ruins of the abbey at Saint-Evroult. All the existing work dates from the fourteenth century. The site of the cloister lies in the field beyond the masonry.

had turned to God? Or did Robert become a monk because he knew that his role as a co-founder of the monastery, as well as his place in society, would ensure that he rose rapidly through the ranks to a position of authority? His subsequent career certainly suggests that this was the case, and so does his personality. Orderic says that 'he preferred to lead rather than to follow and to command rather than to obey'. By 1059 he was abbot, having hounded the previous incumbent out of office. It seems very likely that other members of the aristocracy turned to the Church for the same reason – it was simply another road to power.

Some men came to regret their decision to become a monk, which was often made when they feared that death was upon them. Orderic tells us stories about these with a degree of relish, for, at least in the examples he provides, they come to an unhappy end. There was, for example, a priest called Ansered who suffered from a severe illness and so begged the abbot of Saint-Evroult to allow him to become a monk in the abbey. He recovered from his illness, however, and returned as far as possible to the lax habits of his life as a secular priest ... Abbot Thierry clearly perceived that his life and conduct were most shocking and that he hated the monastic rule, for he had asked his father and mother to claim him and take him away from the monastery; and fearing that the other brethren might be infected by Ansered's vices ... allowed him to leave the cloister and return to the world. Ansered, heaping sin on sin, kept company with a common woman, and not content with her made love to another called Rosie, with whom he agreed to go to the shrine of St Giles. In this way he hoped to keep his passion for her from his family and friends.

It all worked out badly for Ansered. Before they could even leave for the pilgrimage, Rosie took up with another clerk. As a result, she failed to make her rendezvous with Ansered, who turned back to find out what had kept her. He discovered Rosie in bed with the other man. She warned her unnamed lover that they had been discovered, and he snatched up an axe and struck Ansered on the head, killing him stone dead. The body was put in a sack and buried, but it was uncovered by wild beasts which ate one of his legs. The smell of his rotting corpse attracted the attention of the villagers, and his body was recovered by his parents and buried outside the graveyard. 'What a wretched death this man suffered,' says Orderic with some satisfaction, 'who chose rather to return to worldly vanity than to seek the way to heaven among the servants of God!'

Despite individual cases, recruitment into the Benedictine Order was good. This was fortunate because William's reign saw the foundation of a number of monasteries in Normandy as well as priories that were dependent on them in England after 1066, and they all needed to be staffed. William fitz Osbern founded two houses, at Lyre and Cormeilles. His religious patronage was exceeded by Roger of Montgommery, who founded abbeys at Troarn, Sées and Almenèches. The Tosny family established a house at Conches, Hugh of Avranches founded a monastery at Saint-Sever, and Thurstan Haldup and his son Eudo founded the abbey at Lessay, the glorious church of which still stands today – restored after being severely damaged during the Second World War. William founded three monasteries, two in Normandy and one in England, and the events that led to their establishment illustrate just how varied the reasons for making such foundations might be.

The two Norman houses were constructed at Caen in the Bessin and at Montebourg in the Cotentin. In both cases their foundation was due to more than simple piety. The abbey at Montebourg, founded *c.* 1080, was located in an area where William's rule was relatively weak. The monastery was a bastion of royal authority in the region, as the monks would naturally look to the king for support and would draw others into his orbit, especially as the abbey's estates and thus power would increase over time. Indeed the abbey was initially endowed with only a small number of estates, some of which William had probably taken from Nigel II of the Cotentin in the immediate aftermath of Val-ès-Dunes. These were probably insufficient, and Richard of Reviers —whose father had been planted in the area by William after the battle — later added possessions in the Bessin, Cotentin and England to such an extent that the monastery became as closely associated with him as with the king.[22]

The earlier, and much the more important, of the two Norman houses was the abbey at Caen, dedicated to St Stephen (St Etienne in French) which had been founded as a penance for William's marriage to Matilda. The nave and crossing of the abbey church that went up during William's reign survive. This austere church, with its two towers (higher now than when the church was first built) and severe facade, is a monument in itself to William's wealth and, therefore, power. But it is also a monument to William's political drives. Caen was already a town by 1026, but William decided to make it the centre of his dominion over Lower Normandy. The foundation of a castle as well as the two abbeys there (St Stephen, founded by William, as noted above, and Holy Trinity by Matilda), each with their own boroughs, would make the town all the more important. The duke gave his new abbey lands and rights and, in addition to this terrestrial endowment, donated to it an arm bone, some hairs, and a phial of blood of its patron saint.[23] These would probably have helped the abbey to attract some pilgrims and their offerings, although there is no evidence that the cult ever took off.

Battle Abbey, in contrast, was founded as a thank-offering for William's victory over Harold at Hastings in 1066, and as penance for the Christian blood that had been spilt there. According to the *Chronicle of Battle Abbey*, which was not written until the second half of the twelfth century, immediately before the battle of Hastings, William said to his men:

> I make a vow that on this very battlefield I shall found a monastery for the salvation of all, and especially for those who fall here, to the honour of God and his saints, where servants of God may be supported: a fitting monastery with a worthy liberty. Let it be an atonement: a haven for all, as free as the one I conquer for myself.

The monks who had been entrusted with the construction of the monastery decided that the sloping battlefield was too inconvenient, and so selected a different spot, lower down and towards the western slope of the ridge. When the king enquired how the building was proceeding, he was asked for permission to begin work on this new site. He refused angrily, and demanded that they build where they had been told to do so, on the battlefield, with the high altar placed over the spot where Harold had fallen. They protested, 'without presuming to oppose him', citing the lack of water and good stone for building. The king responded that he would endow the abbey so that 'the supply of wine in it will be more abundant than that of water in any other great abbey', and he also promised to pay for the cost of transporting stone to the site. This successfully overcame the monks' resistance. It should also serve as a warning not to take the king entirely at face value. Battle Abbey may have been in part a penance for the blood spilt during the battle, but it was also a glorious monument to William's victory and a celebration of that achievement.

Like all men, William wanted to save his soul, and his foundations and donations can be interpreted on this personal level. But William also needed to control the Church if he were to impose his authority on his dominions, and he was not prepared to countenance a rival. And for this reason he controlled communications with Rome and kept a tight hold of appointments to bishoprics. In return, William protected the Church from the rapacity of his subjects. But William was not taken to task for this. It was a relationship that the Church itself valued and supported. In the words of the Norman Anonymous:

> For the governance of the Church kings receive power at their coronation to rule and confirm her in justice and judgment and to order her affairs according to the discipline of Christian law. Thus they reign over the Church, which is the kingdom of God.[24]

CHAPTER 7
A KINGLY FIGURE: WILLIAM'S PERSON AND PERSONALITY

There are no accurate, contemporary representations of William. Although he is shown a number of times on the Bayeux Tapestry, there is no attempt at a realistic representation of the king's features or build. The portraits on William's English coins are stylized, as are those on his seal. Without any accurate visual representations we have to rely on written descriptions. William of Malmesbury provides perhaps the fullest of these:

> He was of a proper height, immensely stout, with a ferocious expression and a high bald forehead; his arms extremely strong so that it was often a remarkable sight to see no one able to draw his bow, which he himself, while spurring his horse to a gallop, could bend with taut bowstring. He had great dignity both seated and standing, although his prominent corpulence gave him an unshapely and unkingly figure. He enjoyed good health, for he was never laid up with any dangerous illness except at the end of his life; and he was so devoted to hunting in the forest that ... he ordered that many miles of country should be cleared of their inhabitants and turned over to woodland, in which he could be relieved of all other business and relax his mind.

Of course, William of Malmesbury could not himself have seen the king in person, so this description must be based on the memory of someone who had seen him around 50 years earlier.

A 'proper height' would seem to be something in the region of 5 feet 10 inches. That is William's estimated height, based on the length of his femur (thigh bone), which is the only part of him now lying in his grave at Caen. The complete skeleton was still there in 1522, when William's body was exhumed. He was found to have been a man with unusually long arms and legs, and a picture was commissioned to put the flesh back on the bones. The result was, of course, no more accurate than the portraits in the Bayeux Tapestry. William's body was carefully replaced in the grave, but in the 1570s the Calvinists ransacked the abbey, opened the grave once again and threw out all of the king's remains. Only one thigh bone was recovered (and later measured).

Another description of the king, which is heavily based on the description of Charlemagne in Einhard's *Life* of the emperor, gives us the detail that 'in speech he was fluent and persuasive, being skilled at all times in making clear his will. If his voice was harsh, what he said was always suited to the occasion.'

Eloquence was seen as a virtue, but if William could argue his case, he might also try to terrify his listeners into obedience. William of Malmesbury says that William swore 'by the resurrection and glory of God!' It seems it was his practice 'deliberately to use such oaths, so that the mere roar from his open mouth might somehow strike terror into the minds of his audience'. Oaths in the eleventh and twelfth centuries generally took this blasphemous form, and were all the more offensive for it. Thus William's son, William Rufus, used to swear 'by the Holy Face of Lucca', a miracle-working wooden sculpture of Christ kept at Lucca in Italy but which was used as the model for a great crucifix at Bury St Edmunds; Henry I, so Malmesbury tells us, swore 'by our Lord's death'. This flew in the face of advice of the monk Ælfric of Eynsham, writing at the end of the tenth century, who said that God forbade every oath to Christian folk, but that if words had to be strengthened then they should end with 'believe me'.[1]

If we cannot reconstruct William's features, we do at least have an idea of his appearance. The Bayeux Tapestry depicts William, indeed the Normans in general, as clean-shaven and sporting distinctive haircuts. The back of the head was shaved almost to the crown; the hair at the sides and front was worn longer and was apparently combed forward.[2] This style, if the Normans really wore their hair like this, was to be abandoned by William's sons. They and their peers wore their hair long. This did not gain the approval of the clergy. Eadmer says:

> now at this time it was the fashion for nearly all the young men of the court to grow their hair long like girls; then, with locks well-combed, glancing about them and winking in ungodly fashion, they would daily walk abroad with delicate steps and mincing gait.

These courtiers, so Orderic says, had also abandoned the clean-shaven look of their fathers and grew little beards, like filthy billy goats, revealing by their outward appearance the sinfulness of their souls.

The Bayeux Tapestry, all manner of manuscript illuminations and wall paintings also provide evidence for the cut of Norman clothes. Men usually wore a knee-length tunic, often with the neck opening, cuffs and lower hem picked out in a contrasting colour. Sometimes these edgings were decorated with embroidery or patterned silk. On their legs they wore hose – leggings that were suspended from a belt, like stockings – or trousers which might be held tightly around the leg with leg-bindings or puttees. Men of an adequately high status might also wear a cloak, usually semi-circular in shape, fastened by a brooch which might be worn at the front or over the right shoulder.

'The Normans,' said William of Malmesbury, 'were then, as they still are, well-dressed to a fault.' As King William stood at the very top of society, it is likely that some if not all of his clothes would have been made out of silk. As we have already seen, some time after Earl Roger of Hereford was imprisoned in 1075, William sent him a silken tunic, and other items, which Roger then burned. William would not have sent such items to his prisoner if he were not wearing silk himself. His gift also reveals that such rich dress was by now considered suitable for an earl, not just a king. Silk was readily obtainable both on the continent and in England in the eleventh century – Robin Fleming has suggested, with pardonable exaggeration, that late Anglo-Saxon England was 'awash' with it.[3] And it is also the case that by the second or third decade of the eleventh century, at the latest, entire garments were being made out of silk in western Europe. Emperor Henry II (d. 1024), for example, was crowned in a white silk tunic with red trim. Ladislaus of Hungary (d. 1095) had a silk robe, too, although only the body of it remains.[4] These silks were frequently patterned with lions, elephants, griffins, and so on, or with repeating geometric shapes.

The Conquest of England seems to have introduced at least one further refinement to Norman dress. This was embroidery, often in gold thread, and sometimes with the addition of jewels. Edward the Confessor was dressed by his wife in

> raiments either embroidered by herself or of her choice, and of such a kind that it could not be thought that even Solomon in all his glory was ever thus arrayed. In the ornamentation of these no count was made of the cost of the precious stones, rare gems and shining pearls that were used. As regards

mantles, tunics, boots, and shoes, the amount of gold which flowed in the complicated floral designs was not weighed.[5]

The style was taken up immediately by the Normans. William of Poitiers says that as early as March 1067 they were dressing themselves in this English manner. He notes that the French present at William's courts at Fécamp and Rouen gawped 'at the clothes of the king and his courtiers, woven and encrusted with gold, [and] they considered whatever they had seen before to be of little worth'.

Fur was also a mark of status. William of Malmesbury, in his *Life* of Wulfstan of Worcester, tells a story that gives us some information about the types of fur available. Bishop Geoffrey of Coutances had launched into a series of good-natured witticisms on Wulfstan's attire. He eventually asked why Wulfstan wore only lambskins when he could, and should, use the pelts of sable, beaver or wolf. Wulfstan replied that the skins of such crafty beasts might be suitable for Geoffrey, who was expert in secular matters, but he, who was an innocent soul, was content with lambskins. Geoffrey suggested that at the very least Wulfstan should trim or line his clothes with cat fur, to which Wulfstan retorted: 'Believe me, we sing about the lamb of God more often than the cat of God.' Geoffrey was delighted at the riposte and burst out laughing, acknowledging that Wulfstan had got the better of him.

Aside from sable, beaver, wolf and cat, we know that ermine skins might be worn – Roger of Hereford, along with the silken tunic, burned a mantle of ermine. Marten skins were imported from Ireland. Domesday Book records that the king's reeve at Chester had first choice of all the marten skins imported to that city, and anyone who failed to allow him to make his purchases first was fined 40 shillings. We hear in one diploma of a fox fur being used as a gift – it was presumably worn around the neck.[6] Manuscript illuminations and some documentary sources also reveal that squirrel fur was used as a lining – vair – with the skins sewn together to form an alternating grey and white pattern (the coat of the Eurasian red squirrel turns a blue grey in winter). We are told, in the diploma that records the donation, that when Roger of Montgommery gave his abbey at Troarn the marsh which surrounded it, 'in the presence of many noble men he threw his son, Robert of Bellême, dressed in a miniver [squirrel-skin] cloak, into the water, in witness and memory that the demesne of the abbot and monks extended up to there'.[7] It was an act that was certainly likely to have left the desired impression.

Just as there is little hard evidence of what William looked like, so there is a lack of the information necessary to establish what he was like as a person. This is, of course, inevitable with somebody who lived more than 900 years ago. There are no personal papers or diaries. All that we have are the recollections of a very few people who might or might not have known the king at first hand, and the odd writ or diploma that sheds some light on the man by way of a mnemonic. Those writers in a position to know the king were disinclined to talk about what he was like personally. They were more concerned to emphasize his good points as a ruler, while dwelling only briefly on his bad ones. These descriptions consequently tell us much more about how contemporaries thought about kingship, and the qualities of a good ruler, than about William's personality, but they are all we have to go on.

The Burgundian, Hugh of Flavigny, reports that in 1087, after William's funeral, some of his friends gathered together in a house in Caen. They reminisced about the dead king, and spoke of, among other things, his eloquence, generosity and cheerfulness.

William certainly had a sense of humour. These things are notoriously difficult to interpret, but it seems to have been the sort of humour found among close-knit groups of men. It had a practical, slightly brutal quality. So, for example, Lanfranc, at that time prior of Le Bec, was exiled from Normandy for speaking against the duke's marriage to Matilda. Knowing that the duke was coming, Lanfranc mounted a lame horse and rode out of the abbey gate, straight towards the oncoming duke:

> At first that stately personage, Duke William, turned his face away. But through the working of God's mercy, William soon regarded him pityingly, and with a nod of kindness granted him leave to speak. Then Lanfranc said in fitting jest: 'At your order I am departing from this province on foot, hampered by this useless quadruped. If you want me to be able to carry out your command, give me a better horse.'[8]

The cheek of this remark seems to have tickled the duke, for he smiled and allowed Lanfranc to clear himself of the accusations that had been made against him. He was restored to favour and remained a close adviser for the rest of William's reign. And he continued to use humour to manage the king, as William of Malmesbury explains in his *Gesta Pontificum*:

> What is more, King William needed only a glance from Lanfranc to quell his haughty manner. For his part, Lanfranc managed the king with a holy skill,

not sternly upbraiding what he did wrong, but spicing serious language with jokes. In this way he could usually bring him back to a right mind.

Another of William's closest friends was William fitz Osbern, who nonetheless found himself the butt of one of William's jokes in 1066. The duke affectionately ribbed him by returning to camp from a reconnaissance wearing not only his own coat of mail but carrying his friend's hauberk (chain mail tunic) over his shoulders, too, thereby providing incontrovertible evidence that William fitz Osbern was a weakling.[9] Two further vignettes can be found in William's acts. On one occasion, probably in 1062, he pretended that he was going to hit Hugh the Forester with the shoulder blade of a pig when the latter spoke against a grant he made to Marmoutier. It was a memorable, comedic moment. In a similar vein, in 1069 at Winchester, he pretended that he was going to stab the abbot of the Trinité-du-Mont, outside Rouen, through the hand when confirming a gift to that abbey. 'Thus ought the land to be given,' he joked.[10] Again, the event was memorable, and it was meant to be – again it was used as a mnemonic. And although there is a supposition among recent historians that the abbot would have been scared by William's action, he might equally have laughed about it. At least he was not thrown into a ditch.

The same sort of rough humour is found in the nicknames given to men in this period, which were often of a highly personal nature. Many of them are ambiguous to us today, because we do not know if they were an exaggerated but true reflection of a man's attributes or else a sarcastic inversion. One of the rebels in 1047 was called Haimo Dentatus – Haimo the Toothy – presumably because he had large teeth or, if the name were intended sarcastically, because he had lost them all.[11] Orderic mentions a man known as Ralph Donkey-Head 'because of his huge head and shaggy hair'.[12] The Crispin family took their name from Gilbert Crispin, who was given his nickname because 'in his early youth he had hair that was brush-like and stiff and sticking out, and in a manner of speaking bristling like the needles of a pine tree ... This gave him the nickname of Crispin from "crispus pinus" – "pine hair".'[13] The Mauduit family had a name which meant 'ill-conducted', suggesting that some family member had been unable to behave in a seemly manner or else had always displayed the highest standards of etiquette. Earl Hugh of Chester was known as Hugh the Fat because he was, indeed, very fat. There was even, in the first decade of the twelfth century, a man called Humfrey of the Golden-Balls (*aureis testiculis*), a name now rendered as Orescuilz.[14] How he got his nickname is unknown.

William was, then, a practical joker, and a man whom humour could soften. But he was also a pious man. William of Poitiers says that,

> he was accustomed to lend an eager ear to readings from Holy Writ and to savour their sweetness; he found in them a feast for the soul for he wished to be delighted, corrected, and edified by them. He received and honoured with seemly reverence the Host of salvation, the Blood of our Lord, holding in strong faith to that which true doctrine has ordained ... From a tender age he took part devoutly in religious services, often joining in the celebration of them in the company of a religious community of clerks or monks. To old men this youth shone as a fine example for the daily assiduity with which he attended the sacred mysteries.

William of Malmesbury provides a less inflated view: 'He was a practising Christian as far as a layman could be, to the extent of attending mass every day and every day hearing vespers and matins.' He was a friend to the greatest churchmen of his day. He was close to Lanfranc and also to Anselm, Lanfranc's successor as archbishop. He seems to have appreciated churchmen who had true faith. He received by proxy the blessing of the famous Abbot Hugh of Cluny with ostentatious but apparently genuine humility. But there was a distinction between William's personal piety and his respect for individual bishops and abbots, and his view of the Church as an institution. He did not bow to the pope's will; he appointed the men that he wanted to bishoprics, some of them in return for money or help; and he thought nothing of attempting to purchase monks to staff his abbeys. William desired to make worthy appointments to the abbeys of England, so he wrote to Abbot Hugh of Cluny and sought to purchase six or 12 of his monks whom he might appoint as abbots. He recognized that this would be a great loss to Cluny and so offered to pay £100 per monk per annum to the abbey as a friendly thank-offering. The abbot refused point blank. The monks were not for sale, and he would certainly not sell them into perdition in a strange land.[15] Although he might have been pious, and feared damnation, control of the institutional Church was a matter of policy, not faith, for King William.

Associated with William's piety, perhaps, was his sexual continence, which was seen as something worthy of praise by monastic writers such as William of Malmesbury. Malmesbury's words reveal, however, that others might find this harder to understand and might consequently wonder whether it was due to physical problems rather than genuine continence:

Besides his other virtues, William had such respect for chastity, especially in early manhood, that public gossip told of his impotence. When, however, on the advice of his nobles he married, his conduct was such as to keep him free for many years of any suggestion of misbehaviour ... although there are scandal mongers who maintain that he abandoned his early continence when royal power came to him, and wallowed in the embraces of a priest's daughter, whom Matilda sent packing after having her hamstrung by one of her vassals; the vassal (so the story goes) was deprived of his fief, and Matilda was flogged to death with a horse's bridle. But to believe this of so great a king I regard as lunacy.

Malmesbury's verdict must be right, for William does seem to have had real affection for his wife. Although Matilda roused him to fury when he learned that she was giving financial support to Robert Curthose during his rebellion in *c*. 1078,

that this occasioned no lessening of their affection as man and wife he himself made clear; for when she died, four years before him, he gave her a most splendid funeral, and showed by many days of the deepest mourning how much he missed the love of her whom he had lost.

William's relationship with the rest of his family is harder to divine. Malmesbury notes that William venerated the memory of his father and was engaged in bringing his bones back from Nicaea to Normandy when he died, but the fact that he had left it so long to do this suggests that his veneration was a late development. Malmesbury says too that he treated his mother, Herleva, 'as long as she lived with distinguished generosity'. There is no evidence of this, however, and the small gifts that he gave to the abbey of Grestain, where she was buried, do not indicate great affection.[16] Equally, although his relationship with his half-brother, Count Robert of Mortain, the founder of Grestain, remained good until his death, he fell out with Odo of Bayeux, his other half-brother, in bizarre circumstances in 1082 or 1083 – as we shall see. From 1077 his relationship with his eldest son was increasingly fraught. Robert was lectured in private and then scorned in public, with William pointing out his failings to those who would listen. Robert rebelled in 1077 or 1078 and, although he was reconciled with his father by 1080, the two men fell out for a second time from 1084 to 1087. William's relationship with his younger sons was better, but perhaps this was because they had no expectation of inheritance and so did not bridle at their lack of power. All of this is very impressionistic, because the sources tell us very little indeed about William's relationships with members of his family, unless they impacted directly on the politics of the day. In contrast, there are a number of details in the narratives that evidence Matilda's close relationship with her son Robert.

Others of William's character traits are harder to interpret, because our sources do not distinguish between his character and his kingship. Both William of Poitiers and Orderic Vitalis make the point that the king was especially concerned with justice. But this was something that was expected of a king. It had therefore to be said of William, whether it was true or not. Equally the sources portray William as a strong and stern man. Poitiers talks about his 'strict discipline', the 'E' version of the *Anglo-Saxon Chronicle* says that he was a stern and a hard man, and that during his reign,

> The rich complained and the poor lamented,
> But he was too relentless to care though all might hate him,
> And they were compelled, if they wanted
> To keep their lives and their lands
> And their goods and the favour of the king,
> To submit themselves wholly to his will.
> Alas! That any man should bear himself so proudly
> And deem himself exalted above all other men!

But, again, how much of this is a depiction of William the ruler, and how much of it was William's personality? Or is this a case where personality and kingship shade into each other to such an extent that they cannot now be told apart?

The same is true for the fault about which all the sources are agreed. William, they say, was avaricious. The 'E' version of the *Anglo-Saxon Chronicle* reflects that,

> A hard man was the king
> And took from his subjects many marks
> In gold and many more hundreds of pounds in silver.
> These sums he took by weight from his people
> Most unjustly and for little need.
> He was sunk in greed
> And utterly given up to avarice.

William of Malmesbury, in a position to sum up the general view on William from his vantage point in the twelfth century, remarks that, the only point on which he is rightly criticized is his passion for money, which no scruples restrained him from scraping together by seeking opportunities in all directions, doing and saying much – indeed everything – that was unworthy of so great a monarch where dawned a glittering hope of gain. Nor is there any other excuse I can suggest, except that, as someone said, 'he must fear many men, whom many fear'. For it was fear of his enemies that drove him to squeeze the money from his provinces, with which either to slow up their attacks or even to drive them off entirely; very often, as happens in human affairs, when strength failed he secured the loyalty of his opponents by largesse.

This avarice looks to have been a matter of state. It is not at all clear from what the *Chronicle* and Malmesbury say that William personally was greedy. His unpopular demands for money were the result of the need to defend his dominions and thereby fulfil the functions of a good ruler. When it comes to William's personality, then, we can be sure of only one thing: that we must pause to consider the nature of the sources, what they are telling us and why, before even thinking of condemning William as stern or avaricious.

This cheerful, pious, perhaps stern man, decked out in silk and warmed by his fur-trimmed cloak, lived in a number of different residences that were scattered across Normandy and England. In Normandy the king had castles and palaces at, for example, Rouen, Fécamp, Lillebonne, Bonneville, Caen, Cherbourg and Lyons-la-Forêt. Some of these, such as the castles at Rouen and Lillebonne, were impressive edifices made of stone. The hall at Lillebonne, which probably dated to William's reign, was demolished in the 1830s. Pictures of it show a two-storeyed building, with a covered arcade below and a room lit with a series of two-light windows above.[17] At Caen the footings of William's palace remain to give an idea of the size and layout of the buildings. There was a hall (16m × 8m) and a separate chamber block, as well as a chapel. There was also a kitchen and a bakery. This accommodation rapidly became too small, and Henry I built a new hall to the south-west which still stands and is known as the *salle de l'Echiquier* (31m × 11m). To the north of the palace there was a gate tower, similar to the later one at Ludlow, which provided the chief strong point.[18]

In England William had residences at, for example, London, Winchester, Windsor and Gloucester, all of them in the south of the country. Of these the most famous – and the most intact – is the White Tower of the Tower of London, which was begun in around 1075 but not finished until around 1100, owing to a break in construction between *c.* 1080 and *c.* 1090. By that point

31. The footings of William's palace at Caen, with Henry I's
salle de l'Echiquier to the right.

the chapel of St John had been begun but not completed, and it is unlikely that more than the entrance-level rooms could be used by the king and his court. William, then, did not live to see the completion of one of the monuments most closely associated with him[19]

These buildings were not glazed, but had shutters to keep out the worst of the weather, although they would also have cut out the light. Some buildings, such as the White Tower, had fireplaces and garderobes built into the thickness of the walls. In other halls a fire was lit in a hearth in the middle of the floor, and the smoke would slowly leave the room through louvres in the roof. The walls may have been painted, and in the grandest residences they might have been broken by blind arcades, perhaps with capitals at the tops of the pillars depicting various animals or stories. Blind arcading survives in William fitz Osbern's hall at Chepstow, which must date from before 1071, while nine decorated capitals survive from the hall that William Rufus built at Westminster in the 1090s. These are in rather poor condition, but one of them shows an attack on a castle, one a hunt, and two depict tales from Æsop's Fables.[20] There is no evidence that the Normans shared the English taste for wall hangings before 1066, however. These hangings appear in English wills of the tenth and eleventh centuries, and some of them were very large – they might have been used to partition rooms. It may be that the Normans developed a similar taste for such decoration after the Conquest. We know that Adela of Blois, William's daughter, had a tapestry in her chamber that showed her father's Conquest of England, and Henry of Huntingdon says that when William died, his treasure included hangings.

William of Malmesbury, in a well-known passage, said of the English that 'in small mean houses they wasted their entire substance, unlike the French and the Normans, who in proud great buildings live a life of moderate expense'. Malmesbury does not mean that there was barely a stick of furniture in Norman houses, however. When William was holding court, his throne might have been the only piece of furniture in the room – although in one scene the Bayeux Tapestry shows Odo sitting alongside his brother on a similar stool. But it is certain that William's castles and palaces were comfortably furnished. The sorts of things that could have been found in them are suggested by the lists of items in the ninth-century capitulary, *De Villis*.[21] This was sent by the Emperor Charlemagne to his estate managers, and it sets out precisely what should be available at each of the emperor's residences. With regard to furniture, it says that each house should have in its storerooms, beds, mattresses, pillows, bed-linen, table-cloths and seat covers. Tenth- and eleventh-century English wills also mention seat covers, table covers and bed curtains,[22] while the description of Edward the Confessor's palace in the *Life of King Edward* reads: 'The throne, adorned with coverings embroidered with gold, gleamed in every part; the floors were strewn with precious carpets from Spain.'

Oddly, beds are particularly well attested. The Bayeux Tapestry shows Edward the Confessor on a bed, with the two legs at its foot ending in carved dragons' heads, and with curtains around it. He is covered by a decorated quilt and his head is propped up on a large pillow. Henry I lies on a similar bed in John of Worcester's *Chronicle*, where he dreams of being attacked by the three orders of society in turn – the labourers, the knights and the clergy. An act of William's son, Henry I, tells us what went on his bed. Roland of Oissel held land in Oissel, on the Seine, in return for 'finding straw for use in my chamber and a down quilt for my bed when I come to my house at Oissel and a lodging for my butler and to keep the quilt until I return'.[23]

William's residences, although they did have a private chamber, were

32. The chapel of St John in the White Tower. In William's day, it is likely that the work had gone no higher than the tops of the columns.

more public than private. They were used not only as a place for the king and his court to rest their heads at night, but as the venues for courts and communal eating. The Bayeux Tapestry shows men at table, drinking from bowls and horns; drinking horns decorated with gold at both ends were taken to Normandy in 1067. Some of these utensils survive to the present day. Excavations have uncovered pottery pitchers, glass beakers, wooden plates, spoons and knives.

William is said to have been temperate in his drinking. But when feasting, and at other times too, his drink of preference would have been wine. As noted above, Poitiers says that when the duke was waiting for his fleet to find him in the Channel, he 'partook of an abundant meal, accompanied by spiced wine, as if he were in his hall at home'. Indeed the Bayeux Tapestry shows stores of arms and armour being assembled for William's invasion of England, and in this same scene there is a cart, pulled by two men, on which there is a large barrel. The caption above the scene reads: 'and here they pull a cart with wine and arms'. There were vineyards in Normandy, with the best of the Norman wine coming from the area around Argences and along the Seine valley. We hear, now and again, of grape presses being destroyed during periods of violence.

Cider was also known in Normandy. One monk from the abbey of Saint-Benoit-sur-Loire complained of the ubiquitous presence of this drink in the duchy.[24] Beer, on the other hand, was probably more an English drink. A number of Cambridgeshire manors paid a rent in malt in 1086, which would have been used to make beer. But wine was known there too, even before the Conquest. Henry of Huntingdon recounts an argument between Harold Godwinson and his brother Tostig. He says that afterwards Tostig angrily went to Hereford, where Harold had prepared a royal banquet. 'There he dismembered all his brother's servants, and put a human leg, head, or arm into each vessel for wine, mead, ale, spiced wine, wine with mulberry juice, and cider.'

In both Normandy and England, food was a social marker.[25] The rich ate more meat than the poor, and the trend in the eleventh and twelfth centuries was towards the consumption of more beef and pork at the expense of mutton. Game animals, such as red, roe and fallow deer, would also regularly feature on the menu. As to birds, the canons of Harold Godwinson's foundation at Waltham ate blackbirds, plovers, partridges and pheasants. Geese were also consumed by the well-to-do. Indeed William of Malmesbury says that Wulfstan of Worcester was so distracted by the delicious smell of roasting goose that 'his soul melted in delight'. He was, though, called away on urgent business before the bird was ready. Leaving with an empty stomach, Wulfstan turned the matter over in his mind and ended up taking a vow never again to feast on food of that kind. For those living close to the coast, there was also the opportunity to eat fresh fish — in these days before refrigeration, those living inland could only have sea fish that had been salted. Porpoise was among the most luxurious of fishes; herrings and eels too were upper-class delicacies, and vast quantities of these fish might be owed as rents. So, for example, in 1086 the church at Blytheburgh in Suffolk paid 3,000 herrings to the king; the miller at Isleham in Cambridgeshire paid the bishop of Rochester 300 eels as well as a money rent of 2s. 8d. The English monk Ælfric, in his *Colloquy*, which was used to teach Latin to young monks, has his fisherman explain that he took eels, pike, minnows, burbot, trout and lampreys from the river, while from the sea he took herrings, salmon, porpoises, sturgeon, oysters, crabs, mussels, winkles, cockles, plaice, flounder, lobster and suchlike.

Aside from listing the furnishings to be kept in store at the emperor's residences, the capitulary *De Villis* sets out obligations and requirements about what would now be called the home farm, next to the castle or palace. It provides a massive amount of detail about the animals kept, the vegetables and herbs grown, and the foodstuffs made. It provides a glimpse into the life, admittedly at the highest social level, of the ninth century. It was a life that was probably not that different from that of the eleventh century. It commands that the custodians of these royal manors should ensure that the fishponds were kept in good repair and enlarged; that on each of the estates there should be as many cowsheds, pigsties, sheepfolds and goat-pens as possible; that the houses should be guarded at all times; that 'anything which they do or make with their hands – that is lard, smoked meat, sausage, newly salted meat, wine, vinegar, mulberry wine, boiled wine, garum, mustard, cheese, butter, malt, beer, mead, honey, wax and flour – that all these are made or prepared with the greatest attention to cleanliness'; that the woods and fields should be well maintained; that there should always be fatted geese and chickens available; that there should always be swans, peacocks, pheasants, ducks, pigeons, partridges and turtle doves 'for sake of ornament'. It may be remarked here that a peacock is shown in the top margin of the Bayeux Tapestry, above William's palace in the scene where Harold is brought to him, and the number of peahens in England certainly increased after the Conquest.

In the later part of the twelfth century, and possibly already in William's day, those who dined in the hall with their lord were supposed to follow a detailed set of rules that set out what behaviour was and was not acceptable. These were written down by Daniel of Beccles, who seems to have compiled his book – *The Civilized Man* – during the reign of Henry II (1154–89).[26] Some of Daniel's ordinances are as follows: do not pick your fleas when the lord is present; if you wish to belch, remember to look up at the ceiling; no one is allowed to urinate in the hall, except for the lord; do not attack your food like a dog; do not fart noisily for fun; do not sit with your legs crossed as this is the mark of haughty pride; do not put too large a piece of food in your mouth; do not talk with your mouth full; do not overload your spoon; do not blow on hot pottage (presumably because it might spray those nearby); do not lick your fingers; if you clean out your nose into your hand, do not let people see what comes out; and, when dining, face your superiors and have your back to inferiors. In addition, Daniel also notes that when a lord was sitting on the toilet, his servant need not kneel as he handed over the pieces of straw or hay with which he would wipe his bottom.

Above the noise of the belching and serious farting of the diners would come the sound of the singing and playing of minstrels. Men like Bishop Guy of Amiens and Geoffrey Gaimar composed poems which must have been intended for performance, and if the Normans could sing the *Song of Roland* as they rode into battle at Hastings, then they must have heard it sung – and more than once. There is a mention of girls and women singing songs about Hereward, too, and minstrels certainly sang in the presence of Archbishop Thomas of York (1070–1100). They would have been accompanied on the harps and other stringed instruments depicted in manuscripts, while bone flutes have been recovered in excavations. There might even have been a dramatic or performance element to songs. This is suggested by the Bayeux Tapestry, where at least some of the gestures employed by the characters depicted reflect those used by actors on stage, as found in manuscripts of Terence, the Roman comic dramatist of the second century BC.[27] But these snippets of information are all that we have; the tunes and the details of the performance are all lost.

When the torches in the hall were finally extinguished, the king and queen would go to their separate chambers, complete with beds and down quilts. Some of the greatest might leave the hall and go to billets in houses nearby, but most would doss down in the hall. The more important of them – or just the most nimble – might sleep on the tables and benches; the less important (or more restless sleepers) would have to make do with the floor. Talking of Thomas Becket's hospitality while chancellor, one of his biographers remarks that,

> he ordered his floors to be covered every day with new straw or hay in the winter, fresh bulrushes or leaves in the summer, so that the multitude of knights, who could not all fit on the stalls, could find a clean and pleasant space and leave their precious clothes and beautiful shirts unsoiled.[28]

At William Rufus's court, all manner of things might go on during the night. Indeed the king had all the lights left unlit, so that courtiers could move around with anonymity. This seems not to have been the case in the Conqueror's day, however. William's piety and morality, as well as his continence, seem to have ensured that his court remained a wholesome place during the hours of darkness.

No portrait of William would be complete without reference to his love of hunting. William of Poitiers remarks on William's enthusiasm for falconry. The sieges of Domfront and Alençon did not constitute unrelieved military exercise. While attempting to reduce these towns, William found the time to relax. 'Often,' says Poitiers, 'he delighted in flying his falcons, or more often his sparrowhawks' in this 'thickly wooded region'.

The flying of hawks, falcons and other birds of prey was an aristocratic activity because only the rich could afford them. Edward the Confessor was another who delighted in hawks and hunting. On the Bayeux Tapestry, Harold Godwinson is shown riding with a hawk on his left hand. We may note too that the Angevin kings seem always to have taken their hawks with them whenever they crossed the Channel. Falconers are mentioned in Domesday Book, and some shires were obliged to provide birds. The value of a hawk might be £10. In contrast, a mail hauberk might fetch between £7 and £9 *livres* of Rouen – in sterling that was between £1 5s and £2 2s. – and a packhorse cost £1.[29]

But more even then falconry, William loved the hunt. So much so that much of the obituary poem found in the 'E' version of the *Anglo-Saxon Chronicle* is taken up with criticism of this passion, and of the lengths to which William went to maintain his hunting preserves:

> He set apart a vast deer preserve and imposed laws concerning it.
> Whoever slew a hart or a hind
> Was to be blinded.
> He forbade the killing of boars
> Even as the killing of harts.
> For he loved the stags as dearly
> As though he had been their father.
> Hares also he decreed should go unmolested.

The most well known of William's forests is the New Forest – a name which itself reveals that the creation of royal hunting grounds did not begin with the Conquest. William of Malmesbury states that the New Forest,

> was a region which … William, with villages abandoned, had reduced for thirty miles and more to 'woodland glades and lairs for the wild beasts'. It is indeed a dreadful sight: where in old days human society and divine worship flourished, now red deer and roe and suchlike animals wander insolently, not even available to men at large for their benefit.

But the 'vast deer preserve' of the *Chronicle* probably meant not only the New Forest but also the various forests scattered across the country in Berkshire, Oxfordshire, Surrey, Essex and the Welsh marches. By the end of the twelfth century these took up about one quarter of all the land in the country, but they had not reached this extent in William's day.

In these verdant playgrounds, William would hunt deer and boar – animals that he reserved to himself and his successors. The king's monopoly was protected by the notorious forest law, which covered all of the forests and also those areas that bordered them. These laws protected both the game and also the vegetation which provided the animals with shelter and food. The law consequently forbade not just the unlawful poaching of deer but also the felling of trees, excessive grazing, the clearance of land or burning of the undergrowth.

There were two different methods of recreational hunting (as opposed to the professional trapping of animals and birds). The first was to hunt the quarry on horseback, following the hounds – the sort of hunt that is taking place in the lower margin of the Bayeux Tapestry where messengers announce Harold's capture by Count Guy to Duke William. The second involved driving the deer along a set route in the forest, thereby allowing dismounted archers to shoot at them as they ran past their position.[30] In 1086 there were three 'hedges for catching the roebuck' at Lingen in Herefordshire, and there were two more in neighbouring Lye. In Warwickshire, one of these hedges was half a league square. It was while out hunting in this manner that William Rufus was accidentally shot dead by Walter Tirel. Indeed William Rufus was only the most famous of a number of William's family who met their end in the New Forest. 'There,' says Orderic, 'he lost two sons, Richard and William Rufus, and his grandson Richard ... and visions appeared in many terrible forms to various men by which the Lord plainly showed his anger that consecrated buildings had been given over to be a habitation for wild beasts.'

✝

CHAPTER 8

STORMS OF TROUBLES, 1076–87

According to Orderic Vitalis, William's luck was transformed after 1076. Before that year he had always triumphed over his enemies; after it he suffered defeat and disaster. Orderic blamed this change of fortune on the execution of Earl Waltheof. This was perhaps because he had visited Crowland Abbey in the Fens where the earl was buried, and had taken the Waltheof legend to heart. But although William did suffer setbacks after 1076, he suffered them only in Normandy. In England resistance to his rule was virtually at an end – although in 1085 it did look as though he would face another Danish invasion. It is not, then, entirely arbitrary to give these last 11 years of the reign a chapter of their own.

Normandy	England
After May 1076–autumn 1080	
	autumn 1080–autumn 1081
autumn 1081–autumn 1082	
	autumn 1082–spring 1083
spring 1083–85	
	1085–summer 1086
summer 1086–9 September 1087	

Table 2. William's Channel Crossings, 1076–87.

After William had put down the rebellion of the earls in England, he crossed to Normandy. His aim was to finish off Ralph of Gael who had fled to his estates in Brittany and was now ensconced at Dol. William besieged the castle in September or October 1076. But he was not successful. Word reached him that King Philip was approaching with a large army. Ralph and his garrison remained ignorant of this, however, and so William seized the opportunity to negotiate a strategic withdrawal. So rapid was his departure that he left behind him tents and baggage, vessels, arms and furnishings of all kinds, worth in total, says Orderic, £15,000.

William's failure before Dol increased the confidence of his other enemies. Count Fulk of Anjou judged that William was weak and that the time to recover Maine had arrived. At the beginning of 1077 he attacked the lands and castles of John of La Flèche, who was, says Orderic, 'particularly obnoxious to him because of his friendship for the Normans'. John received intelligence of the planned attack, and sent to William for help. Norman troops, commanded by William of Moulins-la-Marche and Robert of Vieux-Pont, were sent to assist John, and they garrisoned his fortresses.

There now seems to have been a stand-off for four years. It was not until 1081 that Count Fulk finally struck at the very heart of John's power – the castle of La Flèche. Nor did he strike alone. By the time his invasion was put in train, he had enlisted the help of Count Hoel of Brittany – at one time William's ally. When William received news of the investment of La Flèche and of the involvement of both Fulk and Hoel, he mustered an army of his own and marched south. The Angevins and Bretons, however, remained confident and did not retreat at news of William's advance. Instead they crossed the River Loire and then burned their boats to make a retreat impossible. That is what Orderic says, at least, but he seems to have forgotten that a retreat to Brittany would not be hindered by the lack of boats. The two armies prepared for battle but the fighting was averted by 'a certain cardinal priest of the Roman church'. He brought the two sides to the negotiating table: 'Parleys took place; various terms were proposed; there was a battle of words.' The upshot of all of this was that the count of Anjou recognized Robert Curthose's right to Maine, with the whole of the fief that he had received from Count Herbert when he was betrothed to Margaret. In return Robert did homage for Maine to Count Fulk. As part of the agreement, John of La Flèche and other of the Manceaux barons were reconciled to Fulk. This settlement ushered in a period of peace with Anjou that was to last until William's death, even if the

33. The cathedral at Bayeux. Parts of the west towers are Bishop Odo's work.

same was not true of his relations with the Manceaux.

William might have had a brief respite from his troubles in 1077, however. In that year, four of the greatest Norman churches were dedicated. These were the cathedral at Evreux, which was to be burned down by King William's son, Henry I, in 1119; Bayeux Cathedral, constructed by Bishop Odo and of which only the two west towers and crypt now remain; and the abbey church of Saint-Etienne in Caen, the Conqueror's own foundation, and the church in which he was buried. In addition, the abbey church of Le Bec was dedicated, too, just a year before the death of its saintly founder, Herluin. William was not present at that occasion, however. Orderic says that the dedications were carried out by Archbishop John of Rouen in the presence of the two English metropolitans; Robert and William, the king's sons; and a great multitude of people. These solemn occasions, and the feasts which no doubt followed, would have allowed William to demonstrate his majesty and wealth at a time when his power was almost at its nadir.

It is possible that these celebrations, with the associated splendour, the fawning on the king and his central part in the proceedings, made his son, Robert, bitter and jealous. Robert Curthose had been born in around 1051. By 1077 he was about 26. According to Orderic, he was 'talkative and extravagant, reckless, very courageous in battle, a powerful and sure archer with a clear, cheerful voice and fluent tongue. Round-faced, short and stout, he was commonly nicknamed "fat-legs" and "curt-hose"'.[1]

Robert thought that he, not his father, should be the reigning duke of the Normans. He had almost certainly been nominated as William's successor in 1066, immediately before the Hastings campaign.[2] He had received the homage of the Normans, just as his father had done when Robert the Magnificent went on pilgrimage to Jerusalem. But whereas Robert had not come back, William triumphed at Hastings and did return to the duchy. And while William lived, he denied Robert Curthose any political power or any independent means to support himself or his household. Even Maine remained entirely in William's power. Both Orderic and John of Worcester are very clear that it was Curthose's frustrated ambition that led him to rebel against his father. Orderic pictures a stand-up row over the subject. William told Robert, at great length, not to press his demands and to be patient. He responded:

> 'My lord king, I did not come here to listen to a lecture, for I have had more than enough of these from my schoolmasters and am surfeited with them. Give me instead a satisfactory answer about the honour due to me, which I am awaiting so that I may know what kind of life I may live. On one thing I am unshakeably resolved and wish all to know: that I will no longer fight for anyone in Normandy with the hopeless status of a hired dependant.' On hearing this the king exclaimed in anger, 'I have already told you plainly enough and have no scruples in telling you again even more plainly that I will never agree as long as I live to relax my grip on my native land of Normandy.

Moreover, I do not choose to divide the kingdom of England, which I won with such great pains, in my lifetime ... Let no one doubt this for one moment: as long as I live I will surrender my duchy to no one, and will allow no living man to share my kingdom with me.'

Robert had probably been on the brink of rebellion for some time. He was finally brought to it late in 1077 or early in 1078 as a result of an incident at the frontier town of L'Aigle. The king was preparing to launch an expedition against the men of the Corbonnais, an area that lay immediately to the south of the duchy. He and his sons were lodged in the town. Robert had taken up residence in the house of a burgess called Roger Cauchois. He was joined there by his brothers, who went upstairs and began to play dice in the upper room 'as knights do'. They made a great deal of noise, became drunk and soon began to 'pour down water' (apparently a monkish euphemism for 'urinate') on Robert and his sycophants beneath. Ivo and Aubrey of Grandmesnil, two of Robert's companions, were outraged. They confronted Curthose and spurred him into action. Robert dashed up the stairs in a rage and started a fight. The noise was so loud that the king was quickly there. He forced his sons to patch up the quarrel. On the next night, Robert, who must have been humiliated by these events and his father's reaction to them, left L'Aigle and headed for Rouen with the intention of seizing the castle. But Roger of Ivry, the castellan, had been warned and was ready. He refused to surrender to Robert and he also sent messengers to the king to tell him what was happening. The king flew into a terrible rage and commanded that the conspirators should be seized. Most of them, including Robert Curthose, fled into exile.

They went first to Robert the Frisian, count of Flanders.[3] Curthose next sought the help of King Philip of France, and the king sent him to the castle of Gerberoy on the frontier with Normandy. From here he could do serious mischief on the Norman border. During his stay at Gerberoy, Curthose assembled a collection of common knights from Normandy and promised them, and many French barons besides, 'more than it was in his power to give'. In the meantime King William fortified his frontiers, putting garrisons in his castles to prevent Robert and his allies from plundering across the border. But he was unable to tolerate the presence of his enemies so close to his frontier for very long. And so towards the end of 1078 he raised an army and marched against his errant son and his miscreant friends who were still at Gerberoy. His luck deserted him once more. Robert's forces sallied out of the castle and joined battle. Robert attacked his own father and wounded his hand or arm. William's

34. The thirteenth-century oak effigy of Robert Curthose in Gloucester Cathedral.
He died, the prisoner of his brother Henry I, at Cardiff in 1134.

horse was then killed beneath him. According to John of Worcester, it was
only then that Robert realized just who he was fighting. 'As soon as Robert
recognized William's voice, he quickly dismounted, and ordered his father to
mount his horse, and in this way allowed him to leave.' The 'D' version of
the *Anglo-Saxon Chronicle* tells a different story. According to the chronicler,
an Englishman, Toki, son of Wigod of Wallingford, brought up another horse
for William, but was immediately killed by a crossbow bolt for his trouble.
Orderic, on the other hand, fails to mention the episode altogether.

William returned to Rouen to lick his wounds and nurse his grievances
against his son. He was not at all pleased when a collection of lords, including
such luminaries as Roger of Montgommery, Earl Hugh of Chester and Roger
of Beaumont, pressed him to make peace with Robert. But despite the king's
displeasure, his nobles continued to urge him to resolve matters with his son
and nominated heir. They were joined by the bishops and clergy and even,
if we are to believe Orderic, by representatives of the king of the French.
Eventually, faced with no other choice, the king gave way and was reconciled
to his son. Shortly afterwards, on 8 May 1080, Pope Gregory VII wrote to

Curthose, advising him to show proper obedience to his father and reminding him that he would inherit all William's power and estates at the proper time:[4]

> because we have heard through our son Hubert that you have agreed to your father's counsels and have altogether banished those of wicked men, we are rejoicing. Moreover we counsel and in a fatherly way beseech that it may ever be graven upon your mind that whatever your father may possess with so strong a hand and with such widespread renown he seized from the mouth of his enemies, knowing, however, that he would not live forever but so manfully pressing forward with this in his mind: that he would pass it on to some heir of his own.

In August 1079, taking advantage of William's problems in Normandy, King Malcolm of Scots invaded England and burned his way through Northumberland as far south as the Tyne. John of Worcester reports that he 'killed many people, took captive many more, and returned home with a great booty'. For now, William was unable to punish this apparently unprovoked attack.

The next year Bishop Walcher of Durham was murdered as the result of a local feud. The chief protagonists, aside from the bishop himself, were Ligulf, a local English nobleman, and Leobwine, Walcher's archdeacon. The story reveals just what could happen when the petty jealousies of any great man's household got out of control. To cut a long story very short, Bishop Walcher died simply because Leobwine was jealous of Ligulf's position, and took offence when Ligulf responded robustly to his jibes. This is the kernel of the story, as reported by John of Worcester:

> One day, when Ligulf had been asked by the bishop for his advice, and had decided on whatever was right and just, Leobwine opposed him pig-headedly and exasperated him with insulting remarks. But because Ligulf had answered him with greater vehemence than usual, Leobwine left the court and summoned Gilbert, a man to whom the bishop, who was his kinsman, had entrusted the administration of the county placed under his control. Leobwine clearly asked Gilbert to avenge him and kill Ligulf as soon as possible. Gilbert willingly agreed to Leobwine's evil request, and gathering together the bishop's and Leobwine's knights, went one night to the township where Ligulf was staying, and unjustly killed him in his residence with nearly all his household.

When Bishop Walcher heard of this he distanced himself from Leobwine and attempted to meet with Ligulf's family to settle the feud before more blood was spilt. They met at Gateshead, but Walcher was unable to convince Ligulf's kinsmen that he had played no part in the murder. The result was that Leobwine, the bishop and almost all his household were killed by the mob. The insurgents then marched on Durham and besieged the castle for four days before they dispersed. Simeon of Durham reports that,

> as soon as the intelligence of this transaction was circulated, Odo, bishop of Bayeux, who was second only to the king, and many of the chief nobles of the kingdom, came to Durham with a large body of troops, and in revenging the bishop's death they reduced nearly the whole land into a wilderness. The miserable inhabitants who, trusting in their innocence, had remained in their homes were either beheaded as criminals or mutilated by the loss of some of their members.

Simeon also notes that a magnificent pastoral staff, encrusted with sapphires, speedily disappeared after Bishop Odo had transferred it from the church to the safety of the castle.

King Malcolm of Scots had taken the opportunity presented by the death of the bishop, who was also earl of Northumbria, to invade the north of England again. But this time he was not allowed to escape scot-free. An army marched north under the command of Robert Curthose. He invaded Scotland and ravaged all of Lothian, so that Malcolm was brought to terms at Falkirk. The king of Scots renewed the terms of the treaty reached at Abernethy in 1072, and gave Robert hostages for his good behaviour. There is a sense, at least in the sources that originate at Durham, that the campaign had not been an outstanding success, but the Scots did not invade England again during William's reign. Robert had one further act to perform. He paused on his way back from Scotland on the north bank of the Tyne. There, across the river from Gateshead, where Walcher had been murdered, he built a new castle at the place now known as Newcastle. It was, at that time, the most northerly royal castle in England. Its construction reveals how little control William then had over Northumberland, and that he intended to change that state of affairs. It was to be a base for further Norman expansion, and it was soon handed over to a new Norman earl of Northumbria. This man, Aubrey, about whom almost nothing is known, was earl for a little less than a year. He was succeeded by Robert of Mowbray, a nephew of Bishop Geoffrey of Coutances. Orderic says that he was strong and dark and hairy and rarely smiled. He was to rebel against William Rufus in 1095.

In 1081 a battle was fought in the west of Wales at an unidentified place known as Mynydd Carn. The rival claimants for north and south Wales joined battle. Gruffydd ap Cynan and Rhys ap Tewdwr emerged as the victors, and as unopposed kings of Gwynedd (north Wales) and Deheubarth (south Wales) respectively. It can be no coincidence that King William made a journey to St Davids, in the far south-west of Wales, later the same year. This so-called pilgrimage clearly had a more political purpose. To begin with, the king did not go alone. The 'E' version of the *Anglo-Saxon Chronicle* says, 'In this year the king led levies into Wales, and there freed many hundreds.' The Welsh source, the *Brut y Tywysogion* or *Chronicle of the Princes*, describes the king as making a pilgrimage to St Davids, but three of the manuscripts add that he went with 'many Frenchmen'. Such pilgrimages were a political tool, and William's intention was not to show due respect to St David but rather to overawe Rhys ap Tewdwr. And it may be supposed that Rhys, unwilling to bring down on his head the wrath of William's army, made all the right noises. He submitted to William's power and agreed to pay a farm – an annual payment – of £40 for south Wales. The payment was subsequently recorded in Domesday Book, although whether Rhys ever actually paid over the money is unknown.

There was no need to make such an expedition in force to north Wales. Gruffydd ap Cynan might have emerged victorious at Mynydd Carn, but his triumph was shortlived. One of his own barons, Meirion Goch, arranged for his capture by the Norman earls of Chester and Shrewsbury at Y Rug in Edeirnion, and he was taken back to Chester where he was held for 12 years.[5] Earl Hugh of Chester must have been delighted by this turn of events. He had been pushing west, along the coast of north Wales, since he had been given the earldom in *c.* 1071, and Gruffydd had been a thorn in his side for many years. He had even stormed and burned the castle at Rhuddlan in 1075, although he had not been able to take the keep. With Gruffydd now in prison, and with no other Welshman available to take his place, the Normans made great strides. Earl Hugh and his lieutenant Robert of Rhuddlan crossed the River Conwy soon after Gruffydd's capture and built castles at Abergwyngregyn, at the western end of the Roman road through the coastal mountains of north Wales, at Bangor, Caernarfon and at Aberlleiniog on Anglesey. A Breton bishop of Bangor, Hervé, was appointed in 1092, although he was unable to hold on to his see after the Welsh revolt of 1094 and eventually became the first bishop of Ely in 1109. And whereas Rhys ap Tewdwr paid

35. The motte at Rhuddlan, constructed by Earl Hugh of Chester and
Robert of Rhuddlan in *c.* 1073.

£40 for south Wales in 1086, it was a Norman, Robert of Rhuddlan, who paid
the £40 due for north Wales.

Bishop Odo of Bayeux had been one of the props of William's regime ever
since he was made bishop late in 1049 or early in 1050. He was the only one
of William's regents to have free rein to act as he saw fit, without the necessity
to wait for William's orders. The shock of his betrayal in either late 1082 or
early 1083 must have been violent; no wonder that William was so reluctant
to release the bishop, his half-brother, from prison even as he lay on his death
bed. But what form did Odo's betrayal take? It is something that is shrouded
in mystery; something which has been described by David Bates, for good
reason, as 'bizarre'.[6] It seems, on the later evidence of Orderic, William of
Malmesbury and the twelfth-century source known as the Hyde Chronicle,
that Odo was trying to purchase the papacy for himself. Orderic says that,

> certain soothsayers at Rome, in an attempt to discover who would succeed
> Hildebrand in the papacy, ascertained that Odo was to be pope in Rome after
> Gregory's death. When the news reached Odo, bishop of Bayeux, who with
> his brother King William ruled the Normans and English, he counted all the

power and wealth of the western kingdom for nothing, wishing only to have authority as pope over the Latins and all the peoples of the earth. Sending to Rome, he bought himself a palace, secured the alliance of the leading Roman families by scattering lavish gifts, and embellished his palace at great expense with superfluous furnishings. He sent for Hugh, earl of Chester, and a great force of distinguished knights, invited them to set out with him for Italy and recklessly backed up his request with lavish promises.

King William heard of these plans at the eleventh hour – how Odo had managed to conceal them for so long is a mystery in itself – and was furious. Quite why he reacted so violently is not explained. However, it may be surmised that William was concerned that Odo would denude the country of knights, exposing both England and Normandy to invasion. Orderic also suggests that the king was concerned about Odo's oppression of the Church and people of England. In any event, William determined to prevent Odo leaving for the continent and to bring him to trial. He surprised Odo on the Isle of Wight and arrested him personally – none of the other lords dared lay a hand on the mighty prelate. As a churchman, Odo could claim immunity from prosecution in a secular court. William swept such argument aside, declaring that he was trying not the bishop of Bayeux but the earl of Kent. Odo was found guilty, presumably of treason, and was imprisoned at Rouen for the remainder of William's reign.

William suffered an even greater loss in November 1083. His wife Matilda died. She had been William's regent in Normandy and had also, perhaps, been a moderating influence on him. Orderic noted that the king experienced bad luck after her death, and this would explain why. Her body was taken to her abbey of the Holy Trinity at Caen, and there laid to rest. The monument that Orderic says was erected over her grave has disappeared, but the eleventh-century tombstone remains. An epitaph was engraved on it, 'in letters of gold', and although all the gold is now gone, the words still remain:

> The lofty structure of this splendid tomb
> Hides great Matilda, sprung from royal stem;
> Child of a Flemish duke, her mother was
> Adela, daughter of the king of France,
> Sister of Henry, Robert's royal son.
> Married to William, most illustrious king,
> She gave this site and raised this noble house,
> With many lands and many goods endowed,
> Given by her, or by her toil procured.

Comforter of the needy, duty's friend;
Her wealth enriched the poor; left her in need.
At daybreak on November's second day,
She won her share of everlasting joy.

At some time after 9 January 1084 Robert Curthose rebelled against his father for the last time. On this occasion there was to be no reconciliation. But equally, this time Curthose did not cause his father trouble on his borders. Instead Robert toured the courts of Europe, wandering through France and Germany. He might even have gone to Italy to attempt to win the hand of Countess Matilda of Tuscany. If he did try, however, then he failed.

About three years after William had reached his agreement with Count Fulk of Anjou over Maine, some of the Manceaux took up arms against him one last time. Hubert, the *vicomte* of Maine, gathered an army at his castle of Sainte-Suzanne, strategically sited on a crag above the River Erve, and then unleashed his strength against the Normans who were stationed in the county. The citizens of Le Mans, who were targeted by Hubert, appealed to William for help. But he could not storm the castle and nor could he block-ade it. He therefore built a castle in the valley of the River Beugy to restrict Hubert's ability to move across the county, and returned to Normandy. But all that happened was that the castle in the valley was attacked time and time again by the rebel garrison on the crag above. Its stocks were plundered and its defenders captured. But if William could not defeat Hubert, then Hubert could not vanquish William. In the end it was Hubert himself who brought the rebellion to a close. Growing tired of the insecurity that was of his own making, he allowed himself to be talked into peace.

For the most part, William had not been personally involved in the fight-ing in Maine. Instead he had been taking stock in Normandy and preparing for another crisis that he could see looming. At the beginning of 1084 he sent messengers into England demanding the collection of a Danegeld at an extremely high rate of 6s. for every hide of land. The large sum might have been due to the war in Maine and to fear of the trouble that Curthose might provoke. Alternatively, or additionally, William intended to use the money to hire the large army that he took to England in 1085. But what was this crisis that necessitated such dramatic action? The *Anglo-Saxon Chronicle* tells us in its annal for 1085, and also records what William did with the army he had collected:

36. Sainte-Suzanne above the River Erve. The castle is on the right, and the
considerable remains of an eleventh-century keep are still
preserved within the curtain wall.

In this year men reported and declared it to be true that Cnut, king of
Denmark, son of King Swein, was on his way here, determined to conquer
this country with the help of Count Robert of Flanders, since Cnut had
married Robert's daughter. When King William learned of this – he was
then residing in Normandy because he owned both England and Normandy
– he returned to England with a vast host of horse and foot from France and
from Brittany which was greater than any that had ever come to this country.
It was so vast that men wondered how this land could feed such a host. The
king, however, had the host spread over the whole country, quartering them
with each of his vassals, according to the produce of his estate. Men suffered
great hardship during this same year, for the king gave orders for the coastal
districts to be laid waste, so that if his enemies landed they would find
nothing which could be quickly seized.

This, then, was to be a two-pronged attack, with the Danes landing on the
east coast in Lincolnshire or Yorkshire, and the count of Flanders attacking the coast of Kent or Essex. It is not the grand alliance against William
portrayed by David Douglas, but it was still dangerous.[7] William needed to
be prepared.

The king awaited the arrival of the Danes throughout 1085, but they did
not come. In fact Cnut was murdered at Odense in 1086, and the invasion
never materialized. But the crisis had evidently exposed weaknesses in the
English administration. Questions had arisen about the number of knights
and the amount of tax that might be raised from England's resources. And so
William, at the end of his Christmas court at Gloucester,

had important deliberations and exhaustive discussions with his council about this land, how it was peopled, and with what sort of men. Then he sent his men all over England into every shire to ascertain how many hundreds of 'hides' of land there were in each shire, and how much land and livestock the king himself owned in the country, and what annual dues were lawfully his from each shire. He also had it recorded how much land his archbishops had, and his diocesan bishops, his abbots and his earls and – though I may be going into too great detail – what or how much each man who was a landholder here in England had in land or in livestock and how much money it was worth. So very thoroughly did he have the inquiry carried out that there was not a single hide, not one virgate of land, not even – it is shameful to record it, but it did not seem shameful to him to do – not even one ox, nor one cow, nor one pig which escaped notice in his survey.

The Anglo-Saxon chronicler is here describing the inquests that resulted in the creation of Domesday Book. It may be supposed that this was just one of the surveys carried out at this time, however, for the calculation of the military strength of England, mentioned by Orderic, John of Worcester and others must have comprised a separate record which is now lost.

The making and meaning of Domesday Book is a complicated business, where several different interpretations of almost any aspect of the survey are possible. Nonetheless, it is possible to sketch how Domesday was made, and what it contains.

The first thing that had to be done was collect the information. The country was divided into seven circuits (see Map 5). Teams of commissioners were then dispatched to each of the circuits. These commissioners were all men of high rank, but they were also unconnected with the shires that they surveyed, in order to ensure that they would be impartial. Bishop William of Durham, for example, was one of the commissioners on Circuit II (the south-west), while the commissioners for Circuit V (the west midlands) were Bishop Remigius of Lincoln, Henry of Ferrers, Walter Giffard and Adam fitz Hubert of Ryes.[8] The survey only covered those parts of the country that were under Norman control. Durham and Northumberland were untouched by the work, while the survey of north Lancashire and Cumbria records only the land held by the king and by Roger the Poitevin and Hugh fitz Baldric. The commissioners held sessions in the shire courts, and perhaps some of the hundred courts too, where they were given the answers to a series of questions including: how much land was there in the manor, how many households were there, how much was the manor worth? The information was double-

Map 5. The Domesday circuits.

checked and written down. The reports produced by each set of commissioners were then taken to the king.

The findings of the survey were summarized in the register that was already known as Domesday Book by the end of the twelfth century. Despite the name, there are in fact two Domesday Books, known as Great Domesday and Little Domesday. Little Domesday has in fact more pages than Great Domesday, but is called Little Domesday because it contains the results for only three counties, Norfolk, Suffolk and Essex. Great Domesday contains the information for all the other English counties. It is now generally agreed that Little Domesday was produced first, which explains why it contains far more information for each of the manors in it than Great Domesday. It must have been apparent to the single scribe who was responsible for the production of the Great Domesday Book that it would take him years to complete the register if the same information were to be incorporated for every county. And so he pruned his material as he went, and did so more and more drastically as the work progressed, so that although there is an overall pattern to the whole, some areas of the country are less fully described than others.

The result was a digested mass of information. The following entries, from Kent and Surrey respectively, give a flavour of precisely what can be found within the folios of Great Domesday:

> The archbishop of Canterbury holds Orpington. In the time of King Edward it answered for 3 sulungs, and now for 2 sulungs and a half. Land for [...]. There are 2 ploughs in demesne and there are 46 villans with 25 bordars holding 23 ploughs. There are 3 mills at 16s. 4d. and 10 acres of meadow and 5 denes of woodland for 50 pigs. In total it was worth in the time of King Edward £15 and when acquired £8 and now £25 and, however, it pays £28. There are two churches.

> The archbishop holds Cheam, for the supplies of the monks. In the time of King Edward it answered for 20 hides and now for 4 hides. There is land for 14 ploughs. There are 2 ploughs in demesne and 25 villans and 12 cottars with 15 ploughs. There is a church there and 5 slaves and 1 acre of meadow. Wood for 25 pigs. In the time of King Edward and after it was worth £8. Now £14.

As these two examples demonstrate, the entries provide information about ownership, the amount of geld that the land owed (based on the number of hides or sulungs in the manor), the amount of arable land (which would produce the money to pay the tax), the number and type of inhabitants (again to establish tax liability, because villans, cottars and bordars would have their tax paid for them), and any other revenue-producing items in the manor, such as churches, mills, fishponds and salt pans. And having established these things, the entries conclude with the value of the manor – the money that it produced every year for its lord. Usually three values are given: the value during King Edward's reign; the value of the manor when it was given to its new, usually Norman, lord; and the value at the time the survey was made in 1086. These values can be used to assess the disruption caused by Norman settlement or, for example, the extent of the harrying of the south and the north.

One thing that all historians can agree on is that having gone to all this trouble, the information in Domesday Book must mean something. Trying to establish exactly what it means is where the arguments begin.[9] Frederick

William Maitland thought that Domesday was a geld book, not a register of land holding. V.H. Galbraith, on the other hand, argued that the geographical arrangement was a hindrance to establishing how much each person owed in tax. He therefore concluded that Domesday was a feudal register. It established who held what. Sally Harvey has opined that the geographical arrangement reflected the sheriffs' rolls, and so it *was* related to the geld. But she thought that it was intended to be the basis for a new fiscal rating that would replace it. Paul Hyams has argued that title was a primary consideration, so Domesday was indeed a register. Nicholas Higham thinks that Domesday is concerned with billeting arrangements and was intended to make the manner in which troops were billeted on the population fairer, once the crisis of 1085 had shown that this might be necessary. David Roffe, in a controversial work, has gone so far as to divorce entirely the survey from the book. Perhaps Domesday was supposed to do all these things. It was certainly soon used as evidence of title, even if that had not been its original purpose. Indeed it was this use that gave the book its name. Richard fitz Nigel explains in his *Dialogue of the Exchequer* that,

> this book is called by the English 'Domesday', that is, by metaphor, the day of judgement. For just as the sentence of that strict and terrible Last Judgement cannot be evaded by any art or subterfuge, so, when a dispute arises in this realm concerning facts that are there written down, and an appeal is made to the book itself, the evidence that it gives cannot be set at naught or evaded with impunity. For this cause we have called this same book 'Domesday', not because it passes judgement on any doubtful points raised, but because it is not permissible to contradict its decisions, any more than it will be those of the Last Judgement.

All of this was done quite quickly, for the returns, if not Domesday Book itself, were ready by the summer of 1086 when they were presented to William during a great court held at Old Sarum at Lammastide (1 August). He was joined there by his council, 'and all landholders who were of any account throughout England no matter whose vassals they might be'. All of them became his men and did him homage.[10] And as homage was given in return for land, it may be supposed that these men were, in turn, confirmed in their estates, as recorded in the survey. The Salisbury oath, then, seems in some ways to have made a formal end to the Norman Conquest of England, although the oath might have been intended to ensure that William had the support of all the men who mattered throughout England — or at least that part of England covered by the survey – should the threat of another Danish invasion arise again in the future.

From Salisbury, William went to the Isle of Wight, and from there he crossed to Normandy. During his absence in England, King Philip had taken the opportunity to attack the diocese of Evreux, ravage the lands of William of Breteuil and Roger of Ivry around Pacy, and drive away herds of cattle and prisoners. His actions roused King William to a fury. He demanded that the whole of the Vexin, including Pontoise, Mantes and Chaumont, should be restored to him – Orderic claims that it had been given to Robert the Magnificent by King Henry I in thanks for restoring him to his kingdom in 1033 – and he uttered dire threats about what he would do should Philip not bow to his will. It took some time for William to make good his threats, however, because he fell ill and took to his bed at Rouen. King Philip of France, making fun of William's corpulence, joked that the king of the English was keeping to his bed 'like a woman who has just had her baby'. This personal insult drove William to still further fury, and, according to Malmesbury,

> he called his army together and entered France with hostile intent. He laid it all low, he ravaged everything; nothing could pacify his furious resolve to avenge, by injuring many, the insult he had received. Eventually he set fire, with flaming missiles, to the city of Mantes and burned St Mary's church there; one recluse, who even in such an emergency thought she ought not to leave her cell, was burnt to death, and all the possessions of the citizens were destroyed. Encouraged by this success, he was urging his troops too rashly to add fuel to the fire, when he went too close to the flames, and the heat of the blaze with the exceptional warmth of the autumn brought on an illness. Some say that his horse, in jumping a steep ditch, ruptured its rider's internal organs because his stomach projected over the forward part of the saddle. Overcome by the pain, he sounded the retreat and retired to Rouen where, as the malady increased daily, he took to his bed. The doctors who were consulted inspected his urine and foretold certain death.

William lay ill for between two and six weeks at Rouen.[11] In the twelfth century, only a few years after the end of William's reign, it was

> a populous and wealthy city, thronged with merchants and a meeting place of trade routes. A fair city set among murmuring streams and smiling meadows, abounding in fruit and fish and all manner of produce, it stands surrounded by hills and woods, strongly encircled by walls and ramparts and battlements, and fair to behold with its mansions and houses and churches.

37. The bottom half of folio 30v of the Great Domesday Book, showing the beginning of the account of the archbishop of Canterbury's lands in Surrey. The third of these is for Cheam, one of the entries transcribed above.

It was a bustling and noisy place – too noisy by far for the man who was dying there in 1087. And so William commanded that he should be taken out of the city and carried up to the church of St Gervase which stood on a hill to the west. 'A small dwelling' was quickly built for him, and it was there that the king spent the last days of his life, surrounded by his physicians and some of the most important of his subjects: Archbishop William of Rouen; Count Robert of Mortain, his half-brother; Gerard, his chancellor; and two of his sons, William and Henry, both of whom were to succeed him in turn as kings of the English.[12] Knowing that his end was approaching he commanded Count Robert to summon the officials of his household to his bedside. According to an anonymous tract, written within a year or two of William's death, when they were present he ordered them, to enumerate one by one all the things which were in his household, namely crowns and arms, vessels and books, and ecclesiastical vestments. And as it seemed good to him he declared what ought to be given to churches, to the poor, and finally to his sons.

His duchy he reluctantly left to his eldest son, Robert, who was in arms against him at the time. England, however, he left to God, while making it clear that he hoped his second son, William, would succeed him there. Indeed he gave him the crown and other insignia, as well as a letter addressed to Archbishop Lanfranc of Canterbury, to make certain that no obstacle should stand in the way of God's will. The king also gave orders that all his political prisoners should be released. He was eventually persuaded that the amnesty should include his own half-brother, Bishop Odo of Bayeux, whom William had kept in prison for the previous four years. But he yielded reluctantly and told all those urging him to release the prelate that they would regret it.[13]

On the morning of Thursday 9 September 1087, just as the bells of the cathedral were ringing for prime (the divine office held at approximately 6 o'clock in the morning), William the Conqueror raised his eyes to heaven, commended his soul to St Mary, and died.

> The physicians and others present, who had watched the king as he slept all night without a sigh or a groan, and now realized that he had died without warning, were utterly dumbfounded and almost out of their minds. But the wealthier among them quickly mounted horse and rode off as fast as they could to protect their properties. The lesser attendants, seeing that their superiors had absconded, seized the arms, vessels, clothing, linen, and all the royal furnishings, and hurried away leaving the king's body almost naked on the floor.

In Rouen the citizens reacted to the news with panic, rushing around and asking each other what they should do, now that their protector was dead. Eventually, however, the city's clergy, both canons and monks, regained their senses and processed together to the church of St Gervase. There they commended the king's soul to God according to Christian rites. King William had decided that he wanted to be buried in the abbey he had founded at Caen, rather than lie alongside his ancestors at Rouen or Fécamp. Arrangements had to be made to convey the body there, and these were left to a 'country knight' (a term of abuse) called Herluin. He accompanied the body on its way, by road and water, to its final resting place.

38. Rouen from St Catherine's Hill.

Abbot Gilbert of Caen – who is said to have been a glutton, indulging in secret meals while urging his monks to fast, and thus so fat as to look like a pregnant woman[14] – had come in procession with the monks of the abbey to meet the cortege, along with the clergy and most of the population of the town. But while prayers were being said, a fire began to rage through the town. Seeing smoke and fireballs rising into the sky, the assembled multitude rushed away to help extinguish the flames before the whole of Caen was set ablaze. Only the monks were left to complete the service and bring the body into their convent. Nor was this the end of the drama. After the great and good of Normandy had assembled in the abbey, Bishop Gilbert of Evreux preached a sermon, which took as its theme the king's righteousness and love of justice. He concluded by asking the congregation to forgive the king, if he had ever done them any wrong.

Then Ascelin fitz Arthur came forward from the crowd, and made this complaint in a loud voice, in the hearing of all: 'This ground where you stand was the site of my father's house, which this man for whom you intercede, when he was still only duke of Normandy, violently took away from my father. Refusing him all redress, he founded this church in the fullness of his power. Therefore I lay claim to this land and openly demand it, forbidding in God's name that the body of this robber be covered by earth that is mine or buried in my inheritance.'

When the bishops and other magnates heard these words, and learned from the testimony of neighbours that he had spoken the truth, they had the man brought to them and, far from treating him roughly, appeased him with gentle words and made peace with him. For the place of burial alone they offered him 60 shillings on the spot, and for the rest of the land that he claimed they promised a sum of equivalent value.

But, with the unseemly dispute settled, a final indignity was still to come. When it was time to place the king's body in the stone sarcophagus that had been prepared for it, the monks discovered that it had been made too short. The corpse was, consequently, doubled up and thrust into its stone container so forcefully that,

the swollen bowels burst, and an intolerable stench assailed the nostrils of the bystanders and the whole crowd. A thick smoke arose from the frankincense and other spices in the censers, but it was not strong enough to conceal the foul ignominy. So the priests made haste to conclude the funeral rights, and immediately returned, trembling, to their own houses.

It was a wretched end to the life of a great king, or so at least Orderic Vitalis, who provides us with much of this information, would have it. In his version of events he was keen to draw an allegorical meaning from the episode. The lessons he drew concerned the empty vanity of the world: the rich and powerful lay abandoned when they died; the man who had once been wealthy had to borrow money in order to be laid to rest; and the king had eaten well when he was alive so that his bowels burst, revealing thereby the vain glory of the flesh. Rich and poor alike die, he concludes, so trust not in false princes but in the living God. Orderic is an excellent raconteur, but like any good monk of his time he was inclined to moralize whenever given the opportunity.

Those living closer in time to events provided much less drama. The anonymous account of the king's last days provides no hint of the mishaps before and during the funeral. Equally the anonymous writer of the 'E' version of the *Anglo-Saxon Chronicle*, viewing events from across the Channel, mentions only the facts of William's death and his burial at Caen without elaboration. But as he was a religious man, and a Benedictine monk to boot, the chronicler was unable to resist the chance to moralize, and did so in words of identical import to Orderic's:

Alas! How deceitful and transitory is the prosperity of this world. He who was once a mighty king and lord of many a land was left of all the land with nothing save seven feet of ground; and he who was once decked with jewels lay then covered over with earth.

39. The modern memorial slab over William's grave in Saint-Etienne of Caen.

LEGACY

What was the legacy of William the Bastard, duke of the Normans and king of the English? The answer to that question depends on whether we are concerned with the short or the long term, and whether we are concerned with politics, culture, economics or society.

The immediate aftermath of the reign, politically speaking, was not good. William's decision to divide his cross-Channel 'empire' on his death resulted in turmoil. William had given his greatest lords lands on both sides of the Channel, and they quickly realized that it would be difficult, if not impossible, for them to serve two masters. Orderic has Bishop Odo complain that:

> Now that our old leader is dead two young men have succeeded him, and now they have suddenly divided the government of England from that of Normandy. How can we provide adequate service to two lords who are so different and live so far apart? If we serve Robert, duke of Normandy as we ought we will offend his brother William, who will then strip us of great revenues and mighty honours in England. Again, if we obey King William dutifully, Duke Robert will confiscate our inherited estates in Normandy.

The result was a rebellion. Bishop Odo, Roger of Montgommery, Count Robert of Mortain and others rose against William Rufus in favour of Robert Curthose, in the hope of reuniting the 'Norman empire' under the more pliant of the two brothers. They failed to achieve their aim, with the result that Bishop Odo was exiled from England (he was to die at Palermo in 1096, *en route* to Jerusalem with Duke Robert). Another rebellion in favour of Curthose followed the succession of Henry I to the throne in 1100. Again it failed to topple the king. This time it was Robert of Bellême who lost his English estates and was exiled.

The failure of the rebels to reunite England and Normandy might have been due to the ineptitude of Robert Curthose. Although Orderic acknowledged his abilities as a soldier, he writes that the duke was too soft to maintain order in Normandy, and so the greatest lords of the duchy slowly fell away from his allegiance and either allied themselves with Rufus or Henry or took power for themselves. Robert of Bellême, for example, made himself almost an independent ruler in the Hiémois and Bellême after 1094, only now and then acknowledging Curthose's authority. In the Cotentin, Robert's youngest brother, Henry, carved out a lordship for himself and although Robert tried to recover his authority there in 1091, Henry was back within a year or two and became stronger than ever. In 1106, six years after he had become king of the English, he took Normandy from his brother at the battle of Tinchebray and imprisoned him for the rest of his life. Robert Curthose died at Cardiff in 1134.

Henry was a strong king, in the image of his father, and his experiences in England, and of the English administration, led to the routine use of the writ in Normandy and to other innovations in government and justice. In many ways, however, the duchy and the kingdom remained as separate as they had been during his father's life. But although Henry succeeded in reuniting his father's dominions, and ruled them successfully until his death in 1135, his legacy was less than his father's. Unlike the Conqueror, Henry left no male heir to succeed him. His only legitimate son, William, died in the wreck of the White Ship off Barfleur in November 1120 and, despite a rapid second marriage, no more children were forthcoming. As such, when he died there was a struggle for power between his nephew, Stephen, and his daughter, Matilda. Normandy was conquered in 1144 by Count Geoffrey of Anjou, Matilda's husband. In 1151 their son, Henry, became duke in his stead. And in 1154 this same Henry succeeded to the throne of England as Henry II. Thus ended the line of Norman kings. Henry II was the first of the Plantagenets.

In political terms William's legacy was thus somewhat fraught. But in social and cultural terms it was both richer and longer lasting. In England the Normans and the English grew closer together. The English fought for Rufus against Curthose in 1088, while, according to Frank Barlow, 'by 1100 most of the immediate post-Conquest tensions had gone out of English Benedictine monasticism. The English and Norman traditions had fused.'[1] The two peoples fused, too. Despite the fact that French was the language of the aristocracy, the English language adopted hundreds of French words to become an altogether richer language. Sometimes the words adopted reflect the class divisions. Thus the English peasants husbanded their animals and French lords consumed them, and this is reflected in English words for animals like cow and sheep, and French words for the meat they produce like beef and mutton. Normans married Englishwomen to legitimize their claim to their estates and offices (Henry I was one of them). The Normans took on English habits; they grew their hair long and adopted luxurious clothes and foods. The English gave their children Norman names. They began to identify themselves with the conquerors, and vice versa. By the end of the twelfth century, writers such as Gerald of Wales might write of an English conquest of Ireland. A generation earlier, these men would have been called French.

All of this is at odds with modern attitudes to the Conquest. Many English people today identify more readily with the Anglo-Saxons than the Normans, despite the fact that the English are the product of both peoples and cultures. Indeed the queen to this day retains the title of duke of Normandy – and rules the Channel Islands in that capacity. There is a sense that somehow the Conquest is unfinished business. It is a sentiment reflected in the memorial at Bayeux and in the fact that the 'Normans' are always booed at the annual re-enactments of the battle of Hastings. This is not a new phenomenon. In the middle of the nineteenth century, Thomas Carlyle could write: 'England itself, in foolish quarters of England, still howls and execrates lamentably over its William the Conqueror, and rigorous line of Normans and Plantagenets; but without them, if you will consider well, what had it ever been?'

Such attitudes do, at least, reveal that the Conquest still means something today. But the impact of William's conquest goes deeper than the collective beating of the national breast. It was the Normans who took England into Europe. There had been strong connections between the two before the Conquest, certainly, but after 1066 England was integrated into the political and cultural life of Europe as never before. The cathedrals and the castles that dot today's landscape were built or rebuilt by the Normans in a new, continental, Romanesque style. Much of their work survives – witness the castles at Chepstow or Rochester or the stone bulk of the castle and cathedral above the river at Durham. The English Church adopted continental manners. England now looked to the continent and not to Scandinavia and continued, and continues, to do so. And the traffic soon began to flow in both directions. The *Song of Roland* might have been introduced to England after the Conquest, but in 1139 Geoffrey of Monmouth launched his *History of the Kings of Britain*, and with it King Arthur, onto a receptive world. By 1154 Nicholas Brakespear had become the only Englishman ever to be pope (as Adrian IV). Whether this reorientation of England and, indeed, Britain, to face the continent was a good or bad thing remains very much a subject for debate, of course – but it is a debate that probably would not happen at all were it not for the Norman Conquest.

✝

NOTES

Preface

1. There are a limited number of endnotes in this book. That they are limited means that they do not comprise a complete scholarly apparatus. In particular, although the source for the quotations embedded in the text is usually given, there is not usually an endnote providing their precise location in the edition used. Instead the notes are intended to acknowledge, and direct readers to, the work of modern historians that I have used in writing this biography. The Further Reading will, I hope, fill any remaining gaps. I have also used the notes to highlight some of the differences between the primary sources and the arguments offered by historians, as well as to explain and develop some of the ideas, words or phrases found in the text.

Prologue

1. The Latin text of William fitz Stephen's *Life* of Becket can be found in *Materials for the History of Thomas Becket, Archbishop of Canterbury*, ed. J.C. Robertson, Rolls Series, vol 3 (London, 1887), pp 1–154. Some extracts, translated into English, have recently become available in *The Lives of Thomas Becket*, trans. M. Staunton (Manchester, 2001). This extract, however, which is only a part of fitz Stephen's famous description of London, is from *English Historical Documents, II. 1042–1189*, ed. D.C. Douglas and G.W. Greenaway (London, 1953), pp 956–7 (no. 281).
2. Henry of Huntingdon, *Historia Anglorum*, ed. and trans. D. Greenway (Oxford, 1996), p 446.
3. There are a number of different versions of the annals known jointly as the *Anglo-Saxon Chronicle*. Three of them cover the events of William's reign, in whole or in part. Scholars have labelled them 'A', 'D' and 'E'. The 'C' version, which mentions the dedication of the abbey, ends on the eve of the battle of Hastings. The different manuscripts were compiled at different places and sometimes reflect different political sympathies. The annals covering the period 1035–66

in the 'C' version of the *Chronicle*, for example, were probably written in Mercia and demonstrate a sympathy for the earls of Mercia and some antipathy to the house of Godwin (see S. Baxter, 'MS C of the Anglo-Saxon Chronicle and the politics of mid-eleventh century England', *English Historical Review*, 122 (2007), pp 1189–1227), whereas the annals of the 'D' chronicle that cover the period around the Conquest of England were compiled by someone working close to Archbishop Ealdred of York (see P. Wormald, 'How do we know so much about Anglo-Saxon Deerhurst?', Deerhurst Lecture (1991)).

4. Both J.L. Nelson, 'The rites of William the Conqueror', *Proceedings of the Battle Conference*, 4 (1982), pp 117–32, and Michael Lapidge are in favour of the Third Ordo; George Garnett prefers the Second Ordo: G. Garnett, 'The third recension of the English coronation ordo: the manuscripts', *The Haskins Society Journal*, 11 (2003), pp 43–71.

5. For Orderic's career, see below, pp 126–7.

6. For more on Poitiers and his work, see below, p 90.

Chapter 1. Fire and Sword Everywhere, *c.* 1027–47

1. For the view, adopted here, that Herleva was the daughter of an undertaker rather than a tanner see E.M.C. van Houts, 'The origins of Herleva, mother of William the Conqueror', *English Historical Review*, 101 (1986), pp 399–404.

2. William of Malmesbury, *Gesta regum Anglorum*, ed. and trans. R.A.B. Mynors, R.M. Thomson and M. Winterbottom, vol. 1 (Oxford, 1998), p 426 (para 229). Orderic, in contrast, says that William was eight: Orderic Vitalis, *The Ecclesiastical History of Orderic Vitalis*, ed. and trans. M. Chibnall, 6 vols (Oxford, 1969–80) (henceforth 'Orderic'), ii.10 and iv. 82.

3. Ralph Glaber, *Five Books of Histories*, ed. and trans. J. France (Oxford, 1989), p 204.

4. D.C. Douglas, *William the Conqueror: The Norman Impact upon England* (London, 1964), p 44 ('it is indeed a matter of some wonder that the young duke survived the troubles of his minority'); D. Bates, 'William I (1027/8–1087)', in *Oxford Dictionary of National Biography From the Earliest Times to the Year 2000*, ed. H.C.G. Matthew and B. Harrison, 60 vols (Oxford, 2004), lix. 46.

5. Suetonius, *The Twelve Caesars*, trans. R. Graves, revised by J.B. Rives (London, 2007), p 1.

6. This is also suggested by the act that reveals Osbern was not the only casualty that night. This reads: 'At that time when Osbern *dapifer* (= steward) *was killed by his enemies* (my emphasis), Gulbert the son of Erchembald the *vicomte*, his faithful man, was gravely wounded with him. He, concerned for the salvation of his soul, inspired by the grace of God, was made a monk of the Holy Trinity by the Lord Abbot Isembert. On the day, therefore, when he assumed the habit of religion, he gave the Holy Trinity le Val-Richer and the meadows at le Vaudreuil,

with the consent of his brothers Croco and Erchembald. William, count of the Normans, praised and confirmed this deed by the sign of his own hand' (*Recueil des actes des ducs de Normandie de 911 à 1066*, ed. M. Fauroux (Caen, 1961), no. 95).

7. Some historians, such as David Crouch and Pierre Bauduin, have argued that Henry attacked Tillières because Gilbert Crispin had given shelter to the rebel Count Waleran of Meulan. Henry's siege was not, therefore, aimed at Duke William directly (D. Crouch, *The Normans: The History of a Dynasty* (London, 2002), p 62; P. Bauduin, *La première Normandie (Xe–XIe siècles). Sur les frontières de la Haute Normandie: Identité et construction d'une principauté* (Caen, 2004), p 191). That interpretation, however, is undermined by Henry's subsequent sack of Argentan and his aggressive reconstruction of the castle at Tillières, which appear to be part of the same campaign.

8. D. Bates, 'The Conqueror's adolescence', *Anglo-Norman Studies*, 25 (2003), pp 3–4.

9. The identities of the men who stood closest to William, both as duke and king, are indicated by the documents produced at William's court. The diplomas, notices and other acts (Latin = *acta*) were signed by the duke and by those in attendance who were considered either suitably important or were concerned with the business that the document dealt with. Thus it is possible to gain a picture of those who were frequently at court, and thus who were, it may be supposed, intimates of the duke. The relevant acts here are *Recueil des actes des ducs de Normandie*, ed. Fauroux, nos. 94, 99, 105, 107, 113, 120 and possibly 69 (Montgommery); 96, 99, 113, 117, 118, 119, 120 (William fitz Osbern); 73, 88, 96, 106 (Beaumont). That does not mean, however, that simply counting the number of times a person appears in ducal or royal *acta* is enough to establish their importance at court. We do not know how many documents have been lost, and the few that chance to survive may well distort the original picture. Thus the documentary evidence must be supported by the narratives produced by Poitiers, Orderic and others, which can add some useful details, as well as explicitly confirm the picture presented by the *acta*, as when Poitiers lists the 'shining luminaries' of Normandy (see below, p 61).

10. See, among others, W.L. Warren, *King John* (second edition, London, 1978), pp 228–9; J.C. Holt, *The Northerners: A Study in the Reign of King John* (Oxford, 1961), especially ch. 11.

11. King Henry's support for Duke William has been put down to an obligation to reciprocate the help afforded him by Duke Robert the Magnificent in 1033, which allowed him to keep his throne, or simply to the bond between lord and man, although William's relationship with Henry is by no means clear. In addition, the king was concerned about the growth of Angevin power at this time, as is revealed by the campaign he launched against Count Geoffrey in

1048, on which William was present (see p 22). The king would have guessed that if William were defeated by the rebels, the count of Anjou would seize the opportunity to extend his influence toward and even into Normandy. That Henry might also have been concerned about the situation in Burgundy is suggested by the fact that the chief rebel was Guy of Burgundy. Guy was the son of Count Reginald of Bourgogne-outre-Sâone, who was himself the son of Otto-William. After the death of Duke Henry of Burgundy without direct heirs in 1002, his step-son Otto-William had claimed the duchy, but had been defeated by Robert the Pious by 1016. King Robert then established his son Henry as duke, and when Henry became king in 1031 he handed the duchy to his brother, Robert (J. Dunbabin, *France in the Making 843–1180* (Oxford, 1991), p 180). Count Reginald lived on, however, and the possibility that Guy might gain control of Normandy might have worried King Henry – Guy and Reginald together, with their rival claim on Burgundy, could well have threatened his brother's hold on that duchy. Neither the Norman nor Burgundian sources say anything about this, of course, because in the event the rebellion failed, but such a concern would have given the king another solid reason to support William.

12. For more on the rebellion and its causes, as well as the advance of ducal authority into the west of Normandy, see M. Hagger, 'How the west was won: the Norman dukes and the Cotentin, *c.* 987–1087', *Journal of Medieval History*, 38 (2012), pp 20–55.

Chapter 2. The Undefeated Duke, 1047–66

1. For what follows see William of Jumièges, Orderic Vitalis and Robert of Torigny, *Gesta Normannorum ducum*, ed. and trans. E.M.C. van Houts, 2 vols (Oxford, 1992–95) (henceforth 'Jumièges'), i. xxxii–xxxv and E.M.C. van Houts, 'Jumièges, William of (*fl.* 1026–1070)', *Oxford Dictionary of National Biography*, xxx. 828.

2. Malmesbury, *Gesta regum Anglorum*, p 494 (para 267). Historians have not been able convincingly to establish precisely how William and Matilda were related. One of the suggestions put forward is that Adela, the daughter of King Robert of France I who married Count Baldwin V of Flanders, had been married, or at least betrothed, to Duke Richard III of the Normans first. That seems unlikely, however, as William of Jumièges says that she was still in her cradle when she was betrothed to Baldwin (Jumièges, ii. 52). Douglas, *William the Conqueror*, pp 76–7 and Appendix C notes some of the other theories surrounding their relationship, but concludes that they all have their problems. D. Bates, *William the Conqueror* (London, 1989), p 32 suggests that the obscurity of their kinship is 'probably an important point'.

3. The prohibition on marriage within 'seven degrees' was based on Roman Law. The idea was to avoid incestuous relationships. To do this, Roman Law forbade

marriages within 'four degrees', 'and had computed degrees by counting from one prospective spouse up to the common ancestor and then down to the other partner. Hence a father and daughter were considered related within the first degree, and a brother and sister within the second'. In the ninth century, the number of degrees was increased from four to seven, and the way in which these degrees were counted also changed, so that instead of going up to the common ancestor and then down again, 'one computed degrees by counting generations back *only* to the common ancestor' (see on this topic C.B. Bouchard, 'Consanguinity and noble marriages in the tenth and eleventh centuries', *Speculum*, 56 (1981), pp 268–87, especially pp 269–71 where there is also a table illustrating how the law worked). This meant that the number of unions that would be considered incestuous increased dramatically – couples could not get married if they shared great-great-great-great grandparents. It is no surprise, then, that this law was often and openly flouted, although it also gave couples the opportunity to dissolve their marriages on grounds of consanguinity should it prove politically convenient to do so. The most famous examples of such a manipulation of the law are Eleanor of Aquitaine's two marriages, the first to Louis VII of France and the second to Henry II of England.

4. Noted in Douglas, *William the Conqueror*, p 78; H. Tanner, *Families, Friends and Allies: Boulogne and Politics in Northern France and England, c. 879–1160* (Turnhout, 2004), p 87.

5. Douglas, *William the Conqueror*, p 58. Bates says that they had both been held from Richard II (Bates, *William the Conqueror*, p 33), but there is no evidence that the dukes of the Normans held Domfront in Fauroux's *Recueil*, nor in any of the chronicles.

6. The chronology followed here is that first suggested by David Douglas in 1964 (*William the Conqueror*, Appendix B). The order of events had to be established because the narratives put them in different orders, and do not provide dates. Thus Jumièges puts William of Arques's rebellion before the rebellion that led to Val-ès-Dunes, which cannot be right as the count continued to attest William's *acta* after 1047.

7. The Roman Law offence of *maiestas* (treason by undermining the ruler and his commands) is found in Normandy on a few occasions in this period, although it is given its Roman name only once, in a document that was drafted at the abbey of Mont-Saint-Michel. See M. Hagger, 'Secular law and custom in ducal Normandy, *c.* 1000–1144', *Speculum*, 85 (2010), pp 827–67, especially pp 835–7.

8. Jumièges, ii. 8; Orderic, ii. 316.

9. Caesar, *Gallic War*, 8.44; trans. C. Hammond (Oxford, 1996), p 217.

10. *Recueil des actes des ducs de Normandie*, ed. Fauroux, nos. 100, 103, 108, 124; Bates, 'The Conqueror's adolescence', p 12.

11. Jim Bradbury seems to suggest that the knights carried their saddles because their horses had died during the siege (J. Bradbury, *The Medieval Siege* (Woodbridge, 1992), p 65). In fact the carrying of saddles was symbolic of surrender, and a ritual sign of submission, known as *harmiscara*. See M. DeJong, 'Power and humility in Carolingian society: the public penance of Louis the Pious', *Early Medieval Europe*, 1 (1992), pp 29–52, at pp 45–50, and J. Hemming, '*Sellan gestare*: saddle-bearing punishments of medieval Europe and the case of Rhinnon', *Viator*, 28 (1997), pp 45–64.

12. A letter from the monks of Fécamp to William, written after 1066, reveals the existence of a *vicomte* who had taken lands away from the abbey (Bates, *Normandy before 1066*, p 206).

13. Suger of Saint-Denis, *The Deeds of Louis the Fat*, trans. R. Cusimano and J. Moorhead (Washington DC, 1992), pp 87–8.

14. Orderic, ii. 90.

15. See D. Bates, 'Lord Sudeley's ancestors: The family of the counts of Amiens, Valois and the Vexin in France and England during the 11th century', in *The Sudeley – Lords of Toddington* (Thetford, 1987), pp 34–48, and M. Hagger, 'Kinship and identity in eleventh-century Normandy: the case of Hugh de Grandmesnil, *c*. 1040–1098', *Journal of Medieval History*, 32 (2006), pp 212–30.

16. Bates, *Normandy before 1066*, p 83.

17. See K. Thompson, 'Family and influence to the south of Normandy in the eleventh century: the lordship of Bellême', *Journal of Medieval History*, 11 (1985), p 222, and 'The Norman aristocracy before 1066: the example of the Montgomerys', *Historical Research*, 60 (1987), pp 260–2. On the family generally, see G. Louise, *La seigneurie de Bellême Xe–XIIe siècles: dévolution des pouvoirs territoriaux et construction d'une siegneurie de frontière aux confins de la Normandie et du Maine de la charnière de l'an mil*, La Pays Bas-Normand, 2 vols, 3 and 4 (1990) and 1 and 2 (1991).

18. See B. Golding, 'Robert of Mortain', *Anglo-Norman Studies*, 13 (1991), pp 119–44.

19. See D. Spear, *The Personnel of the Norman Cathedrals during the Ducal Period, 911–1204* (London, 2006), p 90, J. Le Patourel, 'Geoffrey of Montbray', *English Historical Review*, 59 (1944), pp 129–61, and M. Chibnall, 'La carrière de Geoffroi de Montbray', in *Les évêques normands du XIe siècle*, ed. P. Bouet and F. Neveux (Caen, 1995), pp 279–93. Both Le Patourel and Chibnall say he became bishop in 1049 (although Chibnall depends on Le Patourel here). This, however, as Spear notes, goes against the dating in the narrative known as the *De statu huius ecclesiae* which was produced at Coutances just after the bishop's death (*Gallia Christiana*, vol 11 (Paris, 1759), *Instr.* col. 217–24).

20. *Recueil des actes des ducs de Normandie*, ed. Fauroux, no. 157; translation from Bates, *Normandy before 1066*, p 57.

Chapter 3. William the Conqueror, 1066

1. See E.M.C. van Houts, 'Edward and Normandy', in *Edward the Confessor: The Man and the Legend*, ed. R. Mortimer (Woodbridge, 2009), pp 67–75.
2. Jumièges, ii. 76–8; *Recueil des actes des ducs de Normandie*, ed. Fauroux, nos. 69, 70, 73 (with 111), 76 (king), 85 (king). See also S. Keynes, 'The æthelings in Normandy', *Anglo-Norman Studies*, 13 (1991), pp 186–94.
3. C.P. Lewis, 'The French in England before the Norman Conquest', *Anglo-Norman Studies*, 17 (1994), p 124.
4. P. Stafford, *Unification and Conquest: A Political and Social History of England in the Tenth and Eleventh Centuries* (London, 1989), pp 92–3, and also Barlow, *Edward the Confessor*, pp 106–9. Bates, however, says that there is broad agreement that Edward offered William the throne (Bates, *William the Conqueror*, p 59). For other views on Edward's promise, and its nature, see E. John, 'Edward the Confessor and the Norman succession', *English Historical Review*, 94 (1979), pp 241–67; A. Williams, 'Some notes and considerations on problems connected with the English royal succession, 860–1066', *Proceedings of the Battle Conference*, 1 (1978), pp 144–67; A. Williams, 'Land and power in the eleventh century: the estates of Harold Godwineson', *Proceedings of the Battle Conference*, 3 (1981), pp 171–87; and S. Baxter, 'Edward the Confessor and the succession question', in *Edward the Confessor: The Man and the Legend*, ed. R. Mortimer (Woodbridge, 2009), pp 77–118.
5. William of Poitiers, *Gesta Guillelmi*, ed. and trans. R.H.C. Davis and M. Chibnall (Oxford, 1998) (henceforth 'Poitiers'), p 118. This is questioned by George Garnett, who points out that the only source for this principle is Poitiers himself (G. Garnett, *The Norman Conquest: A Very Short Introduction* (Oxford, 2009), pp 33–4), although he does acknowledge that there is some English evidence for a deathbed bequest of the throne in January 1066. There was, however, no reason for Poitiers to have made this custom up, especially as he then had to explain why it should not count against William's own claim.
6. This survey of Godwin's career follows F. Barlow, *The Godwins: The Rise and Fall of a Noble Dynasty* (London, 2001), pp 37–43.
7. Discussed in E.M.C. van Houts, 'The ship list of William the Conqueror', *Anglo-Norman Studies*, 10 (1988), pp 159–83.
8. Poitiers, p 104.
9. *Recueil des actes des ducs de Normandy*, ed. Fauroux, no. 231. Cecilia's oblation is mentioned again in 1077, perhaps because she was then old enough to be professed (Orderic, iii. 8).
10. B. Bachrach, 'Some observations on the military administration of the Norman Conquest', *Anglo-Norman Studies*, 8 (1986), pp 1–25.
11. R.H.C. Davis, 'The warhorses of the Normans', *Anglo-Norman Studies*, 10 (1988), p 80 does not accept the figures relating to the horses. But as J. Gillingham,

'William the Bastard at war', in *Studies in Medieval History Presented to R. Allen Brown*, ed. C. Harper-Bill et al. (Woodbridge, 1989), p 158 points out, we do not need to accept these figures to know that the general point is right.

12. H. Tsurushima, 'The eleventh century through fish-eyes: salmon, herring, oysters, and 1066', *Anglo-Norman Studies*, 29 (2007), p 204.

13. C. Grainge and G. Grainge, 'The Pevensey expedition: brilliantly executed plan or near disaster?', in *The Battle of Hastings: Sources and Interpretations*, ed. S. Morillo (Woodbridge, 1996), pp 137–9.

14. A notice recording a gift to the abbey of La Trinité-du-Mont outside Rouen of land at Sotteville-lès-Rouen reveals that Roger fitz Turold was one who died during the voyage – perhaps at this time (*Regesta Regum Anglo-Normannorum, the Acta of William I (1066–1087)*, ed. D. Bates (Oxford, 1998) (henceforth '*Regesta*'), no. 231).

15. This is an example of how food might be used to reveal something of a person's state of mind in medieval narratives. Indeed food might also be used to reveal status (see below, pp 146, 176–7) and to create communities. The Bayeux Tapestry shows the Normans lunching shortly after their arrival at Pevensey, and it is likely that this image is intended to imply all of these elements. For a discussion, see M. Hagger, 'Lordship and lunching: interpretations of eating and food in the Anglo-Norman world, 1050–1200, with reference to the Bayeux Tapestry', in *The English and Their Legacy, 900–1200. Essays in Honour of Ann Williams*, ed. D. Roffe (Woodbridge, forthcoming 2012) and, more generally, C. Neuman de Vegvar, 'Dining with distinction: drinking vessels and difference in the Bayeux Tapestry feast scenes', in *The Bayeux Tapestry: New Approaches*, ed. M.J. Lewis et al. (Oxford, 2011); D. Bullough, *Friends, Neighbours and Fellow-drinkers: Aspects of Community and Conflict in the Early Medieval West*, Chadwick Papers, 1 (1990); B. Effros, *Creating Community with Food and Drink in Merovingian Gaul* (Basingstoke, 2002); C.W. Bynum, *Holy Feast and Holy Fast: The Religious Significance of Food to Medieval Women* (Berkeley, Los Angeles and London, 1987); *Food in Medieval England: Diet and Nutrition*, ed. C.M. Woolgar, D. Serjeantson and T. Waldron (Oxford, 2006); and C.M. Woolgar, 'Food and the Middle Ages', *Journal of Medieval History*, 36 (2010), pp 1–19. Archaeological excavations have been revealing what sorts of food were consumed in the Middle Ages (and sometimes how they were consumed) for many years. See, for example, C. Lee, *Feasting the Dead: Food and Drink in Anglo-Saxon Burial Rituals* (Woodbridge, 2007); N. Sykes, 'Zooarchaeology of the Norman Conquest', *Anglo-Norman Studies*, 27 (2005), pp 185–97; N. Sykes, *The Norman Conquest: A Zooarchaeological Perspective*, BAR (Oxford, 2007); and *Food, Craft and Status in Medieval Winchester. The Plant and Animal Remains from the Suburbs and City Defences*, ed. D. Serjeantson and H. Rees (Winchester, 2009). For an anthropological perspective see, for example, M. Jones, *Feast: Why Humans Share Food* (Oxford, 2007).

16. The 'D' version of the *Anglo-Saxon Chronicle* says that William sailed 'from Normandy into Pevensey' on 28 September. I take that to mean that he left Normandy on Michaelmas eve. The 'E' version says he arrived on 29 September, which, if I am right, would mean that both texts are in agreement. Poitiers, however, seems to suggest that he *left* Normandy on 29 September (Poitiers, p 168). Jumièges provides no date at all. Malmesbury was of the view that William landed in England on 28 September, although he makes this clear only when recounting the events leading to the battle at Tinchebray on 28 September 1106, and might have 'mis-remembered' for effect (Malmesbury, *Gesta regum Anglorum*, p 722, para 398).

17. Suetonius, *The Twelve Caesars*, trans. Graves, revised by Rives, pp 28–9.

18. M. Bloch, *Feudal Society, II. Social Classes and Political Organization*, trans. L.A. Manyon (London, 1962), pp 293–4, quotes the Carolingian proverb: 'He who has stayed at school till the age of twelve and never ridden a horse is fit only to be a priest.'

19. Davis, 'The warhorses of the Normans', p 80; Amatus of Montecassino, *The History of the Normans*, trans. P.N. Dunbar (Woodbridge, 2004), p 84.

20. The *Song of Roland* is an epic romance that tells the tale of Roland who commanded the rearguard of Charlemagne's army in Spain in 778 and was killed, with his companion, Oliver, in a battle below the pass through the Pyrenees at Roncesvalles. The story was widely known across western Europe, perhaps because of the continuing attempt to reconquer Spain from the Moors, and the growing popularity of the pilgrimage to Santiago de Compostela, so that Roland and Oliver may be found flanking the main door of the cathedral at Verona. The continuing popularity of this poem in the Anglo-Norman *regnum* after 1066 is suggested by the fact that the earliest surviving copy of the poem comes from England (Oxford, MS Digby 23, part 2). This rather unexceptional manuscript is reproduced online (http://image.ox.ac.uk/show?collection=bodleian&manuscript=msdigby23b).

21. *Carmen de Hastingae Proelio of Guy Bishop of Amiens*, ed. and trans. F. Barlow (Oxford, 1999), p 24; Henry of Huntingdon, *Historia Anglorum*, ed. and trans. Greenway, p 392; Wace, *Roman de Rou*, trans. G.S. Burgess (Woodbridge, 2004) (henceforth 'Wace'), p 182.

22. S. Morillo, 'Introduction', in *The Battle of Hastings: Sources and Interpretations*, ed. S. Morillo (Woodbridge, 1996), p xxvi.

23. See Lucan, *Civil War*, trans. S.H. Braund (Oxford, 1992), p 150. Jumièges, ii. 170 implies that William did this, but it is the *Carmen* (p 34) and Wace (p 191) that say so explicitly.

24. Poitiers, p 140. The *Carmen*, too, says that Harold's body was buried on the summit of a cliff to be the guardian of shore and sea (p 34), which suggests that this was the earliest version of the story and the one perhaps most likely to be

true. On the other hand, *The Waltham Chronicle*, ed. and trans. L. Watkiss and M. Chibnall (Oxford, 1994), pp 50–4 and Wace, p 192 say that Harold was buried at his foundation at Waltham Abbey.

25. The origin of the idea that God would punish a people because of their sins can be traced back to the Old Testament story of Noah and in the punishment meted out to the cities of Sodom and Gomorrah (Genesis, 6:5–9:29; 18:20–19:25). It was developed by, among others, St Augustine in his *On the City of God against the Pagans* and Orosius in his *Seven Books of History against the Pagans*. The idea can be found in the time of King Alfred when England was suffering from a wave of Viking attacks (R. Abels, *Alfred the Great: War, Kingship and Culture in Anglo-Saxon England* (London, 1998), pp 220–1). The remarks in the *Anglo-Saxon Chronicle*, as well as the passage quoted from Malmesbury, demonstrate that the idea was still current in the eleventh and twelfth centuries.

26. Morillo ('Introduction', p xx) attributes this comment to Gillingham and implies that it was made in his 'William the Bastard at War', but it is not found there and I have not been able to trace its origin.

27. *Carmen de Hastingae Proelio*, ed. and trans. Barlow, p 36, says he remained at Hastings for a fortnight.

Chapter 4. I See God! Ritual and Government

1. It is worth noting that William was not only styled duke but also count and *princeps* in the *acta* produced during his reign. These titles were given to him by his subjects, rather than being officially sanctioned. William's seal, cut after he became king, and presumably reflecting his own preference, styles him *patronus* (patron or advocate) of the Normans rather than *dux* (duke).

2. The form of the ceremony is described by both Dudo of Saint-Quentin, who was writing *c.* 1010, and William of Jumièges (Dudo of Saint-Quentin, *History of the Normans: Translation with Introduction and Notes*, trans. E. Christiansen (Woodbridge, 1998), pp 60, 98, 171; Jumièges, i. 72, 88, 134; ii. 80). William of Jumièges says only that the lords of Normandy acclaimed the heir and swore fealty to him, omitting the reference to relics found in Dudo's work. By the end of the twelfth century, the Church had become much more clearly involved. The soon-to-be King Richard I was invested as duke of Normandy in 1189 by the archbishop of Rouen: 'Count Richard came to Rouen and was girded with the sword of the duchy of Normandy by Walter the archbishop of Rouen, in the presence of the bishops, earls, and barons of Normandy ... Having then received the oaths of fealty from the clergy and people of the duchy of Normandy he gave to Geoffrey son of Count Rotrou of the Perche his niece Matilda ... in marriage' (Roger of Howden, *Chronica Magistri Rogeri de Houedene*, ed. W. Stubbs, Rolls Series, vol 3 (London, 1870), p 3). There is no evidence that such a ceremony had been performed previously.

3. Thegns were an English equivalent to knights or barons, depending on their precise status. See A. Williams, *The World Before Domesday: The English Aristocracy, 900–1066* (London, 2008), Introduction.

4. M. Biddle, 'Seasonal festivals and residence: Winchester, Westminster and Gloucester in the tenth to twelfth centuries', *Anglo-Norman Studies*, 8 (1986), pp 51–63. Biddle thinks that the chronicler might be right about the location of the crown-wearings, but his own Appendix A (p 64) indicates that this can only be demonstrated for the years after *c.* 1080.

5. For example, a lawsuit involving the rights of the canons of Bellême in the diocese of Sées makes reference to William's 'royal authority', and so too does an act for Mont-Saint-Michel whereby another plea was decided by a group of judges to whom William's 'royal authority' was delegated (*Regesta*, nos. 29 and 214). The canons of the council of Lillebonne of 1080 also speak of the king's *vicomte* and the king's commands operating in the duchy (Orderic, iii. 26–36).

6. The *Life of Lanfranc* is translated by S. Vaughn, *The Abbey of Bec and the Anglo-Norman State* (Woodbridge, 1981), pp 87–111 with the passage in question at p 107. The translation here, however, follows (for the most part) Nelson, 'The rites of the Conqueror', *Proceedings of the Battle Conference*, 4 (1981), p 131.

7. Ruler portraits comprise a stylized representation of a ruler, depicted with certain attributes. Thus the well-known portrait of the Emperor Otto III shows him seated on a throne, wearing a crown and holding a sceptre. Edward the Confessor was depicted on his seal, and on the Bayeux Tapestry, in much the same way; he is again seated on a backless throne, with a crown and sceptre. Suger of Saint-Denis wrote about what these insignia meant when describing the coronation of Louis VI in 1106: '[Louis] took from [the archbishop of Sens] the sword of secular knighthood, girded him with the ecclesiastical sword for the punishment of evildoers, and joyfully crowned him with the diadem of the kingdom. With the approval of the clergy and the people, he devoutly handed him, along with the other royal insignia, the sceptre and rod that symbolise the defence of the churches and the poor' (*The Deeds of Louis the Fat*, trans. Cusimano and Moorhead, p 63). On ruler portraits generally see C.E. Karkov, *The Ruler Portraits of Anglo-Saxon England* (Woodbridge, 2004), Introduction.

8. See on this generally J. Hudson, 'Henry I and counsel', in *The Medieval State: Essays presented to James Campbell*, ed. J.R. Maddicott and D.M. Palliser (2000), pp 109–26.

9. Ibn al-Athir. *The Chronicle of Ibn al-Athir for the Crusading Period from l-Kamil fi'l Ta'rikh. Part 1. The Years 491–541/1097–1146: The Coming of the Franks and the Muslim Response*, trans. D.S. Richards (Aldershot, 2005), p 13.

10. C.P. Lewis, 'The early earls of Norman England', *Anglo-Norman Studies*, 13 (1990), pp 216–17.

11. *Ibid.*, pp 219–20.

12. *Ibid.*, pp 217–18; D. Bates, 'The character and career of Odo, bishop of Bayeux, 1049/50–1097', *Speculum*, 50 (1975), p 6, and for his estates see p 10; Le Patourel, 'Geoffrey of Montbray', p 152.

13. On this topic see F. West, *The Justiciarship in England, 1066–1272* (Cambridge, 1966) and D. Bates, 'The origins of the justiciarship', *Proceedings of the Battle Conference*, 4 (1982), pp 1–12. Bates sees the arrangements made as being more formal than is suggested here.

14. The king's words are put into his mouth by Orderic, iv. 42.

15. J.A. Green, *English Sheriffs to 1154* (London, 1990); M. Hagger, 'The Norman vicomte, c. 1035–1135: what did he do?', *Anglo-Norman Studies*, 29 (2007), pp 65–83.

16. *Regesta*, no. 129; translation from *English Historical Documents, II. 1042–1189*, ed. Douglas and Greenaway, pp 431–2 (slightly amended).

17. A. Williams, 'A vicecomital family in pre-Conquest Warwickshire', *Anglo-Norman Studies*, 11 (1989), pp 286–92.

18. Personal names changed as a result of the Conquest, with surviving members of the English aristocracy taking Norman names: R. Bartlett, *England under the Norman and Angevin Kings 1075–1225* (Oxford, 2000), pp 538–41; H.M. Thomas, *The English and the Normans: Ethnic Hostility, Assimilation, and Identity 1066–c. 1220* (Oxford, 2003), pp 97–100.

19. R. Sharpe, 'Address and delivery in Anglo-Norman royal charters', *Charters and Charter Scholarship in Britain and Ireland*, ed. J.A. Green and M.T. Flanagan (London, 2005), pp 32–3; M. Hagger, 'The earliest Norman writs revisited', *Historical Research*, 82 (2009), p 183. Writ-charters, too, are discussed in the second of these articles and also in R. Sharpe, 'The use of writs in the eleventh century', *Anglo-Saxon England*, 32 (2003), pp 247–91.

20. Translation from *English Historical Documents, II. 1042–1189*, ed. Douglas and Greenaway, p 399.

21. There has been some controversy concerning the existence of a chancery, or rather a writing office, before 1066. Pierre Chaplais was convinced that there was no such office until the later years of William's reign (P. Chaplais, 'The Anglo-Saxon chancery: from the diploma to the writ', in *Prisca Munimenta: Studies in Archival and Administrative History presented to Dr A. E. J. Hollaender*, ed. F. Ranger (London, 1973), pp 43–62; the article was reprinted there from *Journal of the Society of Archivists*, 3 (1965–69), pp 160–76). In contrast, Florence Harmer, who edited the surviving pre-1066 English writ-charters, thought that there *was* a writing office (F. Harmer, *Anglo-Saxon Writs* (Manchester, 1952), pp 57–61), and so too did Simon Keynes (S. Keynes, 'Regenbald the chancellor (*sic*)', *Anglo-Norman Studies* 10 (1988), pp 213–21). Its existence is suggested by the use of similar words and phrases in the king's writs, as well as by the addition to beneficiary-drafted diplomas of *signa* in different hands and inks (which can,

of course, only be seen in the few cases where these documents survive as originals) which suggests that they were 'officially' added when the document was authenticated. David Bates seems to concur that there was indeed a writing office, not least because there were chancellors who, presumably, intervened in the production of documents (*Regesta*, pp 96–102).

22. The question of a Norman writing office is less controversial than for its English equivalent. Most authorities are agreed that William had neither a chancellor nor a writing office in Normandy before 1066 (see *Recueil des actes des ducs de Normandie*, ed. Fauroux, pp 41–7; Bates, *Normandy before 1066*, pp 154–5; C. Potts, 'The early Norman charters: a new perspective on an old debate', in *England in the Eleventh Century*, ed. C. Hicks (Stamford, 1992), p 36). Only R.A. Brown has disagreed: 'Some observations on Norman and Anglo-Norman charters', in *Tradition and Change: Essays in Honour of Marjorie Chibnall presented by her Friends on the Occasion of her Seventieth Birthday*, ed. D.E. Greenway, G. Holdsworth and J. Sayers (Cambridge, 1985), pp 152–63. It is possible, however, that there had been a writing office for a short period of time in the 1020s, which probably collapsed in the turmoil that followed the death of Duke Richard II.

23. *Regesta*, no. 200.

24. The three documents in question are *Regesta*, nos. 209, 208 and 202 respectively.

25. *The Letters of Saint Anselm of Canterbury*, trans. W. Frölich, vol. 1 (Kalamazoo, 1990), p 266 (no. 110).

26. As a result, during the time that Henry I ruled Normandy (1106–35), writs were issued, for example, by Count Stephen of Mortain (Caen, Archives Départementales du Calvados, 1 J 41 (cartulary of Saint-Etienne, Caen), fo. 23r), Count Amaury of Evreux (Caen, Archives Départementales du Calvados, H 7761 (original writ), Evreux, Archives Départementales de l'Eure, G122 (cartulary of the canons of Evreux), p 37, no. 75) and Robert of la Haye-du-Puits; (Bibliothèque nationale de France, MS lat. 10087 (cartulary of Montebourg abbey), p 113, no. 307). The French Count Theobald of Blois, who was Henry I's nephew, also used a writ on at least one occasion (*Cartulaire de Saint-Jean-en-Vallée de Chartres*, ed. R. Merlet (Chartres, 1906), p 31, no. 51).

27. *La France Romane au temps des premiers Capetiens (987–1152)* (Paris, 2005), p 79.

28. Much has been written on the duties of rulers in the Middle Ages. For an overview see J. Canning, *A History of Medieval Political Thought 300–1450* (London, 1996). Orderic Vitalis also sets out his own views on what the dukes should do and how they should behave at various points in his *Ecclesiastical History* (Orderic, iv. 150; vi. 56, 62, 86, 96). For ducal law-making see G. Davy, *Le duc et la loi: héritages, images et expressions du pouvoir normatif dans la duché de Normandie, des origins à la mort du Conquérant (fin du IXe siècle–1087)* (Paris, 2004) and Hagger, 'Secular law and custom in ducal Normandy', pp 827–67, at pp 838–49.

29. M. de Bouard, 'Sur les origines de la trêve de Dieu en Normandie', *Annales de Normandie*, 9 (1958), pp 169–89, at pp 172–4; Bates, *Normandy before 1066*, pp 163–4. For a more general study see H.E.J. Cowdrey, 'The Peace and the Truce of God in the Eleventh Century', *Past & Present*, 46 (1970), pp 42–67.

30. The feud was legitimate in William's Normandy, but it was also a threat to peace as it might get out of control. Consequently, William and his successors attempted to limit the way that a feud was prosecuted. In 1075 William forbade private vengeance in cases of murder (i.e. a feud) unless the victim was either a father or son (Bates, *Normandy before 1066*, p 164; Hagger, 'Secular law and custom in ducal Normandy', pp 838–9). He also seems, at least on occasion, to have treated homicide as a breach of his peace, and thus as treason. He could thus involve himself in the prosecution of the offence and bring the trial into his own court. This is what he did following the murder of Mabel of Bellême in 1077 (Orderic, iii. 160–2).

31. Orderic, vi. 354.

32. This is reported in the inquisition on the lands of the bishopric of Bayeux held in 1133, which thus explained how his estates came to be held by the bishop (*Recueil des Historiens des Gaules et de la France*, par Dom. M. Bouquet, nouvelle édition publiée sous la direction de M. Léopold Delisle, 24 vols (Paris, 1738–1904), xxiii. 702). Grimoult's crimes and subsequent loss of estates for himself and his heirs is also mentioned in the act by which William granted them to the cathedral, which dates from 1074 (*Regesta*, no. 27). It is only Wace, however, who says precisely what it was that Grimoult planned to do (see above, p 10).

33. The report of the case may be found in R.C. van Caenegem, *English Lawsuits from William I to Richard I*, Selden Society, 106 (1990), 50–1 (no. 19).

34. Some of the surviving Anglo-Saxon lawcodes, the *Leges Henrici Primi*, and even Glanvill tell us that English laws differed between the three kingdoms of Wessex, Mercia and Northumbria, and even between the shires. Judgement by the suitors of the hundred and shire courts is exactly what we would expect to see in these circumstances. It is likely that these regional variations only developed after King Edgar, followed by his successors, commanded that cases should be heard in the first instance at the hundred and shire level (III Edgar, 2, English translation in *English Historical Documents I, c. 500–1042*, ed. D. Whitelock (London, 1955), pp 394–7 (no. 40) at p 396) – presumably so as to keep the amount of business coming before the kings down to a minimum. This delegation of justice to the localities, and the lack of any central check on what the courts were doing, was probably the reason why these variations had developed in the first place. Once they had appeared, however, the role of the local courts in English justice became entrenched – although that is not to say that cases were never heard before the king either before or after the Conquest.

35. In the late Roman empire, if a party to a dispute could show that they had

held the property in question undisturbed for 30 years, then any rival claim was defeated. This 30-year rule was continued under the Merovingians and Carolingians (J.L. Nelson, 'Dispute settlement in Carolingian west Francia', in *The Settlement of Disputes in Early Medieval Europe*, ed. W. Davies and P. Fouracre (Cambridge, 1986), pp 50–1), and survived to be enforced in the courts of north-western France into the eleventh and twelfth centuries (See, for example, *Cartulaire de l'abbaye de Saint-Père de Chartres*, ed. B. Guérard, 2 vols (Paris, 1840), i. 236–7 (ch. 11); *Cartulaire de Saint-Vincent du Mans*, ed. R. Charles and S. Memjot d'Elbenne (Mamers-Le Mans, 1886–1913), pp 54–5 (no. 74). There is clear evidence of the use of a similar rule in Norman lawsuits, where the decisions in the pleas between the abbey of La Trinité-du-Mont and the bishop of Evreux and the monks of Lonlay and Saint-Florent of Saumur, among others, depended in part on the existence of such a custom (*Regesta*, nos. 235 and 267. II).

36. *Recueil des actes des ducs de Normandie*, ed. Fauroux, nos. 24, 113, 191.
37. *Regesta*, no. 241. The best introduction to this topic remains M. Chibnall, 'Military service in Normandy before 1066', *Anglo-Norman Studies*, 5 (1983), pp 65–77.
38. On this subject see R. Abels, 'Bookland and fyrd service', *Anglo-Norman Studies*, 7 (1985), pp 1–25 and, on landholding before the Conquest more generally, Williams, *The World Before Domesday*, chs. 4 and 5.
39. *Regesta*, no. 131.
40. A. Williams, 'A bell-house and a *burh-geat*: lordly residences in England before the Conquest', in *Anglo-Norman Castles*, ed. R. Liddiard (Woodbridge, 2003), pp 23–33.
41. G. Beresford, 'Goltho manor, Lincolnshire: the buildings and their surrounding defences c. 850–1150', *Proceedings of the Battle Conference on Anglo-Norman Studies*, 4 (1982), pp 13–36, quotation at p 33.
42. Only a few Norman castles of this period have been excavated, and so there is a limited amount of information about their appearance. The small fortification at Mirville (Seine-Maritime) comprised an almond-shaped enclosure of 22m x 10m, surrounded by a ditch that was 3m deep. Within the enclosure, the excavators found an apsidal wooden hall as well as the stone footings of a small tower, which was later removed (J. le Maho, 'Note sur l'histoire d'un habitat seigneurial des XIe et XIIe siècles en Normandie: Mirville (S. Mme)', *Anglo-Norman Studies*, 7 (1985), pp 214–23). The short-lived mid-eleventh-century castle at Grimbosq (Calvados) was essentially a fortified manor house, with the addition of a motte topped by a wooden tower (J. Decaëns, 'Le motte d'Olivet à Grimbosq (Calvados): résidence seigneriale du XIe siècle', *Archéologie Médiévale*, 11 (1981), pp 167–201 and see also the model pictured in *La France Romane: au temps des premiers Capétiens (987–1152)*, pp 68–9, no. 14). In contrast, the castle

at Le Plessis-Grimoult was enclosed by a stone wall with a wall-walk and two gate-towers. The earthworks and fragments of the masonry, with distinctive herringbone construction, may still be seen (E. Zadora-Rio, 'L'enceinte fortifié du Plessis-Grimoult (Calvados). Contribution à l'étude historique et archéologique de l'habitat seigneurial au XIe siècle', *Archéologie Médievale*, 3–4 (1973–74), pp 111–243).

43. These are the *Consuetudines et iusticiae* printed in Haskins, *Norman Institutions*, Appendix D, pp 281–4. The translation is taken from R.A. Brown, *The Norman Conquest of England: Sources and Documents* (Woodbridge, 1984), p 153. Haskins suggested that the list of customs dated from 1091, but Bill Aird has recently suggested that 1096 fits the facts better, and he has a strong case even if it cannot be conclusively proven (W.M. Aird, *Robert Curthose, Duke of Normandy (c. 1050–1134)* (Woodbridge, 2008), p 164).

44. J.O. Prestwich, 'War and finance in the Anglo-Norman state', *Transactions of the Royal Historical Society*, fifth series, 4 (1954), pp 19–43, reprinted in *Anglo-Norman Warfare*, ed. M. Strickland (Woodbridge, 1992), pp 59–83, at p 76.

45. J.A. Green, *The Government of England under Henry I* (Cambridge, 1986), pp 55 (royal estates), 69 (Danegeld), 80 (pleas and murdrum).

46. The tax known after 1066 as 'Danegeld' and before 1066 as 'heregeld' was first levied in 1012, and should not be confused with the tribute (*gafol*) used to pay off Danish raiders which was raised for the first time in 991. The *Anglo-Saxon Chronicle* 'D', s.a. 1051 therefore rightly states that Edward remitted the 'heregeld' (army-tax) 'thirty-nine years after it was first imposed'. Either he or William subsequently re-imposed it. I would like to thank Ann Williams for these comments.

47. Williams, *The English and the Norman Conquest*, p 12 and n. 42 which cite II Cnut 79, Hemming's Cartulary and her own '"Cockles amongst the wheat": Danes and English in the west midlands in the first half of the eleventh century', *Midland History*, 11 (1985), p 13.

48. M. Archibald, 'Coins', *English Romanesque Art, 1066–1200* (London, 1984), pp 320–8; P. Grierson, 'The monetary system under William I', in *Domesday Book Studies*, ed. R.W.H. Erskine and A. Williams (London, 1987), pp 75–9.

49. For the contents of this paragraph see F. Dumas, 'Les monnaies Normandes (Xe–XIIe siècles)', *Revue Numismatique*, 21 (1979), pp 84–140.

Chapter 5. Stern Beyond Measure, 1066–76

1. The table is based on the itinerary provided by David Bates in *Regesta*, pp 76–84.

2. Orderic, ii. 282. The use of the word 'game' has been taken as evidence for early tournaments, before that term was coined. See, for example, D. Crouch, *Tournament* (London, 2005), pp 1–12.

3. Orderic says 20 February (ii. 282) but Chibnall notes that 22 February was more

likely (at n. 5, referring to the foundation charter of St Peter's, Cassel). Bates does not commit himself (*William the Conqueror*, p 85); D. Nicholas, *Medieval Flanders* (London, 1992), p 52 says 22 February.

4. Lewis, 'The early earls of Norman England', p 217. John of Worcester says he was made earl in Herefordshire (John of Worcester, iii. 4), which Lewis discusses.

5. Williams, *The English and the Norman Conquest*, p 9 and n. 14.

6. D. Bates, 'The Conqueror's earliest historians and the writing of his biography', in *Writing Medieval Biography 750–1250: Essays in Honour of Frank Barlow*, ed. D. Bates, J. Crick and S. Hamilton (Woodbridge, 2006), p 132.

7. J. Gillingham, 'William the Bastard at war', in *Studies in Medieval History Presented to R. Allen Brown*, ed. C. Harper-Bill et al. (Woodbridge, 1989), p 141.

8. The story is a good example of how justice was seen in the eleventh century. Justice meant, amongst other things, punishment according to one's just deserts, even if that meant a very severe punishment indeed. Medieval writers, such as Gregory the Great in his *Moralia in Job*, thus tended to urge the use of temperance and mercy, so as to soften the harshness of justice.

9. Simeon of Durham says that Copsi had previously been Tostig's deputy (Symeon of Durham, *Libellus de exordio atque procursu istius, hoc est Dunhelmensis, ecclesie. Tract on the Origins and Progress of this the Church of Durham*, ed. and trans. D. Rollason (Oxford, 2000), p 180).

10. Williams, *The English and the Norman Conquest*, pp 16–17.

11. *Anglo-Saxon Chronicle* 'D', s.a. 1067; trans. Garmonsway, p 202; John of Worcester, iii. 6 says she went straight to Flanders. See also Williams, *The English and the Norman Conquest*, pp 19–21.

12. *Anglo-Saxon Chronicle* 'D', s.a. 1068 and John of Worcester both say that William built both castles at York at this time. John adds that he garrisoned them with 500 knights (John of Worcester, iii. 6).

13. Lewis, 'The early earls of Norman England', pp 219–20.

14. John of Worcester says Eadric made peace with William in 1070 (John of Worcester, iii. 14).

15. William of Jumièges discusses the attack and William's response, but he seems to conflate the events of 1068 and 1069 (Jumièges, ii. 180).

16. John of Worcester provides the figure of 240 ships (John of Worcester, iii. 8). The *Anglo-Saxon Chronicle* gives 300 ('E', s.a. 1069; trans. Garmonsway, p 202).

17. Richard fitz Nigel, *Dialogue of the Exchequer*, in *English Historical Documents, II. 1042–1189*, ed. Douglas and Greenaway (1953), p 528. On 'waste' see H.C. Darby, 'The Geography of Domesday England', in *Domesday Book Studies*, ed. R.W.H. Erskine and A. Williams (London, 1987), pp 32–3.

18. See Darby, 'The geography of Domesday England', p 33, fig. 13.

19. A map may be found in T. Rowley, *The English Heritage Book of Norman England*

(London, 1997), p 47.

20. Vegetius, *De re militari*, quoted in Gillingham, 'William the Bastard at war', p 151.

21. For accusations of genocide, see, for example, P. Rex, *The English Resistance: The Underground War against the Normans* (Stroud, 2006), p 108.

22. F. McLynn on P. Rex, *The English Resistance*. Bates also suggests that William's actions would now be treated as a 'war crime' (Bates, *William the Conqueror*, p 84). But this is to miss the point. In 1069–70 his actions were not criminal, nor even unorthodox. William was behaving entirely in accordance with the conventions of his time, and within the limitations they set down.

23. *The Letters of Lanfranc, Archbishop of Canterbury*, ed. and trans. H.M. Clover and M. Gibson (Oxford, 1979), pp 36–9 (no. 2); *English Episcopal Acta 14: Coventry and Lichfield 1072–1159*, ed. J.M. Franklin (Oxford, 1997), pp xxvii–xxviii.

24. *Fasti Ecclesiae Anglicanae 1066–1300. 2: Monastic Cathedrals*, ed. D. Greenway (London, 1971), p 29 and notes.

25. D. Knowles, *The Monastic Order in England* (Cambridge, 1940), p 111 and n. 4.

26. F.X. Martin, 'John, lord of Ireland, 1185–1216', and J. Lydon, 'The expansion and consolidation of the colony, 1215–54', in *A New History of Ireland II. Medieval Ireland 1169–1534*, ed. A. Cosgrove (Oxford, 1987), pp 152–3, 158.

27. The *Anglo-Saxon Chronicle* says that Edwin was killed before Morcar made his way to Ely ('D' and 'E', s.a. 1071; trans. Garmonsway, pp 206–7).

28. *Liber Eliensis: A History of the Isle of Ely from the Seventh Century to the Twelfth*, trans. J. Fairweather (Woodbridge, 2005), p 205 provides the evidence for the causeway and fortification of peat; in contrast John of Worcester, iii. 20, says that there was a bridge rather than a causeway.

29. Orderic, ii. 258 states that Beaumont was his gaoler. Lewis, 'The early earls of Norman England', p 215, n. 45 notes that Morcar attested one of Roger's acts in 1086 (printed in F. Lot, *Etudes Critiques sur l'abbaye de Saint-Wandrille* (Paris, 1913), no. 41).

30. Lewis, 'The early earls of Norman England', p 219 notes the breakup of Mercia after Edwin's death. Orderic notes, too, that after the defeat of the earls King William divided up the land. Hugh of Avranches was given Chester (ii. 260) and Hugh of Grandmesnil and Hugh of Ferrières were given Leicester and Tutbury respectively (ii. 264).

31. *Regesta*, nos. 1 (1066 × 1078); 12 (1066 × 1084); 66 (1070 × 1087); 80 (1066 × 1087); 98 (1066 × 1084); 130 (1066 × 1087); 184 (1066 × 1087); 189 (1085 × 1087); 288 (1068 × 1083); 337–40 (1070 × 1087). Bates overlooks the possibilities advanced by his own dates, holding that 'it is as good as certain that the large-scale production of Old English writs ended abruptly. 1070 seems to be the likely year, with the writs which marked the appointment of Lanfranc to the archbishopric of Canterbury and Bishop Walkelin to Winchester, being

among the last to survive and – perhaps – to be written' (*Regesta*, p 50).

32. Only Æthelstan had done more, advancing to Dunottar, south of Aberdeen, in 934: S. Foot, *Æthelstan: The First King of England* (New Haven and London, 2011), pp 164–7.

33. See the first of Lanfranc's letters to Roger, printed below, p 108.

34. In contrast John of Worcester says that Waltheof went immediately to Lanfranc who absolved him of his oath, and then went to William in Normandy, to tell him everything and place himself in his mercy (John of Worcester, iii. 24). Given what happened, this seems unlikely. The *Anglo-Saxon Chronicle* implies that he only did this after the conspiracy was discovered ('D', s.a. 1075; trans. Garmonsway, p 211).

35. Williams, *The English and the Norman Conquest*, p 63 and n. 84.

36. According to John of Worcester he was released in 1087 (see below, p 202n.13).

37. Orderic (ii. 322) says that after the execution the body was thrown into a ditch and buried there, hence the delay of a fortnight. John of Worcester says that he was 'thrown into the earth' at the spot where he was beheaded and then removed to Crowland (John of Worcester, iii. 28).

Chapter 6. William and the Church

1. F. Barlow, *The English Church, 1066–1154* (London, 1979), p 25.

2. Orderic, ii. 200; Bates, *Normandy before 1066*, p 202.

3. Gregory VII was one of the greatest popes of the Middle Ages, although a controversial figure. His battles with Henry IV comprise what is commonly known as the Investiture Contest, which was the result of a desire by a reforming party in the Church to make ecclesiastical appointments entirely independent of secular rulers. As the Church was also a great landholder across Europe, that proved a difficult pill for rulers to swallow. William the Conqueror managed to evade these issues during his lifetime, but they did have an impact during Henry I's reign. A compromise was worked out in 1107, which formed the model for the agreement that finally ended the equivalent dispute between the Empire and Papacy, known as the Concordat of Worms 1122 (see H.E.J. Cowdrey, *Pope Gregory VII, 1073–1085* (Oxford, 1998) for an up-to-date study of this pope, and also I.S. Robinson, *The Papacy 1073–1198: Continuity and Innovation* (Cambridge, 1990) for a modern overview of the whole period).

4. F. Stenton, *Anglo-Saxon England* (Oxford, 1943), p 667.

5. H.E.J. Cowdrey, *The Register of Pope Gregory VII 1073–1085: An English Translation* (Oxford, 2002), no. 9.5, p 405.

6. Bates, 'William I (1027/8–1087)', *Oxford Dictionary of National Biography*, lix. 56; Bates, *William the Conqueror*, pp 173–4. Barlow, *The English Church*, p 280 says that in 1086 William recognized Clement but then adopted a neutral position between the two rivals.

7. F. Neveux, 'Les diocèses normands aux XIe et XIIe siècles', in *Les Evêques normands du XIe siècle*, ed. P. Bouet and F. Neveux (Caen, 1995), pp 13–14; Bates, *Normandy before 1066*, pp 11, 30, 192.

8. See above, p 184n.19.

9. Bates, 'The character and career of Odo', p 5; *Recueil des historiens des Gaules et de la France*, xxiii. 699–702.

10. *Leges Henrici Primi*, ed. and trans. L.J. Downer (Oxford, 1972), pp 100–1, paras 7.2, 7.3.

11. Barlow, *The English Church 1066–1154*, p 160; J. Hudson, *The Formation of the English Common Law: Law and Society in England from the Norman Conquest to Magna Carta* (London, 1996), pp 72–3. The surviving records suggest that the ordeal was not much used in Normandy. There is evidence for only three cases in the time of William and his sons. One of them was held to determine whether William Pantulf was an accessory to the murder of Mabel of Bellême (Orderic, iii. 160), while the other two concerned questions of paternity (Regesta, no. 162; Orderic, v. 282). This was not unusual, according to R. Bartlett, *Trial by Fire and Water: The Medieval Judicial Ordeal* (Oxford, 1986), pp 19–20, whose book also provides a useful overview of the subject. For the use of the judicial ordeal, and the duel too, in other parts of western France see also S. White, 'Proposing the ordeal and avoiding it: strategy and power in western French litigation, 1050–1110', in *Cultures of Power: Lordship, Status, and Process in Twelfth-Century Europe*, ed. T.N. Bisson (Philadelphia, 1995), pp 89–123; B. Lemesle, *Conflits et justice au moyen âge: normes, loi et résolution des conflits en Anjou au XIe et XIIe siècles* (Paris, 2008), pp 157–76; and H. Teunis, *The Appeal to the Original Status: Social Justice in Anjou in the Eleventh Century* (Hilversum, 2006), Appendix.

12. Translation from *The Lives of Thomas Becket*, trans. Staunton, pp 112–13.

13. Bates, 'The character and career of Odo', p 2. Bates opines that Odo was born c. 1030 at the earliest, or after 1035.

14. Bates, *Normandy before 1066*, p 211.

15. Lanfranc is one of the towering figures of William's reign. William of Malmesbury provided a biography in his *Gesta pontificum* (William of Malmesbury, *Gesta pontificum Anglorum. Volume 1: Text and Translation*, ed. and trans. M. Winterbottom (Oxford, 2007), pp 48–108), and a *Life* was also written at Le Bec in the twelfth century, which was based on Milo Crispin's *Life* of Herluin of Le Bec (see below, p 200n.8). He has also been the subject of two detailed modern biographies: M. Gibson, *Lanfranc of Bec* (Oxford, 1978) and H.E.J. Cowdrey, *Lanfranc: Scholar, Monk and Bishop* (Oxford, 2003).

16. On the councils see, for example, R. Foreville, 'The synod of the province of Rouen', in *Church and Government in the Middle Ages: Studies Presented to C.R. Cheney on His 70th Birthday*, ed. C.N.L. Brooke, D.E. Luscombe, G.H. Martin and D. Owen (Cambridge, 1976), pp 19–39; Bates, *Normandy before 1066*, p 199; Bates,

William the Conqueror, p 145. On the canons of the council of 1072 see, most conveniently, Barlow, *The English Church 1066–1154*, p 125.

17. For the Norman Anonymous see G. Williams, *The Norman Anonymous: Towards the Identification and Evaluation of the So-Called Anonymous of York* (Cambridge, MA, 1951). The Latin text of the various tracts that make up the Anonymous's work are now available online at http://normananonymous.org/ENAP/. Parts of three of the tracts have been translated into English in *English Historical Documents, II. 1042–1189*, ed. Douglas and Greenaway, pp 675–7 (no. 113) and Barlow, *The English Church 1066–1154*, p 294.

18. The canons were copied into his *Ecclesiastical History* by Orderic (Orderic, iii. 26–34).

19. For what follows see L.K. Little, *Benedictine Maledictions: Liturgical Cursing in Romanesque France* (1993), pp 8–9.

20. *Liber Eliensis*, trans Fairweather, pp 252–3.

21. Abels, *Alfred the Great*, pp 220–1.

22. Although Orderic Vitalis claimed that the abbey was founded by Richard of Reviers (Orderic, iv. 220 and vi. 144–6) a confirmation issued by Richard and signed by Henry I reveals that the real founder was King William (*Charters of the Redvers Family and the Earldom of Devon, 1090–1217*, ed. R. Bearman (Exeter, 1994), pp 57–9, no. 5). Robert of Torigny's suggestion that Baldwin of Reviers was the founder (Jumièges, ii. 134) can probably be discounted altogether. For more on the establishment of William's power in the Cotentin see Hagger, 'How the west was won'. For a different view of the abbey and its foundation, see E. van Torhoudt, 'L'"énigme" des origines de l'abbaye de Montebourg', in *De part et d'autre de la Normandie médiévale: recueil d'études en hommage à François Neveux*, ed. P. Bouet et al. (Caen, 2009), pp 331–46, particularly pp 339–46.

23. Discussed by Lucien Musset in his *Les Actes de Guillaume le Conquerant et de la reine Mathilde pour les abbayes Caennaises* (Caen, 1967), pp 17–18.

24. *English Historical Documents, II. 1042–1189*, ed. Douglas and Greenaway, p 676 (no. 113a).

Chapter 7. A Kingly Figure: William's Person and Personality

1. Ælfric of Eynsham, 'The decollation of St John the Baptist', in *The Homilies of the Anglo-Saxon Church: The First Part Containing the Sermones Catholici or Homilies of Ælfric in the Original Anglo-Saxon with an English Version*, ed. and trans. B. Thorpe (London, 1844), pp 481–5. Robert Bartlett considers oaths only briefly in his *England under the Norman and Angevin Kings*, pp 579–80.

2. A fragment of an Old English letter, printed in *English Historical Documents I, c. 500–1042*, ed. Whitelock, p 825 (no. 232), complains (inter alia) about 'abandoning English practices which your fathers followed' and 'loving the practices of heathen men' by dressing 'in Danish fashion with bared necks and

blinded eyes'. This would seem to be a reference to the sort of haircut worn by the Normans in the Tapestry, suggesting that this style was seen as a Danish fashion generally by the English, thereby providing a further indication that the Tapestry was produced in England (I would like to thank Ann Williams for the reference and the suggestion). It might also suggest that the intended audience was English, because illustrations in Norman manuscripts do not portray figures in this way, as might be expected if the hairstyle was widely worn in the duchy.

3. R. Fleming, 'Acquiring, flaunting and destroying silk in late Anglo-Saxon England', *Early Medieval Europe*, 15 (2007), p 128.

4. Fleming, 'Acquiring, flaunting and destroying silk', p 137 and notes.

5. *Life of King Edward*, p 24.

6. *Le Cartulaire de l'Abbaye Bénédictine de Saint-Pierre-de-Préaux (1034–1227)*, ed. D. Rouet (Paris, 2005), pp 155–7 (A169); E. Zack Tabuteau, *Transfers of Property in Eleventh-Century Normandy* (Chapel Hill and London, 1988), p 116.

7. From an act for Troarn quoted in Tabuteau, *Transfers of Property*, p 151.

8. '*Life* of Herluin', in S. Vaughn, *The Abbey of Bec and the Anglo-Norman State*, p 76 (slightly amended).

9. Poitiers, p 116.

10. *Regesta*, nos. 200 and 232, respectively.

11. Wace, pp 131, 135 calls him 'long-tooth Haimo' which would perhaps indicate the former.

12. Orderic, iv. 184.

13. *The Normans in Europe*, ed. and trans. E.M.C. Van Houts (Manchester, 2000), p 84.

14. *Cartulaire de l'abbaye de Saint-Vincent du Mans*, eds R. Charles and M. d'Elbenne (Le Mans, 1886–1913), cols. 468–9 (no. 831); *Regesta*, ii. 800.

15. Barlow, *The English Church 1066–1154*, p 185; Bates, *William the Conqueror*, p 150.

16. *Regesta*, no. 158. He gave the abbey the manor of Penton Grafton in Hampshire, and the custom (i.e. revenue) from toll and carriage on or over Grestain's holdings in both England and Normandy.

17. The picture, by John Cotman, may be conveniently found in M.W. Thomson, *The Rise of the Castle* (Cambridge, 1991), p 29.

18. J. Decaens, 'Le premier château de Guillaume le Conquérant à Richard Coeur de lion (XIe–XIIe siècles)', in *Memoires du château de Caen* (Caen, 2000), pp 16–20.

19. R.B. Harris, 'The structural history of the White Tower, 1066–1200', in *The White Tower*, ed. E. Impey (New Haven and London, 2008), pp 29–43.

20. They are displayed in a case on the ground floor of the Jewel Tower.

21. *De Villis* in *Readings in Medieval History*, ed. and trans. P. Geary (Peterborough, Ontario, 1989), p 329 (ch. 42). Capitularies were 'decrees divided into *capitula* (chapters), comprising injunctions and provisions agreed upon by the king and

his advisers or the assembly covering administrative matters in both the secular and ecclesiastical spheres' (R. McKitterick, *The Frankish Kingdoms under the Carolingians, 751–987* (London, 1983), p 102). As might be expected from this, they comprised a form of legislation.

22. *English Historical Documents I, c. 500–1042*, ed. Whitelock, pp 524–5, 536–7 (nos. 116, 122).

23. *Regesta regum Anglo-Normannorum 1066–1154: II. Regesta Henrici Primi 1100–1135*, ed. C. Johnson and H.A. Cronne (Oxford, 1956), no. 1087.

24. Bates, *Normandy before 1066*, p 96.

25. See, for example, R. Fleming, 'The new wealth, the new rich and the new political style in late Anglo-Saxon England', *Anglo-Norman Studies*, 23 (2001), p 5 and those works noted above, p 186n.15.

26. For these see Bartlett, *England under the Norman and Angevin Kings*, pp 584–8; J. Gillingham, 'From *civilitas* to civility: codes of manners in medieval and early modern England', *Transactions of the Royal Historical Society*, 12 (2002), pp 272–8.

27. For example, Oxford, Bodleian Library, MS Auct. F. 2.13 (mid-twelfth century). This manuscript has been digitized and is available online at: http://image.ox.ac.uk/show?collection=bodleian&manuscript=msauctf213. See also G. Owen-Crocker, 'The interpretation of gesture in the Bayeux Tapestry', *Anglo-Norman Studies*, 29 (2007), p 146.

28. *The Lives of Thomas Becket*, trans. Staunton, p 50.

29. This demonstrates that hauberks, although by no means cheap, were not as expensive as is often believed. Horses, on the other hand, might cost more than the annual income of a good-sized manor. The document which mentions the hauberk valued at 7 *livres* (*Recueil des actes des ducs de Normandie*, ed. Fauroux, no. 113, which dates from some point between 1043 and 1048), for example, also mentions a horse valued at 30 *livres*.

30. For hunting see F. Barlow, 'Hunting in the middle ages', in the volume of collected papers: *The Norman Conquest and Beyond* (London, 1983), pp 1–21, and C.R. Young, *The Royal Forests of Medieval England* (Stroud, 1979), chs. 1 and 2.

Chapter 8. Storms of Troubles, 1076–87

1. Orderic, ii. 356.

2. See Aird, *Robert Curthose*, p 58.

3. Although Orderic (ii. 358) says he went to Hugh of Châteauneuf to begin with, he contradicts himself later, writing that he actually went to Count Robert first of all (Orderic, iii. 102). This second version of events is supported by the 'D' version of the *Anglo-Saxon Chronicle* s.a. 1079; trans. Garmonsway, p 213. John of Worcester says only that he went to France and sought the king's aid (John of Worcester, iii. 30).

4. Cowdrey, *The Register of Pope Gregory VII*, no. 7.27, pp 358–9.

5. *A Medieval Prince of Wales: The Life of Gruffydd ap Cynan*, trans. D.S. Evans (Llanerch, 1990), pp 66–70. This *Life* also provides some details of Gruffydd's attack on Rhuddlan in 1075 (p 62), but Robert's career is set out in the greatest detail by Orderic, whose informant was Robert's own brother Arnold. It was Orderic too who inscribed on Robert's tomb in the cloister of Saint-Evroult the best of all his epitaphs (Orderic, iv. 134–46).

6. Bates, *William the Conqueror*, p 168.

7. Douglas, *William the Conqueror*, pp 346–7.

8. H.R. Loyn, 'A general introduction to Domesday Book', in *Domesday Book Studies*, ed. A. Williams and R.W.H. Erskine (London, 1987), pp 3–5.

9. The following survey of the historiography owes much to D. Roffe, *Domesday: The Inquest and the Book* (Oxford, 2000), pp 12–15.

10. John of Worcester (iii. 44) provides a little more detail, saying that William made the knights of his tenants-in-chief (archbishops, bishops, abbots, earls, barons, etc) 'swear allegiance to him against all others'.

11. Malmesbury says that William attacked Mantes at the end of August, which would mean that the king was ill for about a fortnight (Malmesbury, *Gesta regum Anglorum*, p 510, para. 282). Orderic says that William attacked Mantes in the last week of July, and that the king lay ill at Rouen for six weeks (Orderic, iv. 78).

12. The anonymous account of William's death lists Archbishop William, Bishop Gilbert, John the doctor, Gerard the chancellor and Count Robert as present at the king's bedside (Jumièges, ii. 184–90; *English Historical Documents, II. 1042–1189*, ed. Douglas and Greenaway, p 279). Orderic mentions that William called to his bedside William and Henry and 'certain friends' (Orderic, iv. 80).

13. Orderic, iv. 96–100. John of Worcester says that William released Odo, Morcar, Roger of Hereford, Siward Barn and Wulfnoth (John of Worcester, iii. 46).

14. Serlo of Bayeux, in *The Anglo-Latin Satirical Poets and Epigrammists of the Twelfth Century*, ed. T. Wright, Rolls Series, 2 vols (London, 1872), pp 251–3.

Legacy

1. Barlow, *The English Church 1066–1154*, p 195.

† FURTHER READING

General

The most important primary sources for William's reign have all been edited, and a good many are available in translation. I have quoted widely from these sources throughout the book (although I have occasionally tweaked the translations a little) because these witnesses from the eleventh and twelfth centuries are the foundation on which all modern interpretations of William's reign are built.

On the Norman side there are William of Jumièges, Orderic Vitalis and Robert of Torigny, *Gesta Normannorum ducum*, ed. and trans. E.M.C. van Houts, 2 vols (Oxford, 1992–95); William of Poitiers, *Gesta Guillelmi*, ed. and trans. R.H.C. Davis and M. Chibnall (Oxford, 1998); the incomparable Orderic Vitalis, *Historia ecclesiastica*, ed. and trans. M. Chibnall, 6 vols (Oxford, 1969–80); and Wace, *Roman de Rou*, trans. G.S. Burgess (Woodbridge, 2004).

On the English side we have the *Anglo-Saxon Chronicle*, ed. and trans. D. Whitelock, D.C. Douglas and S.I. Tucker (London, 1961) but available in a host of other editions (thus the passages from the *Chronicle* found here are from *The Anglo-Saxon Chronicle*, ed. and trans. G.N. Garmonsway (new edition, London, 1972) which remains the most atmospheric translation); John of Worcester, *The Chronicle of John of Worcester*, ed. and trans. P. McGurk et al., 2 vols (Oxford, 1995–8); William of Malmesbury, *Gesta regum Anglorum*, ed. and trans. R.A.B. Mynors, R.M. Thomson and M. Winterbottom, vol. 1 (Oxford, 1998). Not directly concerned with William's reign, although still of interest, are Thomas of Marlborough, *History of the Abbey of Evesham*, ed. and trans. J. Sayers and L. Watkiss (Oxford, 2003) and *Historia Ecclesie Abbendonensis: The History of the Church of Abingdon*, ed. and trans. J. Hudson, 2 vols (Oxford, 2002–7).

William's acts have also been edited, but they have not been translated from the Latin – although the editors have provided brief summaries in French (for the period before 1066) and English (for the period after 1066). William's ducal *acta* are found in *Recueil des actes des ducs de Normandie de 911 à 1066*, ed. M. Fauroux (Caen, 1961). The documents that William issued while king are found in *Regesta Regum Anglo-Normannorum, the Acta of William I (1066–1087)*, ed. D. Bates (Oxford, 1998). The introduction discusses these documents in detail and also provides an itinerary which is the basis for those set out at the beginning of Chapters 5 and 8. Some of these acts, as well as a selection of other documents (including the *Laws of William the Conqueror*, *The Dialogue of the Exchequer* and extracts from the work of the Norman Anonymous) have been translated into English in *English Historical Documents, II. 1042–1189*, ed. D.C. Douglas and G.W. Greenaway (London, 1953).

The two best biographies of William in English are D.C. Douglas, *William the Conqueror* (London, 1964), which is still the fullest account of the reign, and the shorter D. Bates, *William the Conqueror* (London, 1989). There is also a short biography of the king in the *Oxford Dictionary of National Biography from the Earliest Times to the Year 2000*, ed. H.C.G Matthew and B. Harrison, 60 vols (Oxford, 2004), lix. 45–57, also by D. Bates.

Other more general books that cover the reign include R.A. Brown, *The Normans and the Norman Conquest* (second edition, Woodbridge, 1985); D. Bates, *Normandy before 1066* (London, 1982); J. Le Patourel, *The Norman Empire* (Oxford, 1976); M. Chibnall, *Anglo-Norman England* (Oxford, 1986); M. Clanchy, *England and its Rulers, 1066–1307* (third edition, Oxford, 2006); D. Crouch, *The Normans: The History of a Dynasty* (London, 2002); F. Neveux, *A Brief History of the Normans: The Conquests that changed the Face of Europe*, trans. H. Curtis (London, 2008); and the altogether excellent R. Bartlett, *England under the Norman and Angevin Kings, 1075–1225* (Oxford, 2000). Bartlett has also written and presented a BBC television series called *The Normans*, which aired in the summer of 2010 and is available on DVD. The first and second episodes contain material that relates to William the Conqueror. Finally there is a BBC Radio 4 series called *The Norman Way*, which provides some insights into the Conquest and to the period more generally. The URL is: http://www.bbc.co.uk/radio4/history/normanway_home.shtml.

Prologue

For an outline of Westminster at the end of the eleventh century see G. Rosser, *Medieval Westminster 1200–1540* (Oxford, 1989). For Westminster Abbey see R.D.H. Gem, 'The Romanesque rebuilding of Westminster Abbey (with a reconstruction by W.T. Ball)', *Proceedings of the Battle Conference on Anglo-Norman Studies*, 3 (1981) and three new studies: E. Fernie, 'Edward the Confessor's Westminster Abbey', W. Rodwell, 'New glimpses of Edward the Confessor's abbey at Westminster' and R. Gem, 'Craftsmen and administrators in the building of the Confessor's abbey', all in *Edward the Confessor: The Man and the Legend*, ed. R. Mortimer (Woodbridge, 2009). For the coronation, and the dispute over the Ordo used, see J.L. Nelson, 'The rites of the Conqueror', *Proceedings of the Battle Conference*, 4 (1982) and G. Garnett, 'The third recension of the English coronation ordo: the manuscripts', *The Haskins Society Journal*, 11 (2003).

Chapter 1. Fire and Sword Everywhere, *c.* 1027–47

Outside of the biographies, there is very little written specifically on the earliest years of William's reign. The most important is D. Bates, 'The Conqueror's adolescence', *Anglo-Norman Studies*, 25 (2003), which, like this chapter, considers William's career down to Val-ès-Dunes. For William's family see E.M.C. van Houts, 'The origins of Herleva, mother of William the Conqueror', *English Historical Review*, 101 (1986), and D. Bates and V. Gazeau, 'L'abbaye de Grestain et la famille d'Herluin de Conteville', *Annales de Normandie*, 40 (1990). Work on his two half-brothers may be found in the reading for the following chapters.

Chapter 2. The Undefeated Duke, 1047–66

Most of our information for this period is derived from William of Jumièges, William of Poitiers and William's own acts. For these see the references above. In addition, the relevant part of *The Acts of the Bishops of Le Mans Residing in the City* is available online at http://www.fordham.edu/halsall/source/1081gestaarnaldi.html. One other primary source quoted in this chapter is Suger of Saint-Denis, *The Deeds of Louis the Fat*, trans. R. Cusimano and J. Moorhead (Washington, DC, 1992).

For Normandy in this period generally see D. Bates, *Normandy before 1066* (London, 1982) and also P. Bauduin, *La première Normandie (X^e–XIe siècles). Sur* *les frontières de la Haute Normandie: Identité et construction d'une principauté* (Caen, 2004).

On Normandy's neighbours see O. Guillot, *Le comte d'Anjou et son entourage au XIe siècle* (Paris, 1972); R. Barton, *Lordship in the County of Maine, c. 890–1160* (Woodbridge, 2004); K. Thompson, *Power and Border Lordship in Medieval France: The County of the Perche, 1000–1226* (Woodbridge, 2002); D. Bates, 'Lord Sudeley's ancestors: The family of the counts of Amiens, Valois and the Vexin in France and England during the eleventh century', in *The Sudeley – Lords of Toddington* (Thetford, 1987); and H. Tanner, *Families, Friends and Allies: Boulogne and Politics in Northern France and England, c. 879–1160* (Leiden and Boston, 2004). There are also two important articles by K. Thompson on the Montgommery-Bellême family: 'Family and influence to the south of Normandy in the eleventh century: the lordship of Bellême', *Journal of Medieval History*, 11 (1985) and 'The Norman aristocracy before 1066: the example of the Montgomerys', *Historical Research*, 60 (1987), as well as a study in French: G. Louise, *La seigneurie de Bellême Xe–XIIe siècles: dévolution des pouvoirs territoriaux et construction d'une seigneurie de frontière aux confins de la Normandie et du Maine de la charnière de l'an mil*, La Pays Bas-Normand, 2 vols, 3 and 4 (1990) and 1 and 2 (1991). Cassandra Potts has revised the careers of the earliest counts of Avranches: C. Potts, 'The earliest Norman counts revisited: the lords of Mortain', *The Haskins Society Journal*, 4 (1992). For Count Robert of Mortain in particular see B. Golding, 'Robert of Mortain', *Anglo-Norman Studies*, 13 (1991). Many of the individuals mentioned here also have entries in the *Oxford Dictionary of National Biography* (Oxford, 2004). For the Giroie family, see J.-M. Maillefer, 'Une famille aristocratique aux confins de la Normandie: les Géré au XIe siècle', in *Autour du pouvoir ducal Normand Xe–XIIe Siècles*, ed. L. Musset et al. (Caen, 1985) and P. Bauduin, 'Une famille châtelaine sur les confins normanno-manceaux: les Géré (Xe–XIIIe s.)', *Archéologie Médiévale*, 22 (1992). Some aspects of the history of the Grandmesnil family have been dealt with in M. Hagger, 'Kinship and identity in eleventh-century Normandy: the case of Hugh de Grandmesnil, *c.* 1040–1098', *Journal of Medieval History*, 32 (2006).

On the conduct of war in this period see, for example, J. Gillingham, 'William the Bastard at war', in *Studies in Medieval History Presented to R. Allen Brown*, ed. C. Harper-Bill et al. (Woodbridge, 1989) and more generally M. Strickland, *War and Chivalry: The Conduct and Perception of War in England and Normandy, 1066–1217* (Cambridge, 1996); *Anglo-Norman Warfare*, ed. M. Strickland (1992); and J. Bradbury, *The Medieval Siege* (Woodbridge, 1992).

Chapter 3. William the Conqueror, 1066

There are some primary sources for this chapter that have not been mentioned before. Perhaps the most important, certainly the most focused on the battle, is *The Carmen de Hastingae Proelio of Guy Bishop of Amiens*, ed. and trans. F. Barlow (Oxford, 1999). Mention is also made here of *The Life of King Edward Who Rests at Westminster*, ed. and trans. F. Barlow (second edition, Oxford, 1992); Henry of Huntingdon, *Historia Anglorum: The History of the English People*, ed. and trans. D. Greenway (Oxford, 1996); and *The Waltham Chronicle*, ed. and trans. L. Watkiss and M. Chibnall (Oxford, 1994).

The main English players in the drama of the Conquest, Edward the Confessor and Harold, have been the subject of biographies. The best study by far of Edward the Confessor remains F. Barlow, *Edward the Confessor* (second edition, London, 1972). Harold and his family are examined in F. Barlow, *The Godwins: The Rise and Fall of a Noble Dynasty* (London, 2001) and E. Mason, *The House of Godwine: The History of a Dynasty* (London, 2003). These men also have entries in the *Oxford Dictionary of National Biography* (Oxford, 2004).

The French and Norman influences acting on Edward are described in C.P. Lewis, 'The French in England before the Norman Conquest', *Anglo-Norman Studies*, 17 (1994). His sojourn in Normandy is explored in S. Keynes, 'The æthelings in Normandy', *Anglo-Norman Studies*, 13 (1991) and E.M.C. van Houts, 'Edward and Normandy', in *Edward the Confessor: The Man and the Legend*, ed. R. Mortimer (Woodbridge, 2009). Edward the Confessor's promise of the throne to William is discussed in a number of sources. Those most sceptical of the promise include F. Barlow, *Edward the Confessor* and P. Stafford, *Unification and Conquest: A Political and Social History of England in the Tenth and Eleventh Centuries* (London, 1989). For other views on Edward's promise, and its nature, see E. John, 'Edward the Confessor and the Norman succession', *English Historical Review*, 94 (1979); A. Williams, 'Some notes and considerations on problems connected with the English royal succession, 860–1066', *Proceedings of the Battle Conference*, 1 (1978); A. Williams, 'Land and power in the eleventh century: the estates of Harold Godwineson', *Proceedings of the Battle Conference*, 3 (1981); and S. Baxter, 'Edward the Confessor and the succession question', in *Edward the Confessor: The Man and the Legend*, ed. R. Mortimer (Woodbridge, 2009), which surveys the historiography and provides a new view on Edward's promise of the succession to William.

For the battle and the English and Norman armies there is a collection by Stephen Morillo, *The Battle of Hastings: Sources and Interpretations* (Woodbridge, 1996), which includes a number of the articles cited here as well as his interpretation of the various stages of the battle (complete with maps). Perhaps the seminal article on the battle is R.A. Brown, 'The battle of Hastings', *Proceedings of the Battle Conference*, 3 (1981). Other accounts are found in C.H. Lemmon, 'The campaign of 1066', in *The Norman Conquest: Its Setting and Impact*, ed. D. Whitelock et al. (London, 1966). For the English armies see N. Hooper, 'Anglo-Saxon warfare on the eve of the Conquest', *Proceedings of the Battle Conference*, 1 (1978); R. Abels, 'Bookland and fyrd service', *Anglo-Norman Studies*, 7 (1985); N. Hooper, 'The housecarls in England in the eleventh century', *Anglo-Norman Studies*, 7 (1985); R. Abels, *Lordship and Military Obligation in Anglo-Saxon England* (Berkeley and London, 1988). For the Normans see B. Bachrach, 'Some observations on the military administration of the Norman Conquest', *Anglo-Norman Studies*, 8 (1986); E.M.C. van Houts, 'The ship list of William the Conqueror', *Anglo-Norman Studies*, 10 (1988), which is not entirely convincing with regard to the authenticity of this enigmatic document; H. Tsurushima, 'The eleventh century through fish-eyes: salmon, herring, oysters, and 1066', *Anglo-Norman Studies*, 29 (2007), which provides the suggestion that Harold's fleet disbanded to go fishing for herring; C. Gillmore, 'Naval logistics of the cross-Channel operation, 1066', *Anglo-Norman Studies*, 7 (1985); C. Grainge and G. Grainge, 'The Pevensey expedition: brilliantly executed plan or near disaster?', *The Mariner's Mirror* (1993); R.H.C. Davis, 'The warhorses of the Normans', *Anglo-Norman Studies*, 10 (1988). A more general view of contemporary arms and armour is found in I. Peirce, 'Arms, armour and warfare in the eleventh century', *Anglo-Norman Studies*, 10 (1988) and also in D. Nicolle, *Arms and Armour of the Crusading Era 1050–1350: Western Europe and the Crusader States* (new edition, London, 1999). A survey of continental views on the battle may be found in E.M.C. van Houts, 'The Norman Conquest through European eyes', *English Historical Review*, 110 (1995).

The Norman Conquest is, of course, depicted in the woollen threads of the Bayeux Tapestry. There is a vast literature about this embroidery. Among the most recent publications on the subject are: H.E.J. Cowdrey, 'Towards an interpretation of the Bayeux Tapestry', *Anglo-Norman Studies*, 10 (1988); C. Hicks, 'The borders of the Bayeux tapestry', in *England in the Eleventh Century: Proceedings of the 1990 Harlaxton Symposium*, ed. C. Hicks (Stamford, 1992); W. Grape, *The Bayeux Tapestry: Monument to a Norman Triumph* (Munich, 1994); *The Bayeux Tapestry: Embroidering the Facts of History*, ed. P. Bouet, B.J. Levy and F. Neveux (Caen, 2004); L. Musset, *The Bayeux Tapestry*, trans. R. Rex (Woodbridge, 2005); and *King Harold II and the Bayeux Tapestry*, ed. G. Owen-Crocker (Woodbridge, 2005).

Chapter 4. I See God! Ritual and Government

For the crown-wearings see M. Biddle, 'Seasonal festivals and residence: Winchester, Westminster and Gloucester in the tenth to twelfth centuries', *Anglo-Norman Studies*, 8 (1986); H.E.J. Cowdrey, 'The Anglo-Norman *Laudes regiae*', *Viator*, 12 (1981).

For the government of William's dominions there are C.H. Haskins, *Norman Institutions* (Cambridge, MA, 1918); D. Bates, *Normandy before 1066* (London, 1982); H.R. Loyn, *The Governance of Anglo-Saxon England 500–1087* (London, 1984) and, for the period after William's reign. W.L. Warren, *The Governance of Norman and Angevin England 1086–1272* (London, 1987). In addition, the most accessible work specifically on counsel focuses on the reign of Henry I: J. Hudson, 'Henry I and counsel', in *The Medieval State: Essays presented to James Campbell*, ed. J.R. Maddicott and D.M. Palliser (London, 2000). For those left in charge of England and Normandy in the king's absence see F. West, *The Justiciarship in England, 1066–1272* (Cambridge, 1966) and D. Bates, 'The origins of the justiciarship', *Proceedings of the Battle Conference*, 4 (1982). For sheriffs see J.A. Green, *English Sheriffs to 1154* (London, 1990) and for *vicomtes* see M.Hagger, 'The Norman *vicomte, c.* 1035–1135: what did he do?', *Anglo-Norman Studies*, 29 (2007). For the use of writs there is R. Sharpe, 'The use of writs in the eleventh century', *Anglo-Saxon England*, 32 (2003). See also the introduction (and contents) to *Regesta Anglo-Normannorum: The Acta of William I, 1066–1087*, ed. D. Bates (Oxford, 1998). For the introduction of the writ into Normandy during the reign of Henry I see D. Bates, 'The earliest Norman writs', *English Historical Review*, 100 (1985) and M. Hagger, 'The earliest Norman writs revisited', *Historical Research*, 82 (2009). For Regenbald see S. Keynes, 'Regenbald the chancellor (*sic*)', *Anglo-Norman Studies*, 10 (1988). Anselm's letter to Abbot Henry, along with the rest of the letters he wrote while at Le Bec, may be found in *The Letters of Saint Anselm of Canterbury*, trans. W. Frölich, vol. 1 (Kalamazoo, 1990).

For law and justice in the Anglo-Norman dominions see first of all R.C. van Caenegem, *English Lawsuits from William I to Richard I*, Selden Society, 106 (1990), which has translations into English of all the pleas that survive from

William's reign as king. There is also J. Hudson, *The Formation of the English Common Law: Law and Society in England from the Norman Conquest to Magna Carta* (London, 1996), which provides an accessible introduction to this subject, and P. Wormald, *The Making of English Law: King Alfred to the Twelfth Century. Vol. 1: Legislation and its Limits* (Oxford, 1999). For Normandy there is M. Hagger, 'Secular law and custom in ducal Normandy, *c.* 1000–1144', *Speculum*, 85 (2010) and the rather variable G. Davy, *Le duc et la loi: héritages, images et expressions du pouvoir normatif dans la duché de Normandie, des origins à la mort du Conquérant (fin du IXe siècle–1087)* (Paris, 2004).

For knight service in Normandy see D. Bates, *Normandy before 1066* (London, 1982) but especially M. Chibnall, 'Military service in Normandy before 1066', *Anglo-Norman Studies*, 5 (1983). For military service in England before the Conquest see R. Abels, *Lordship and Military Obligation in Anglo-Saxon England* (Berkeley and London, 1988). For the period after 1066 see J. Gillingham, 'The introduction of knight service into England', *Proceedings of the Battle Conference*, 4 (1982); J.C. Holt, 'The introduction of knight service in England', *Anglo-Norman Studies*, 6 (1984).

On castles generally see, amongst many others, M.W. Thomson, *The Rise of the Castle* (Cambridge, 1991); R A. Brown, *English Castles* (third edition, London, 1976); R. Eales, 'Royal power and castles in Norman England', *Medieval Knighthood III*, ed. C. Harper-Bill and R. Harvey (1990); A. Williams, 'A bell-house and a *burh-geat*: lordly residences in England before the Conquest', *Medieval Knighthood IV*, ed. C. Harper-Bill and R. Harvey (1992). These last two articles are republished, with others that might be of interest, in *Anglo-Norman Castles*, ed. R. Liddiard (Woodbridge, 2003). Williams's article looks briefly at the status of a thegn, as does her *The English and the Norman Conquest* (Woodbridge, 1995) and *The World before Domesday: The English Aristocracy, 900–1066* (London, 2008). For an overview of the excavations at Goltho and the conclusions drawn from them see G. Beresford, 'Goltho manor, Lincolnshire: the buildings and their surrounding defences *c.* 850–1150', *Proceedings of the Battle Conference on Anglo-Norman Studies*, 4 (1982).

For finance see J.O. Prestwich, 'War and finance in the Anglo-Norman state', *Transactions of the Royal Historical Society*, 5th series, 4 (1954). On the Danegeld see J. Gillingham, '"The most precious jewel in the English crown": levels of Danegeld and heregeld in the early eleventh century', *English Historical Review*, 104 (1989); M. Lawson, '"Those stories look true": levels of taxation in the reigns of Æthelred and Cnut', *English Historical Review*, 104 (1989);

M. Lawson, 'Danegeld and heregeld once more', *English Historical Review*, 105 (1990). J. Green, *The Government of England under Henry I* (Cambridge, 1986) considers the tax from a later point of view.

For the Norman coinage, the most important article is F. Dumas, 'Les monnaies Normandes (Xe–XIIe siècles)', *Revue Numismatique*, 21 (1979). The most accessible introductions to the English coinage are M. Archibald, 'Coins', *English Romanesque Art, 1066–1200* (London, 1984) and P. Grierson, 'The monetary system under William I', in *Domesday Book Studies*, ed. R.W.H. Erskine and A. Williams (London, 1987).

For the continuing differences between England and Normandy after 1066, see D. Bates, 'Normandy and England after 1066', *English Historical Review*, 105 (1990).

Chapter 5. Stern Beyond Measure, 1066–76

For warfare see the books cited under Chapter 2; for discussion of the Church and Church councils, as well as Lanfranc's letters, see the reading under Chapter 6. Two new primary sources make an appearance in this chapter: Hugh the Chanter, *The History of the Church of York, 1066–1127*, ed. and trans. C. Johnson (Oxford, 1990), and *Liber Eliensis: A History of the Isle of Ely from the Seventh Century to the Twelfth*, trans. J. Fairweather (Woodbridge, 2005). The latter tells us something of Hereward and his rebellion, and is also the source for the story about Gervase in Chapter 6.

Aside from the biographies, two works of fundamental importance for this period of William's life are R.A. Brown, *The Normans and the Norman Conquest* (second edition, Woodbridge, 1985) and Ann Williams's fine book, *The English and the Norman Conquest* (Woodbridge 1995). For those interested in learning more about the Anglo-Saxon aristocracy before the Conquest there are now S. Baxter, *The Earls of Mercia: Lordship and Power in Late Anglo-Saxon England* (Oxford, 2008) and A. Williams, *The World before Domesday: The English Aristocracy, 900–1066* (London, 2009). Also of importance is C.P. Lewis, 'The early earls of Norman England', *Anglo-Norman Studies*, 13 (1990). For some of the changes wrought in the north there are C.P. Lewis, 'The formation of the honor of Chester, 1066–1100', in *The Earldom of Chester and its Charters: A Tribute to Geoffrey Barraclough*, ed. A.T. Thacker (Chester, 1991) and P. Dalton, *Conquest, Anarchy and Lordship: Yorkshire, 1066–1154* (Cambridge, 1994). For a different view of the harrying of the north to the one presented here see D. Carpenter, *The Struggle for Mastery: Britain 1066–1284* (Oxford, 2003).

In addition, D. Bates, 'The Conqueror's earliest historians and the writing of his biography', in *Writing Medieval Biography 750–1250: Essays in Honour of Frank Barlow*, ed. D. Bates, J. Crick and S. Hamilton (Woodbridge, 2006) provides some interesting thoughts on the work of William of Poitiers and its relationship to the complaints made of William's rule in the 'D' version of the *Anglo-Saxon Chronicle*. See also on this author R.H.C. Davis, 'William of Poitiers and his History of William the Conqueror', in *The Writing of History in the Middle Ages*, ed. R.H. Davis and J.M. Wallace-Hadrill (Oxford, 1981), pp 71–100.

Chapter 6. William and the Church

Two useful primary sources which have been translated into English are H.E.J. Cowdrey, *The Register of Pope Gregory VII 1073–1085: An English Translation* (Oxford, 2002) and *The Letters of Lanfranc, Archbishop of Canterbury*, ed. and trans. H.M. Clover and M. Gibson (Oxford, 1979), which provided the letters addressed to King William and Earl Roger quoted in the previous chapter. The passage from William fitz Stephen's *Life* of Becket may be found, with a great deal else, in *The Lives of Thomas Becket*, trans. M. Staunton (Manchester, 2001). The best general work on the Church in William's England remains F. Barlow, *The English Church, 1066–1154* (London, 1979). For Normandy, D. Bates, *Normandy before 1066* (London, 1982) provides the most accessible overview. A more general introduction may be found in R.W. Southern, *Western Society and the Church in the Middle Ages* (Harmondsworth, 1970). Sir Frank Stenton's comment is taken from his *Anglo-Saxon England* (Oxford, 1943), one of a number of more general books (some of them mentioned above) to include a chapter on the Church.

Lists of the Norman bishops and their archdeacons and clergy can be found in D. Spear, *The Personnel of the Norman Cathedrals during the Ducal Period, 911–1204* (London, 2006). Articles on William's bishops include D. Walker, 'Crown and episcopacy under the Normans and Angevins', *Anglo-Norman Studies*, 5 (1983); and H.R. Loyn, 'William's bishops: some further thoughts', *Anglo-Norman Studies*, 10 (1988).

There are a number of biographies of both Norman and English bishops. Among these are D. Bates, 'The character and career of Odo, bishop of Bayeux, 1049/50–1097', *Speculum*, 50 (1975); J. Le Patourel, 'Geoffrey of Montbray', *English Historical Review*, 59 (1944) and M. Chibnall, 'La carrière de Geoffroi de Montbray', in *Les Evêques normands du XIe siècle*, ed. P. Bouet and

F. Neveux (Caen, 1995); M. Gibson, *Lanfranc of Bec* (Oxford, 1978); H.E.J. Cowdrey, *Lanfranc: Scholar, Monk and Bishop* (Oxford, 2003); and D. Bates, *Bishop Remigius of Lincoln 1067–1092* (Lincoln, 1992). Wulfstan of Worcester, not much noticed here, has been the subject of a number of studies. There is a biography, E. Mason, *St Wulfstan of Worcester* c. *1008–1095* (Oxford, 1990), a recent collection of articles, *St Wulfstan and his World*, ed. J.S. Barrow and N.P. Brooks (Aldershot, 2005), and, more recently still, Wulfstan's *acta* have been edited with a very full introduction in *English Episcopal Acta, 33: Worcester, 1066–1183*, ed. M. Cheyney, et al. (Oxford, 2007).

For the Church councils of William's reign see R. Foreville, 'The Synod of the province of Rouen in the eleventh and twelfth centuries', in *Church and Government in the Middle Ages: Studies Presented to C.R. Cheney on His 70th Birthday*, ed. C.N.L. Brooke, D.E. Luscombe, G.H. Martin and D. Owen (Cambridge, 1976) and *Councils and synods with other documents relating to the English Church, Vol. 1, Pt 2: 1066–1204*, ed. D. Whitelock, M. Brett and C.N.L. Brooke (Oxford, 1981). The penitential ordinance, imposed by the papal legate, Bishop Ermenfrid of Sion, in 1070 is discussed in H.E.J. Cowdrey, 'Bishop Ermenfrid of Sion and the penitential ordinance following the battle of Hastings', *Journal of Ecclesiastical History*, 20 (1969). A translation is provided in *English Historical Documents*, pp 606–7 (no. 81). The battle over the primacy is discussed in the biographies of Lanfranc and in Barlow's book on the English Church.

The description of the procedure to be followed in cases where the ordeal by water was used is taken from J. Hudson, *The Formation of the English Common Law: Law and Society in England from the Norman Conquest to Magna Carta* (London, 1996). For more on the ordeal generally, see R. Bartlett, *Trial by Fire and Water: The Medieval Judicial Ordeal* (Oxford, 1986).

The Fécamp curse is taken from L.K. Little, *Benedictine Maledictions: Liturgical Cursing in Romanesque France* (Ithaca and London, 1993). For miracles see, for example, B. Ward, *Miracles and the Medieval Mind: Theory, Record and Event 1000–1215* (London, 1982); R.C. Finucane, *Miracles and Pilgrims: Popular Beliefs in Medieval England* (London, 1977); and S. Yarrow, *Saints and Their Communities: Miracle Stories in Twelfth Century England* (Oxford, 2006). For a gendered view of contemporary miracles see K.F. Quirk, 'Men, women and miracles in Normandy, 1050–1150', in *Medieval Memories: Men, Women, and the Past in Europe, 700–1300*, ed. E.M.C. van Houts (London, 2001).

For a general introduction to the monastic orders of medieval Europe there is C.H. Lawrence, *Medieval Monasticism: Forms of Religious Life in Western Europe in the Middle Ages* (third edition, London, 2000). The Norman Benedictine houses are discussed in *La Normandie Bénédictine au temps de Guillaume le Conquerant*, ed. L. Gaillard and J. Daoust (Lille, 1967) and much more recently in V. Gazeau, *Normannia Monastica* (Caen, 2007). Monasticism in England is surveyed in the old, but still useful, D. Knowles, *The Monastic Order in England* (Cambridge, 1940) and in J. Burton, *Monastic and Religious Orders in Britain 1000–1300* (Cambridge, 1994). Knowles's book provides the numbers of English abbots still in post during William's reign noted in Chapter 6. For a discussion of the relationship between a monastery and the world outside the cloister see M. Chibnall, *The World of Orderic Vitalis* (Woodbridge, 1984). For William's foundation at Battle see *The Chronicle of Battle Abbey*, ed. and trans. E. Seale (Oxford, 1980); E. Searle, *Lordship and Community: Battle Abbey and its Banlieu, 1066–1538* (Toronto, 1974); and E.M. Hallam, 'Monasteries as "war memorials": Battle abbey and La Victoire', *Studies in Church History*, 20 (1983).

Chapter 7. A Kingly Figure: William's Person and Personality

The capitulary *De Villis* is available in translation in P.J. Geary, *Readings in Medieval History* (Peterborough, Ontario, 1989 and subsequent editions). A small part of the document can also be found in the Internet Medieval Sourcebook at http://www.fordham.edu/halsall/source/carol-devillis.html.

For dress, furnishings, and so on see R. Fleming, 'Acquiring, flaunting and destroying silk in late Anglo-Saxon England', *Early Medieval Europe*, 15 (2007); G. Owen-Crocker, *Dress in Anglo-Saxon England* (revised edition, Woodbridge, 2004); and C. Senecal, 'Keeping up with the Godwinesons: in pursuit of aristocratic status in late Anglo-Saxon England', *Anglo-Norman Studies*, 23 (2000).

As to William's sense of humour, the story concerning Lanfranc's lame horse is found in *The Life of Herluin*, translated in S. Vaughn, *The Abbey of Bec and the Anglo-Norman State* (Woodbridge, 1981). Lanfranc's use of humour to soften William is found in William of Malmesbury, *Gesta pontificum Anglorum. Volume 1: Text and Translation*, ed. and trans. M. Winterbottom (Oxford, 2007). The joke played on William fitz Osbern is found in the *Gesta Guillelmi* of William of Poitiers, while the documents that record the incidents involving Hugh the Forester and the abbot of the Trinité-du-Mont are in the *Regesta Regum Anglo-Normannorum*.

With regard to William's residences see the section on the palace at Winchester in *Winchester in the Early Middle Ages: An Edition and Discussion of the Winton Domesday*, ed. M. Biddle (Oxford, 1976), pp 289–302; R.A. Brown, 'The White Tower of London', in *Castles, Conquest and Charters: Collected Papers* (Woodbridge, 1989); *The White Tower*, ed. E. Impey (New Haven and London, 2008); M. de Boüard, *Le château de Caen* (Caen, 1979); and A. Renoux, 'Le château des ducs de Normandie à Fécamp', *Archéologie Médiéval*, 9 (1979).

For William's piety, in addition to the reading found under Chapter 3, see W. Fröhlich, 'St Anselm's special relationship with William the Conqueror', *Anglo-Norman Studies*, 10 (1988) and F. Barlow, 'William I's relations with Cluny', *Journal of Ecclesiastical History*, 32 (1981).

The passages quoted and paraphrased from Daniel of Beccles are taken from R. Bartlett, *England under the Norman and Angevin Kings, 1075–1225* (Oxford, 2000) and J. Gillingham, 'From *civilitas* to civility: codes of manners in medieval and early modern England', *Transactions of the Royal Historical Society*, 12 (2002). Indeed see Bartlett's book generally for aspects of the life and thought of this period.

On hunting see F. Barlow, 'Hunting in the middle ages', in the volume of collected papers: *The Norman Conquest and Beyond* (London, 1983) and C.R. Young, *The Royal Forests of Medieval England* (Stroud, 1979).

Chapter 8. Storms of Troubles, 1076–87

For much of what is covered in this chapter there are only the sources and the two biographies. In addition, for the career of Odo of Bayeux see the works cited for Chapter 3.

C.W. David, *Robert Curthose, Duke of Normandy* (Cambridge, MA, 1920) was for a long time the only full-length scholarly biography of the Conqueror's eldest son, but it is now replaced by W.M. Aird, *Robert Curthose, Duke of Normandy (c. 1050–1134)* (Woodbridge, 2008). Curthose also has an entry in the *Oxford Dictionary of National Biography* (Oxford, 2004).

For Wales in this period see R.R. Davies, *Conquest, Coexistence and Change: Wales 1063–1415* (Oxford, 1987), republished in paperback as *The Age of Conquest: Wales 1063–1415* (Oxford, 1990); D. Walker, *Medieval Wales* (Cambridge, 1990); A.D. Carr, *Medieval Wales* (Basingstoke, 1995); and *Gruffydd ap Cynan: A Collaborative Biography*, ed. K.L. Maund (Woodbridge, 1996) – with Chris Lewis's article being particularly useful. For English relations with Scotland see J. Green, 'Anglo-Scottish relations, 1066–1174', in *England*

and her Neighbours 1066–1453: Essays in Honour of Pierre Chaplais, ed. M. Jones and M. Vale (London, 1989). For an introduction to Scotland more generally in this period see G.W.S. Barrow, *Kingship and Unity: Scotland 1000–1306* (second edition, Edinburgh, 2003).

There has been a vast amount written about Domesday Book and various aspects of the survey. See, for example: F.W. Maitland, *Domesday Book and Beyond* (Cambridge, 1897); V.H. Galbraith, *Domesday Book: Its Place in Administrative History* (Oxford, 1974); *Domesday Studies*, ed. J.C. Holt (Woodbridge, 1987); S. Harvey, 'Domesday Book and its predecessors', *English Historical Review*, 86 (1971); P. Hyams, '"No register of title": the Domesday inquest and land adjudication', *Anglo-Norman Studies*, 9 (1986); N. Higham, 'The Domesday survey: context and purpose', *History*, 78 (1993); *Domesday Book Studies*, ed. R.W.H. Erskine and A. Williams (London, 1987), reprinted as *The Story of Domesday Book* (Chichester, 2003); R. Fleming, *Kings and Lords in Conquest England* (Cambridge, 1991). Two recent books by D. Roffe have added fresh controversy and stimulated renewed debate: D. Roffe, *Domesday: The Inquest and the Book* (Oxford, 2000) and D. Roffe, *Decoding Domesday* (Woodbridge, 2007). The complete text of the survey, in Latin with an English translation, was published by Phillimore, ed. J. Morris, 34 vols (Chichester, 1975–86). A one-volume translation has more recently been printed: *Domesday Book: A Complete Translation*, trans. A. Williams and G.H. Martin (Harmondsworth, 2002). In addition, there is a complete facsimile of Domesday Book produced by Alecto editions, as well as five CD-ROM databases including: *Domesday Explorer*, ed. J. Morris (2000) and the *Alecto Digital Domesday* (2002).

On Rouen in William's day see D. Bates, 'Rouen from 900 to 1204: from Scandinavian settlement to Angevin "capital"', in *Medieval Art, Architecture, and Archaeology at Rouen*, ed. J. Stratford, The British Archaeological Association Conference Transactions for the Year 1986 (1993). For some observations on royal deaths see S. Church, 'Aspects of the English succession, 1066–1199: the death of the king', *Anglo-Norman Studies*, 29 (2007).

INDEX

Numbers in *italics* refer to illustrations.